WESTMAR COLLEGE LIBRARY

W9-BTP-572

NOTES ON
SOCIAL MEASUREMENT

NOTES ON
SOCIAL MEASUREMENT

Historical and Critical

Otis Dudley Duncan

/05370

RUSSELL SAGE FOUNDATION   NEW YORK

The Russell Sage Foundation

The Russell Sage Foundation, one of the oldest of America's general purpose foundations, was established in 1907 by Mrs. Margaret Olivia Sage for "the improvement of social and living conditions in the United States." The Foundation seeks to fulfill this mandate by fostering the development and dissemination of knowledge about the political, social, and economic problems of America. It conducts research in the social sciences and public policy, and publishes books and pamphlets that derive from this research.

The Foundation provides support for individual scholars and collaborates with other granting agencies and academic institutions in studies of social problems. It maintains a professional staff of social scientists who engage in their own research as well as advise on Foundation programs and projects. The Foundation also conducts a Visiting Scholar Program, under which established scholars working in areas of current interest to the Foundation join the staff for a year to consult and to continue their own research and writing. Finally, a Postdoctoral Fellowship Program enables promising young scholars to devote full time to their research while in residence for a year at the Foundation.

The Board of Trustees is responsible for the general policies and oversight of the Foundation, while the immediate administrative direction of the program and staff is vested in the President, assisted by the officers and staff. The President bears final responsibility for the decision to publish a manuscript as a Russell Sage Foundation book. In reaching a judgment on the competence, accuracy, and objectivity of each study, the President is advised by the staff and a panel of special readers.

The conclusions and interpretations in Russell Sage Foundation publications are those of the authors and not of the Foundation, its Trustees, or its staff. Publication by the Foundation, therefore, does not imply endorsement of the contents of the study. It does signify that the manuscript has been reviewed by competent scholars in the field and that the Foundation finds it worthy of public consideration.

BOARD OF TRUSTEES
Herma Hill Kay, Chair

Robert McCormick Adams
Earl F. Cheit
Philip E. Converse
Thomas C. Edwards
Renée Fox
Carl Kaysen
Patricia King

Gardner Lindzey
Gary MacDougal
James G. March
Frederick Mosteller
John S. Reed
Marshall Robinson
Madelon Talley

HONORARY TRUSTEE
David B. Truman

Copyright © 1984 by Russell Sage Foundation. All rights reserved. Printed in the United States of America. No part of this publication may be reproduced, stored in a retrieval system, or transmitted, in any form or by any means, electronic, mechanical, photocopying, recording, or otherwise, without the prior written permission of the publisher.

Library of Congress Catalog Number: 83–62503
Standard Book Number: 0–87154–219–6
10 9 8 7 6 5 4 3 2 1

FOREWORD

In 1982 the Russell Sage Foundation, one of America's oldest general purpose foundations, celebrated its seventy-fifth anniversary. To commemorate this long commitment to the support and dissemination of social science research, we departed from our customary publishing procedures to commission several special volumes. Unlike most Russell Sage books, which emerge as the end products of various Foundation-supported research programs, these Anniversary volumes were conceived from the start as a series of publications. In tone, they were to be distinctly more personal and reflective than many of our books, extended essays by respected scholars and authors on significant aspects of social research.

As befits an anniversary celebration, several of the volumes will address issues of traditional concern to the Foundation—changing patterns of research on women; the interaction of law and society; the developing techniques of social research itself. Several, too, will be written by scholars whose previous work in these areas the Russell Sage Foundation has been proud to sponsor or publish.

Social measurement, the subject of this first Anniversary volume, has been on the Foundation's research agenda in one form or another for most of our history. Sociologist Otis Dudley Duncan has already made significant contributions to this field, including an important study of social indicators entitled *Social Change in a Metropolitan Community*, published by the Foundation in 1973. As readers of his new Anniversary volume will discover, Dudley Duncan is also uniquely qualified to write the special kind of commemorative volume we had in mind—one that is learned but lively, securely grounded in its author's expertise yet ranging freely and speculatively across theoretical bounds.

These *Notes on Social Measurement* are, as the subtitle suggests, both historical and critical. They offer the combined pleasures of informative synthesis, imaginative reinterpretation, and persuasive argument. This book is a welcome arrival in its own right and an auspicious inaugural volume for the Foundation's "75th Anniversary Series."

MARSHALL ROBINSON
President
Russell Sage Foundation

CONTENTS

1. *Inventing Social Measurement*   1

Some time between Homer and Herodotus the Greeks invented voting to replace earlier methods for ascertaining the collective preference. First contributions to a theory of voting, and the discovery of paradoxes in consequence of such inquiry, emerged only a few years before the French Revolution in an early florescence of mathematical social science in the country that was shortly to revolutionize its system of physical measures. Elections are one kind of apparatus for measurement that has some analogy to weights and measures.

References   10

2. *Historical Metrology*   12

Concern for the accuracy of weights and measures and the attempt to maintain convenient and uniform standards and units are persistent themes in history. Our physical dimensions and techniques for measuring them are social constructs that were invented to solve social problems, and our systems of physical units have evolved through a complex social process that invites investigation by students of social change, class conflict, social movements, bureaucratization, and the sociology of knowledge, as is suggested by observations on the origin and diffusion of the metric system. I propose that the social history of measurement be extended to include social measurement.

References   36

3. *More Inventions*   39

A sociology of invention might identify basic ideas about social measurement and trace the techniques that evolved as elaborations of them. Among the fundamental inventions are several that precede the era of modern science or, at any rate, have their social roots in earlier periods. They include, in addition to (1) voting, (2) counting, to measure the size of the group or functional subdivisions of it, often as an aid to taxation and levying of military forces; (3) valuing goods and services in units of some standard good, which was first accomplished without coins and currency but was later facilitated by monetary systems controlled by central authority; (4) defining and labeling social ranks or degrees, provision for which is found in early Greek and Roman constitutions; (5) appraising the quality of persons or performances by contests, games, examinations, and grading systems, as in the ancient Chinese civil-service examination system and the Greek athletic and poetry contests; (6) making awards or bestowing honors for merit or performance, and meting out punishments for criminal offenses or lesser transgressions when the magnitude of the reward or punishment is somehow calibrated to the degree of excellence, or the gravity of the offense. Modern ideas about (7) chance, conceived as measurable, objective probability, and (8) random selection and allocation, as devices for assuring fairness and/or representativeness, were anticipated in various ways by the ancients. The method by which Athenians designated members of their council (*boule*) in the fifth century B.C., for example, is tantamount to stratified random sampling, although there is no evidence that the Greeks had considered the possibility of calculating probabilities—an innovation made by the seventeenth-century demographer, John Graunt. Among the basic concepts of social measurement are several originating in modern times that are largely due to deliberate scientific investigation, although earlier social roots for some of them could perhaps be found. Index numbers, psychophysical scaling (and other such calibrations of human judgment), utility, measures of statistical distributions, and measures of properties of social networks are salient examples. The variety of uses of time measurement in social organization and social inquiry illustrates how concepts ordinarily taken to be "physical" also are central to quantitative social science.

References   113

4. *On Scales of Measurement*   *119*
   The theory of scale types proposed in 1946 by S. S. Stevens focused on nominal, ordinal, interval, and ratio scales of measurement. Some of his examples of these types—notably those concerning psychological test scores—are misleading. Stevens's equating of scientific classification with measurement on a "nominal scale" and his conse-

quent underemphasis on counting (which actually employs an absolute scale) has mischievous consequences when taken seriously by population scientists. There is no clear place in his theory for the probability scale which, like counting, is central to the population sciences as well as important for some parts of physics. Even an appropriately expanded typology of scales, however, is only one part of a theory of measurement, and that theory, just beginning to emerge, is not always helpful in understanding the attempts to measure made by the empirical or soft sciences.

References   155

5.   Measurement: The Real Thing   157

5.   Measurement: The Real Thing   157

Every science uses physical measures of some kind, most of which can be expressed in terms of the dimensions of length, mass, time, electric current, temperature, luminous intensity, amount of substance, and the plane and solid angles. While standards for the primary units of these dimensions are defined to a very high accuracy, in practice physical measurements (like social measurements) are highly error prone. Moreover, there are still some primitive sectors of physical measurement, like hardness and characteristics of fabricated objects. Still, social science, with the possible exception of economics, has no coherent system of measures, with powerful dimensional properties, like those available to the theoretical physicist.

References   170

6.   Psychophysics   172

6.   Psychophysics   172

The method of magnitude estimation of sensation intensity, due to S. S. Stevens and used by him to establish the "psychophysical law" in the form of a power function relating sensation to stimulus magnitude, has been adapted to measures of values about which there is an approximation to a social consensus, such as the meaning of adjectives, the seriousness of crime, or the prestige standing of occupations. There is also some exploratory work proposing magnitude estimation as an alternative to L. L. Thurstone's method for scaling attitudes. The hope that magnitude estimation can provide a true ratio scale (analogous in its properties to, say, the Kelvin temperature scale) for social values and attitudes has not yet been realized, as is shown by an analysis of the properties of the proposed scales in comparison with scales produced by other methods.

References   197

7. *Psychometrics*   *200*

Social science has made much use of statistical data derived from mental tests and has often adopted the classical psychometric techniques of correlation and factor analysis in constructing instruments. An example is the set of twelve Social Life Feeling Scales of K. F. Schuessler. Research producing them is considered to represent well the current state of the art. Statistics based on scales of this kind unavoidably confound the properties of the measuring device with aspects of the distribution of feelings (or attitudes, et cetera) in the population, thereby violating Thurstone's criteria of invariance and relevance. This is demonstrated with calculations on simulated data derived from a measurement model of Georg Rasch which keeps separate the parameters pertaining to the location of items and persons on the (latent) attitude continuum and those that reflect, as well, the statistical distribution of the population on that continuum.

References   218

8. *Social Measurement: Predicaments and Practices*   *220*

Some distinctive features of social measurement are our dependence on measures and measurement models borrowed from other sciences; the salience of the population concept, which leads to an emphasis on measurement by counting and on the measurement of individual variability; our consequent need for statistical models that recognize real variability as well as measurement error and stochastic behavior, paradoxically coupled with our backwardness in retaining obsolete statistical methods; the fact that the social process itself generates many of our measurements and limits what can be done in basic social science, which creates a set of challenging problems for a sociology of measurement; our willingness to "measure" almost anything that has a name, however thin the theoretical rationale or meager the measurement model; our enforced reliance on "indicators" and "indexes," or symptoms and composites. To understand our measures better, to improve

and rationalize them, we shall have to learn more about the culture of
numbers and what it means for a society whose heritage it is.

   References   239

Acknowledgments   *241*

Name Index   *243*

Subject Index   *253*

Measurement began our might
Yeats

THE ANTIQUITY of several basic concepts and procedures of social measurement (such as voting, counting people, money, social rank, contests, rewards and punishments, and randomization) suggests that their roots are in the social process itself, broadly conceived, and not specifically in the scientific method as it developed in the seventeenth and later centuries. Where social measurement has relied heavily on methods borrowed from psychophysics, psychometrics, and economic index numbers, rather than methods well suited to the population sciences, it has encountered seemingly intractable difficulties, which are only exacerbated by adherence to an inadequate doctrine of scale types. A sociology of measurement, allied with an expanded historical metrology, is needed not less for the improvement of measurement technique than for an understanding of the role of quantification in society.

1

INVENTING
SOCIAL
MEASUREMENT

LYCURGUS, the legendary lawgiver of Sparta, is credited by Plutarch with instituting the senate, or Council of Elders, members of which he at first appointed. Subsequently he provided that each vacancy caused by death would be filled by electing the "most deserving" man over sixty years of age.

The election was made in the following manner. An assembly of the people having been convened, chosen men were shut up in a room near by so that they could neither see nor be seen, but only hear the shouts of the assembly. For as in other matters, so here, the cries of the assembly decided between the competitors. These did not appear in a body, but each one was introduced separately, as the lot fell, and passed silently through the assembly. Then the secluded judges, who had writing-tablets with them, recorded in each case the loudness of the shouting, not knowing for whom it was given, but only that he was introduced first, second, or third, and so on. Whoever was greeted with the most and loudest shouting, him they declared elected (Plutarch, *Lycurgus* xxvi [Perrin 1967, p.285]).

References to which citations are made in each chapter are located at the end of that chapter.

The use of judges to record the volume of applause must represent one of the earliest examples of psychophysical method in the service of social measurement, one of the themes that will concern us later. For the moment, let me call attention to some other features of the example. First, what is at stake here is indeed social measurement, albeit of a crude variety. Interestingly enough, the quantity directly measured (volume of applause or perceived volume of applause) is not the one of interest. Presumably the latter is the collective preference, however vague that concept may have been. (Compare the ordinary thermometer, where we read length of the column of mercury or alcohol to ascertain degree of warmth, another vague concept rendered more precise by the very instrument devised to measure it.) Moreover the reading, while it apparently pertains to a continuous variable, volume of applause, is used only to make a categorical decision—to elect just one of the candidates. (Compare the household thermostat, which reads the continuous variable temperature to make the binary decision, on versus off.)

Unfortunately, we do not know how the judges recorded loudness on their writing tablets or how their records were aggregated, for these procedures too were inventions (albeit ones now lost). Indeed, the passage quoted from Plutarch mentions a number of social inventions that were either brought together from antecedent practice or devised anew by "Lycurgus": the senate, the assembly, the election, the procedure of acclamation, and randomization by lot. Another such invention, mentioned by Herodotus (Book 6) is proxy voting. When Sparta came to have two kings both sat with the Council of Elders and, if they were absent, their nearest kin among the council members cast the two proxy votes as well as their own. Several of these inventions have direct bearing on our topic of social measurement. What I am trying to suggest is that many—and perhaps the most basic—of the procedures natural and social scientists use in measuring were actually invented to solve practical problems. In the beginning, measurement served social purposes only. The scientist may come into the picture when there is a recognized need to improve the measuring instrument. Or, taking the current practice of measurement as his point of departure, he may let his imagination work freely on ideas of amount, extent, magnitude, intensity, duration, numerousness, dimension, scale, and proportion to create abstract conceptual structures and systems of relationships.

The Spartan system evidently persisted in its essentials for some centuries. In his day, Aristotle scorned it as "childish," presumably by contrast with the highly developed procedures of voting and sortition (selection by lot) which he described in *Constitution of Athens*. The somewhat conjectural early history of voting has been nicely summarized by Larsen, who observes (p. 164),

> The practice of taking formal votes in political assemblies and of counting the votes is one of those inventions which, when once made, seem so obvious that they are taken for granted. Consequently, the average observer does not realize that any invention has been necessary; yet it would be hard to point to any single innovation which has influenced more profoundly the development of political institutions. The neglect of the subject by students of Greek history has been particularly unfortunate, for they seem to have before them the key to the invention as far as Western civilization is concerned. . . . there seems to be no trace of the usage in the political institutions of the ancient Near East.

As to timing, Larsen points out that no votes were taken in any of the several meetings of councils and assemblies described in Homer's *Iliad* and *Odyssey*. But voting was apparently in use by the time of the historically attested reforms of Solon (early sixth century B.C.), who transferred the election of magistrates from the *Areopagus* (council) to the popular assembly where, it is supposed, voting was accomplished by show of hands.

Herodotus regularly depicts councils of state or military command reaching their decisions by voting. He does not seem to regard the procedure as novel and, with one exception to be mentioned later, gives few details on the method of voting. According to his Book 6, at the Battle of Marathon (490 B.C.) the Athenian commanders were evenly divided, five in favor of risking a fight and five against. Miltiades then persuaded the commander-in-chief, Callimachus, to cast the deciding vote in favor of engaging the Persians. Book 4 records a unanimous vote of eleven Ionian kings not to destroy a bridge over the Danube, the removal of which would have left the Persians under Darius (died 486 B.C.) at the mercy of the Scythians. In Book 1, the Persian king Cyrus (died 530 B.C.) sought the opinions of his chief officers, but, on hearing from Croesus the Lydian, decided for the course opposite to their unanimous vote. When Darius, who was king of Persia from 522 to 486, and six other conspirators massacred the Magi then ruling Persia, according to Herodotus's story in Book 3, they held a remarkable formal debate on the form the new government should take. Otanes spoke for democratic government arguing, among other things, that equality under the law was promoted when magistrates were appointed by lot. Megabyzus recommended oligarchy and Darius spoke for monarchy. The remaining four voted with him, and he was subsequently selected king when Otanes proposed that the selection be made by drawing lots.

Voting of a sort was practiced in Scythia, according to Herodotus in Book 4. When their king fell sick, three soothsayers named an offender whose false oath was the cause of the malady. When the accused denied it, six more soothsayers deliberated. If they were for conviction the defendant was executed. If not, still more soothsayers were brought in, as many as needed. If in the end the majority found the accused innocent, the original three soothsayers were executed.

Of course all of these accounts may be fiction, as the details of the speeches on democracy, oligarchy, and monarchy would have to be. But it matters little for our present purpose which Persian, Scythian, or Greek, if not Herodotus of Halicarnassus himself, came up with these variations on the idea of voting. His audience in fifth-century Greece could be expected to understand and accept them. His subsequent readers may well have picked up ideas about the exercise of suffrage from the father of history.

There is reason to believe that the secret ballot was used from the times of the earliest formal votes. The "Greek words for voting, for putting a question to vote, and for a decree adopted as the result of a vote" are derived from "*psephos*, the name for a voting token" (Larsen, p. 173). The root, literally "pebble," is preserved in "psephology," a word coined in our time to denote the scientific study of elections. In the fifth century, Pindar in his Eighth Nemean Ode deplored the use of "secret votes" by the Greek chieftains in making the Judgment of Arms that awarded the armor of the slain Achilles to Odysseus (Ulysses) in preference to Aias (Ajax). The incident is dramatically depicted in a painting (c. 490 B.C.) on a cup by Douris that is exhibited in several histories of Greek art (see especially Stanford and Luce, pp. 28–29). On one side of the cup the Greeks are shown dropping their pebbles while the procedure is supervised by a not disinterested

Athena, who anticipates the outcome that will select her favorite.
Although the Judgment of Arms was mentioned in the *Odyssey* (11:
544–546), Homer said nothing about how the decision for Odysseus
was made. By the time of Douris and Pindar it was assumed that a vote
was taken. Not all accounts of the incident agree, however, on this
point (Graves, p. 321), so we are probably safe in surmising that the
versions of Pindar and Douris are anachronistic.

Another of our words that echoes some of the history of Greek
voting is "ostracism." The *ostraka* were bits of broken pottery on which
the Athenian citizen wrote the name of the person he wished to have
expelled from the city. If 6,000 or more votes were cast, the man with
the highest vote had to stay away for a decade. Ostracism was first used
in 487 B.C. and the device was abolished c. 415 B.C.

A mythological justification for the extensive use of voting in legal
proceedings is recapitulated in the *Eumenides* of Aeschylus, a contemporary of Pindar and Douris. Orestes is tried for the murder of his
mother, Clytemnestra (in revenge for her killing of Agamemnon, her
husband and the father of Orestes and Electra). The goddess Athena as
judge goes out to

> . . . choose the noblest of the breed
> Of Athens, and here bring them to decide
> This bloody judgement even as truth is tried.

Athena announces that these proceedings will be the prototype for
future tribunals. Then she charges "these men/ To cast true stones."
Anticipating the divided outcome, she says:

> One judgement still remains. I, at the last,
> To set Orestes free this stone will cast:
> . . . .
>
> Wherefore I judge that here, if equal be
> The votes ye cast, Orestes shall go free.
> Ye judges, haste . . .
> And cast the gathered sea-stones from the urns.

Athena announces the verdict:

> This prisoner, since the stones for ill and good
> Are equal, has escaped the doom of blood.

And to the Chorus of Furies who will, therefore, not be allowed to punish Orestes, she states, "Equal, stone for stone,/ The judgement fell." (Quotations from the Murray translation, lines 485–795)

In chapters 68–69 of *Constitution of Athens* Aristotle describes how in his day (fourth century B.C.) jurors voted in making their decision. Each of them had two brass ballot balls with a stem through the center; the stem of one ball was pierced, the other solid. The pierced stem ballot was used to vote for the plaintiff and the solid one to vote for the defendant. The juror dropped the ball signifying his vote in a brass urn and discarded the other ball in an urn of wood. The brass urn was emptied upon a "reckoning board" for the official counting.

Both Larsen and Staveley find that the system of voting in the assemblies of the Greek city-states was more democratic than the Roman system. In Greece votes were counted by heads, whereas in Rome the vote was taken by curias, centuries, or tribes. The earliest form of the Roman assembly we know about comprised 193 centuries; 80 of these were under the control of the first property class and 18 more were held by the knights, likewise in the first class. If these two groups agreed their position prevailed; they voted first, and it was seldom necessary to call for votes from the remaining four classes. Later developments somewhat broadened electoral participation, but Rome never devised a system that threatened the dominance of a small oligarchy. Group voting per se need not have this effect if the voting strength of the groups is about proportional to their size. In the U.S. presidential elections, for example, the electoral college, although it requires each state to vote as a unit, is based on a sophisticated theory of representation intended to be fair to the whole electorate. In the Roman system however, "although the units might differ as much in their number of voters as our states do, there was no difference in the value of the unit votes" (Taylor, p. 1).

The Roman procedure may have had a persisting influence on ideas about voting. The article on "Electoral Processes" in the 1979 *Encyclopaedia Britannica* describes as "holistic" the conception of representation that prevailed in the Middle Ages and considers that the practice of counting individual votes, which became increasingly prevalent in the seventeenth century, resulted from a conception that was more individualistic. The election of the Catholic bishops and the pope provides a case history of evolutionary change in procedures.

Marc Bloch (p. 351), who tells part of the story, notes that in the twelfth century there was a continuing "reluctance merely to count votes. The decision was considered to belong, not to the majority pure and simple, but, according to the traditional formula, to the fraction which was at once 'the most numerous and the most sound.' . . . Hence the frequency of disputed elections." To the present the conclave, in theory, has an option in regard to the procedure for electing a pope in that the cardinals may choose to elect by inspiration, by compromise, or by ballot. In the latter event, the candidate needs two-thirds of the votes to be elected (Swift, p. 573).

Having located the invention of voting in classical Greece, we would also like to determine the beginnings of the theory of voting. Staveley has many remarks that amount to imputation of implicit theories to those who designed or reformed the Greek and Roman systems. With respect to the group vote, for example, he states (p. 133): "It is tempting to suppose that the principle was deliberately embraced by the governing class . . . to delay the advance of popular sovereignty." The earliest explicit formulation on properties of voting systems I have seen is a letter of Pliny the Younger (A.D. 62?–c. 113) given by Farquharson (1969, *Theory of Voting*, Annexure, pp. 57–60), where the question is raised as to how the outcome may be affected by following different procedures when the Roman senate is confronted with a choice among the alternatives of acquittal, banishment, or death for persons accused of a capital crime. Farquharson's own monograph provides an elegant analysis of the problem which shows, among other things (as Pliny suspected), that what happens under a specified procedure depends on whether the voters vote "sincerely" or are "sophisticated," that is, whether they vote strategically.

This monograph is illustrative of a line of work by contemporary theorists (see also, for example, Arrow 1951; Black 1958; Straffin 1980) that traces back more or less directly to an eruption of mathematical social science in France during the last decades of the eighteenth century. It is not clear whether priority belongs to Borda (see de Grazia 1953, which includes a translation of Borda's paper read in 1770, published in 1781) or Condorcet (1785; excerpts in translation in Baker 1976; commentary in Black 1958) for the observation that in a three-way race where the plurality of votes defines the winner, it is quite possible that either of the other two candidates may actually be preferred to the winner by a majority of voters. This leads to the "first proposal for preferential voting" (Lakeman, p. 298), which is for each voter to rank the candidates. The ranking procedure was also considered further by Laplace (see Todhunter, pp. 546–548), who noted its vulnerability to strategic voting, leading, as he thought, to a bias in favor of mediocre candidates. Laplace indicated that "experience" had led to its abandonment where it had been tried, but gave no details. His analysis of this issue may be one of the precursors of the modern theory of games of strategy, although I have not attempted to establish a historical linkage.

We should note that, although Borda and Condorcet both proposed the use of ranking, they had different ideas about how to pick the winner. Borda is credited with the "method of marks," which amounts to declaring as winner the candidate with the highest mean rank. Condorcet suggested that the candidate, if any, who gets the majority in all pairwise comparisons with each of the others should be elected. But there is no assurance that the electorate's set of rankings will produce a Condorcet winner. Where Condorcet's criterion does select a winner, moreover, it need not be the one chosen on Borda's rule. For example, if six of ten voters rank three candidates A B C and four voters rank them B C A, the Borda winner is B whereas A is the Condorcet winner. Clearly, we cannot insist that both criteria be satisfied without risking an indeterminate election, even though both criteria are attractive. Arrow's monograph, demonstrating a more general impossibility theorem of this kind, has stimulated much work on the compatibility of various rules or criteria for a voting system (or "social welfare function," as Arrow called it).

I wish I knew whether Borda and Condorcet had read Herodotus. In Book 8 of the *History* he records that after the final defeat of the Persian king Xerxes in the battle of Salamis (480 B.C.), and following the distribution of the plunder, the Greek commanders met at the Isthmus to award a prize of valor to the one of their number judged best in terms of his conduct in the whole campaign. They cast votes for first and second place. Each commander felt that he had fought the most bravely, but a majority put Themistocles second. Although no formal award was made, Themistocles had gained the reputation of being the most able. We may, of course, wonder if the account is anachronistic or fictional. But some Greek—Herodotus himself, if not the commanders or an earlier genius—had invented the preferential ballot over two millennia before the French mathematicians.

Gillispie attempts to put the French work into a historical context and indicates that it was Turgot who stimulated Condorcet's and, indirectly, Laplace's interest in "mathematics with civic relevance." Gillispie argues that Turgot and Condorcet were not interested in improving the representativeness of electoral processes. Rather they thought of voting as "a collective device for determining the truth." That Condorcet's paradox has been reinterpreted in accordance with Anglo-Saxon ideas about popular government is one of many nice ironies in the history of measurement. The thrust of Turgot's thinking is made clear in Sewell's summary (pp. 127–128) of the 1774 *Mémoire* which Turgot had intended for Louis XVI. It contemplated "a hierarchy of parish, regional, provincial, and national assemblies" in which votes were restricted to property owners and "allocated in strict proportion to the value of their land." The intention, in Turgot's own words, was to place "the plurality of voices, most often, on the side of those who have received the most education" so as to "render the assemblies much more reasonable than if badly instructed and uneducated people predominated." Fifteen years later, the revolution was under way, with a conflict over voting systems a precipitating factor. The Estates General, called to assemble on 1 May 1789, was to be constituted—as at the last meeting in 1614—in the three separate orders, Clergy, Nobility, and Third Estate, each having the same number of deputies and each voting as a unit. Earlier, however, some provincial assemblies had introduced a modified system in which the Third Estate had double representation and voting was by head. Petitions tendered in late 1788 called for a similar "doubling of the Third." From the beginning of its meetings, the Third tacitly refused to assent to the principle of vote by order; it simply neglected to organize itself to render a unit vote. A month of failure to reconcile the orders produced growing agitation and, after considering various proposals, the Third Estate, on 17 June, voted 491 to 89 to constitute itself the "National Assembly," in which nobles and priests would be seated, but with voting by head without regard to order. On 22 June, Louis XVI declared this and other actions null and void but accepted the idea of vote by head and double representation for the Third in provincial Estates, which were to be elected by order. But this and other concessions were too late. In any event, many nobles continued to insist that they were forbidden by their mandates to vote by head. Mobilization of troops in late June was followed by the reaction of the Parisian masses. The fall of the Bastille on 14 July 1789 later came to symbolize the revolution that already had occurred. (See Lefebvre, especially pp. 29–30, 44–56, 67–79, concerning the issue of voting; also Sewell, pp. 78–85; Stewart, pp. 25–88.) Thus was a controversy over social measurement implicated in a sequence of events with major consequences for physical measurement, as I shall note subsequently.

It remains only to mention that the nineteenth and twentieth centuries have seen a variety of voting schemes suggested. The British mathematician and author of *Alice in Wonderland*, C. L. Dodgson ("Lewis Carroll"), was one of the numerous inventors. He became embroiled in a controversy with the dean of Christ Church (Oxford University), H. G. Liddell (the father of "Alice" in real life), concerning college architecture, and in this context of academic politics issued a series of pamphlets on methods of voting. (The fascinating details are given by Black, Ch. XX.) A more influential literature in political science produced innovations in the electoral systems of many countries during the nineteenth century. For reasons that will become evident, I took special interest in the account of experience with rational election systems by Lakeman, which I quote (p. 9):

Systems of voting and of counting votes are the mechanism by means of which the country records and measures its reactions to the political issues of the day. As with all recording and measuring devices, therefore, it is important that these systems should be as accurate, as reliable, and as impartial as we can make them. To tamper with them—or to tolerate the continuance of their known defects . . . is on a par with using false weights and measures.

REFERENCES

Aristotle. *See* Ross (1921).
Arrow, K. J. *Social Choice and Individual Values*. New York: Wiley, 1951.
Baker, Keith Michael, ed. *Condorcet: Selected Writings*. Indianapolis: Bobbs-Merrill, 1976.
Black, Duncan. *The Theory of Committees and Elections*. Cambridge: Cambridge University Press, 1958.
Bloch, Marc. *Feudal Society*. Chicago: University of Chicago Press, 1961.

Condorcet, Marquis de. "Essay on the Application of Mathematics to the Theory of Decision Making," 1785. *See* Baker (1976).

de Grazia, Alfred. "Mathematical Derivation of an Election System." *Isis* 44 (June 1953): 42–51. Includes translation of Jean-Charles de Borda, "Memoir on Elections by Ballot," 1770/1781.

Farquharson, Robin. *Theory of Voting.* New Haven: Yale University Press, 1969.

Gillispie, Charles Coulston. "Probability and Politics: Laplace, Condorcet, and Turgot." *Proceedings of the American Philosophical Society* 116 (February 1972): 1–20.

Graves, Robert. *The Greek Myths.* Vol. 2. Baltimore: Penguin Books, 1955.

Herodotus. *The Histories.* Trans. by Aubrey de Sélincourt. Harmondsworth: Penguin Books, 1972. (See also *The History of Herodotus*, trans. by George Rawlinson. New York: Tudor, 1956.)

Lakeman, Enid. *How Democracies Vote.* London: Faber and Faber, 1970.

Larsen, J. A. O. "The Origin and Significance of the Counting of Votes." *Classical Philology* 44 (July 1949): 164–181.

Lefebvre, Georges. *The Coming of the French Revolution.* Trans. by R. R. Palmer. New York: Vintage Books, 1947.

Murray, Gilbert, trans. *The Eumenides of Aeschylus.* New York: Oxford University Press, 1925.

Perrin, Bernadotte, trans. *Plutarch's Lives.* Vol. 1 (Loeb Classical Library). Cambridge: Harvard University Press, 1967.

Ross, W. D., ed. *The Works of Aristotle*, Vol. 10. Oxford: Clarendon Press, 1921.

Sewell, William H., Jr. *Work and Revolution in France.* Cambridge: Cambridge University Press, 1980.

Stanford, W. B., and J. V. Luce. *The Quest for Ulysses.* New York: Praeger, 1974.

Staveley, E. S. *Greek and Roman Voting and Elections.* New York: Cornell University Press, 1972.

Stewart, John Hall. *A Documentary Survey of the French Revolution.* New York: Macmillan, 1951.

Straffin, Philip D., Jr. *Topics in the Theory of Voting.* Boston: Birkhäuser, 1980.

Swift, A. "Popes, Election of." *New Catholic Encyclopedia.* New York: McGraw-Hill, 1967.

Taylor, Lily Ross. *Roman Voting Assemblies.* Ann Arbor: University of Michigan Press, 1966.

Todhunter, Isaac. *A History of the Mathematical Theory of Probability*, 1865. Reprint. New York: G. E. Stechert, 1931.

2

HISTORICAL
METROLOGY

THE EARLIEST USE of "metrology" recorded in the *Oxford English Dictionary* is in the title of the book by P. Kelly, *Metrology: or an Exposition of Weights and Measures, chiefly those of Great Britain and France*, 1816. The word may be a borrowing from the French, inasmuch as writing on *métrologie* appeared in France in the late eighteenth century. In its narrowest meaning, metrology has to do with equivalences within and between systems of weights and measures, facilitating conversions required in commerce, the industrial arts, surveying, and so on. In a similarly restricted sense, historical metrology is concerned to establish ratios of obsolete and ancient units to those in current use (see Berriman 1953). Like numismatics, it is one of the auxiliary disciplines to history and archeology. At a high level of scholarship, this kind of work perforce begins to raise sociological questions. Thus Zupko's *British Weights and Measures* (1977, p. xiv) insists on the necessity of examining "all three major components of . . . metrological history; that is, the units of measurement, the physical standards, and the corps of officials who inspected and verified weights and measures and who enforced compliance to the dictates of the law." Unfortunately, much of the literature on historical metrology does not take so modern a point of view; it will require a good many more sociologically sophisticated monographic studies before we can expect to see a good comparative treatise on the sociology of measurement. If we could recover all the lost "constitutions" reputedly prepared by Aristotle and his students, we might have a beginning. In *Constitution of Athens*, at any rate, he reports that *Metronomi* (commissioners of weights and measures) were selected by lot—five for the city proper and five for the port at Piraeus. Their job was to "see that sellers use fair weights and measures" (Ch. 51). There were also *Sitophylaces* (corn commissioners), similarly selected, who watched over prices and the weight of loaves, which they had the power to standardize.

But historical metrology might become broader as well as deeper. Perhaps one of the monographs could look into the standardization of concert pitch. (Today it is usually given as a' = 440 Hz for the violin a-string, although an orchestra noted for its "bright" sound is reputed to tune a bit higher than this. The table given by Lindley and Wachsmann reports variation between 360 and 510 Hz at various times and places during the period 1500–1850.) Or it could trace the social factors that may be implicated in the evolution of the *tactus*, or beat, from a standard based on the human heartbeat—as in the work of a Renaissance composer-performer like Ockeghem—to a calibration in terms of the vibration of a metronome. (You won't find such an analysis where you might expect it—in Max Weber's essay on the "rationalization" of Western music.)

In this as well as other chapters, I mean my title to be taken literally: "notes" on measurement are what I have to offer. But we can at least contemplate the possibility of a metrology generously conceived, in the fashion of the engineer Sydenham (1979, p. 41) as "measurement science, the pursuit of means to convert latent information into meaningful knowledge by rigorous and objective procedures of philosophy and practice"; and by the historian Dupree as a multidisciplinary inquiry into "measurement" as "a social process . . . acting through time . . . which joins man and his environment" (1968, pp. 38–39), an inquiry determined to "see measurement and all who do it as part of human culture" (1979, ms., p. 29). Recognition of such a line of investigation, or discipline, by scientific organizations seems to be quite recent. Sydenham records that an International Committee for Historical Metrology was organized in 1955 and began to hold international conferences in 1975, after becoming a section of the International Union for the History and Philosophy of Science in 1974. The much earlier American Metrological Society, as I shall note below, was not primarily concerned with scholarship.

Historical metrology is one among the many disciplines recognized today that could claim Herodotus as a founder. In Book 6 of his *History*, he noted that Pheidon, a king of Argos, was the ruler who established the system of weights and measures of Peloponnesus, and that gold and silver coinage was invented by the Lydians, who also (in Book 1) introduced retail trade. The Egyptians, Herodotus reported, claimed the discovery of the solar year and its division into twelve parts. He thought the Egyptian calendar of twelve thirty-day months, with five extra days to make the "circuit of the seasons" return uniformly, was superior to the Greek calendar, which intercalated an extra month in every other year (Book 2). He noted that the Egyptian measure of itinerary distance, the *schoenus*, is equivalent to 60 *stades* (sometimes translated "furlongs") whereas the Persian *parasang* is 30 furlongs (Books 2 and 6). His hypothesis was that people who have little land measure it in fathoms, and that the successively larger units, *stades*, *parasangs*, and *schoeni*, are used by peoples with correspondingly larger estates. Although Herodotus attributed surveying and geometry to the Egyptians, he stated that the sundial, the gnomon, and the division of the day into twelve parts were borrowed by the Greeks from Babylonia (Book 2). In his account (Book 3) of the tribute exacted by the Persians from their provinces, Herodotus distinguished between the Babylonian talent used to weigh silver and the Euboean talent, which served as the standard for gold. In reckoning the total tribute he assumed that gold had thirteen times the value of silver per talent. Herodotus takes pride in his own calculations of distances, as in Book 5, where he figures the distance from Ephesus to Susa as 14,040 furlongs. In Book 4 he states that the voyage across the Black Sea along its extreme length takes nine days and eight nights; assuming that a vessel can sail about 70,000 fathoms in a summer day and 60,000 in a night, he finds the total distance to be 1,110,000 fathoms or 11,100 furlongs.

One of the insights contributed by historical metrology is the realization that not only units, but the physical dimensions themselves are social constructs and are not always conceived in the same way. What we think of as area—in dimensional terms, the square of length—was measured by cultivators in southeast Asia by the number of baskets of rice seed required to sow a field. A unit of itinerary distance, the Chinese *li*, was adjusted to the terrain so that a loaded coolie might cover roughly ten *li* per hour in either hilly or flat country. The Chinese even defined a standard vessel for measuring grain and wine in terms of the musical pitch produced when it was struck, so that a pitch pipe, its length measured by millet grains, was substituted for earlier measures of capacity based on the human body. Clock time and calendar time are put onto a common scale late in history. Ancient timepieces—the water clock and the shadow clock—were not very accurate, and the practice was to divide the period of daylight into twelve more or less equal parts, whatever the season. Hence the "hour" had no fixed duration. Moreover, alternative systems of time reckoning could coexist for long periods:

Many religious festivals were by their nature associated with the phases of the moon and therefore fixed in the lunar calendar. . . . Economic life, however, could not operate effectively with months whose exact length it was impossible to foresee for even a relatively short interval of time. Thus both in Egypt and in Mesopotamia civil months of fixed length, 30 days, were used whenever economic estimates or agreements had to be made (Neugebauer 1954, p. 794).

Dupree (1971) notes that a feature of the medieval system of English field measurement which gave it "a massive competitive edge over all its rivals" was that it succeeded in tying together bench, field, and itinerary units of length (distance). But extrapolation of the concept length beyond the limits of ordinary experience raises conceptual as well as technical issues. Thus, in 1928 the distinguished physicist P. W. Bridgman worried about whether, from a strict operationist standpoint, physics was justified in treating as one and the same concept the notion of length pertaining to ultramicroscopic dimensions, the tactual concept suited to everyday life, and the optical concept, which is required for astronomical measures of length. A side benefit of his discussion of the actual experiments in which distances are measured is the reminder that "operations which may be simple from a mathematical point of view may appear complicated from a physical viewpoint" (quoted from reprint in Feigl and Brodbeck, p. 40). A theory of measurement, it would seem, must involve more than mathematics. (Bridgman also has salutary comments on the "restricted accuracy" of astronomical distances, notwithstanding the high accuracy of angle measurement.) The issue broached by Bridgman persists. By reason of a resolution of the General Conference of Weights and Measures we have a new standard for the second, defined by a property of an "atomic clock." Thus, "Until 1967 time was bound up with the classical mechanics of Newton; today it is defined in terms of quantum mechanics, and it is not certain that the two are the same" (Danloux-Dumesnils, p. 64).

A recurrent theme in the co-evolution of dimensions, units, and standards is the need for agreement on what are, after all, mere conventions of measurement and the need for enforcement of uniformity in practice. In Proverbs 11:1 we read, "A false balance is abomination to the Lord; but a just weight is his delight." And, again, in 20:23, "Divers weights are an abomination unto the Lord." The biblical injunction against "divers weights" no doubt reflected a chronic grievance. It proved to be long lasting:

Standard measures of capacity, area, and weight were promised by King John of England when he unwillingly set his seal to the famed Magna Charta, June 15, 1215, at Runnimede. . . . The "measurements" pledge . . . was the thirty-fifth of the sixty-three clauses or pledges to his barons. . . .

Translated from its medieval Latin into modern English, this clause stipulates: "Throughout the kingdom there shall be standard measures of wine, ale, and corn. Also there shall be a standard width of dyed cloth, russet, and haberject; namely [a width of] two ells within the selvedges. Weights [also] are to be standardized similarly" (Klein, pp. 30–31; also Grierson, p. 12).

According to Grierson (p. 32), "The Romans, from Republican days onwards, had primary standards preserved in the temple of Juno Moneta to which secondary standards were supposed to correspond, though many local measures continued in use." But in Britain standardization was achieved slowly and sporadically only in the post-Conquest age. (See also Zupko 1977.)

Early linear measures were created by standardizing units derived from body parts (Skinner 1954). Dupree states (1971, p. 121): "The human body, which was unceremoniously dumped from the measuring systems of Western Europe in the eighteenth century as the least reliable of standards, not only performed reasonably well in terms of accuracy and control as a standard, but it was and is the *only* standard always available in all cultures." A survival of this history, of course, is our "foot" as well as some archaic units like "hand" (still used to measure height of horses) and "span." In the absence of ready access to a standard, an ingenious approximation was available. Jakob Köbel's *Geometrei* (1535), a very successful handbook for surveyors in its time, suggested that "Sixteen men large and small, as they come haphazardly one after another out of church, shall put their shoes one before another. . . . And this length is and shall be a lawful perch" and the sixteenth part of it "the right and lawful foot" (Grierson, pp. 9–10; Klein, p. 66). In the Assize of Weights and Measures of early fourteenth-century Scotland the ell (yard) and inch were defined in a provision that the former should contain 37 inches measured with the thumbs (at the root of the nail) of three men, "that is to say a mekill [large] man and of a man of messurebill statur and of a lytill man." I was surprised to find the width of the fleshy part of my thumb, pressed hard on a ruler, to be very nearly one U.S. inch. Perhaps a second stipulation would apply in my case: "bot be the thoume of a medilkin-man it aw [ought] to stand" (Grierson, p. 9). Not only these anticipations of random and stratified sampling, but also the procedure of averaging are of interest in connection with later discussions.

But Dupree has argued (1968) that such examples of calibration should not be confused with the process of establishing systems of units. A key issue here is that of the ratios of successively larger units. The systems of ancient Rome, ninth-century Europe (as inferred from the plan of the Carolingian monastery of St. Gall), and medieval England share common features based on the arithmetic of doubling or halving. Had the United States first faced the problem of devising a surveying system for its western territories a few years later, we might now be living with a decimal system. In retaining the English mile of 5,280 feet as an itinerary unit and adopting its square as the "section" in a rectilinear grid, the Congress of Confederation, in the Land Ordinance of 1785, set a pattern far-reaching in its consequences for American agriculture, settlement patterns, and population distribution. The section of 640 acres was divided by successive halvings into quarter sections, forty-acre fields, and two-and-one-half-acre townsite blocks, recapitulating the geometric progression discovered by Horn in the Plan of St. Gall (Horn and Born 1979, vol. 1, pp. 77ff.). Dupree concludes:

The actual and continuous existence of the grid opens a new set of perspectives on social history in the Western world. That people had measures, kept them stable, passed them from one generation to another without a single break, and adapted them to changed modes of life gives both shape and continuity to a numbering system running through hitherto unquantified ages. More fundamentally, the Rome-to-America grid ties measurement to the life of people in each age traversed and makes it a part of their language and culture (Dupree, in Horn and Born 1979, vol. 3, p. 137).

The U.S. Constitution provides in Article I, Section 8 that "The Congress shall have Power . . . To coin Money, regulate the Value thereof, and of foreign Coin, and fix the Standard of Weights and Measures." However, the latter prerogative languished during the nineteenth century. In the first presidential message to Congress, 1790, George Washington had stated: "Uniformity in the currency, weights, and measures of the United States is an object of great importance, and will, I am persuaded, be duly attended to." Note, for its relevance to a future discussion, the inclusion of money on the agenda. Toynbee (1954, pp. 293–294) refers to "Generally accepted and effectively operative standard measures of time, distance, length, volume, weight, and value" as "necessities of social life at any level above the most primitive" and as "Social currencies . . . older . . . than governments" but necessities for which the administration "can be turned to account by" governments "for the secondary purpose of moving their public in the direction of their policy."

The first secretary of state, Thomas Jefferson, on 4 July 1790, submitted to the House of Representatives a report on measures, weights, and coins (Boyd 1961, pp. 623–624, 650–675). The report noted the "general approbation, both at home and abroad," for the decimalization of the coinage enacted in 1786 and considered whether it was "in contemplation . . . to extend a like improvement to our measures and weights, and to arrange them also in a decimal ratio," noting the advantages of such a step for the "facility which this would introduce into the vulgar arithmetic." But, confessing his uncertainty as to congressional intent, the secretary asked, "Or, is it the opinion of the representatives that the difficulty of changing the established habits of a whole nation opposes an insuperable bar to this improvement?" Thus, two alternative plans were presented. The more radical one, which Jefferson himself favored, provided for "standards, unchangeable in their nature (as is the length of a rod vibrating seconds, and the weight of a definite mass of rain water)," which "are such as to be accessible to all persons." The weights and measures derived therefrom, "being arranged in decimal ratio, . . . are within the calculation of everyone who possesses the first elements of arithmetic." Despite the support of Washington, Hamilton, and Madison, Jefferson's reform was not adopted. (See "Editorial Note," Boyd, pp. 602–617; also Hellman.)

In 1821 another secretary of state, John Quincy Adams, submitted a "monumental report on weights and measures," a "masterpiece" (Dupree 1957, p. 39) that dealt authoritatively with the history and philosophy of measurement and favorably appraised the principle of the metric system, but stopped short of advising its adoption in this country for a variety of reasons and urged that the Congress take steps to ensure the accuracy and uniformity of the extant U.S. system. (See Dupree 1977.) In any event, neither Jefferson's nor Adams's report had any great effect. In the 1830s the Coast Survey provided sets of weights and measures for the customs houses and the states, although enforcement of standards was left to the states. In the mid-1880s, "Charles Sanders Peirce, head of the office of weights and measures, though better known to posterity as a philosopher . . . testified that the 'office of weights and measures at present is a very slight affair, I am sorry to say' " (Dupree 1957, pp. 271–272). An act of Congress in 1901 created the National Bureau of Standards and gave it responsibility for the custody, preparation, and testing of standards and authorized it to conduct research on problems related to standards, the determination of physical constants and the properties of materials (Dupree 1957, p. 273). (Almost coincidentally, the conduct of the decennial census—the other kind of measurement specifically provided for in the Constitution—was put in charge of a permanent bureau in 1902, "by implication establishing the social sciences as well" [Dupree 1957, p. 279]). In a later discussion I take brief note of the subsequent growth of a national system of scientific measurement.

The most dramatic episode in the documented history of measurement is the instituting of the metric system. The background is "the almost unimaginable confusion in the weights and measures used throughout the world before the French revolution. . . . Inconsistencies were more startling in France than elsewhere" (Langevin, pp. 77–78). According to Langevin, the "chaotic state of mensuration" in France was a consequence of the dissolution of the Roman Empire. Under feudalism, each lord insisted on following his own practices. The hypothesis had been suggested by Bodin (p. 177) at the end of the sixteenth century:

> Now if the power of coining money be one of the rights and marks of Sovereignty; then so is also the power to appoint measures and weights; although that by the customs received there is none so petty a lord, which pretendeth not to have this right. Whereby it cometh to pass, that by the infinite variety of weights and measures, the Commonwealth taketh no small harm.

The French monarchs, despite repeated efforts from the thirteenth century on, were never successful in enforcing standards, apart from those pertaining to the minting of coins. As late as 1778, Jacques Necker reported to Louis XVI:

> I have occupied myself in examining the means which might be employed to render the weights and measures uniform throughout the kingdom, but I doubt yet whether the unity which would result would be proportionate to the difficulties of all kinds which this operation would entail on account of the changing of values which would necessarily be made in a multitude of contracts, of yearly payments, of feudal rights and other acts of all kinds (Quoted by Hallock and Wade, p. 45).

In the decades preceding Necker's report there had been increasingly frequent proposals by scientists concerning the rationale and standards for a new system of measures. The Abbé Gabriel Mouton in 1670 became the first to advocate the principle of decimal divisions; he proposed a "natural" unit of length based on a measured fraction of the length of an arc of meridian (Langevin, p. 85; Moreau, p. 4). Contemporaneously, Christopher Wren put to the Royal Society in London the idea echoed in Jefferson's report, that the unit should refer to the length of a pendulum that swings once in half a second. Evidently, such suggestions gained attention, for in his *The Spirit of the Laws* of 1748 Montesquieu commented sarcastically (pp. 169–170), "There are certain ideas of uniformity, which . . . make an impression on little

souls," mentioning as items in point—in addition to "the same laws
. . . the same religion"—"the same authorized weights, the same
measures in trade." Anticipating a theme of the metric controversy in
such countries as England, the United States, and India, he asked, "Is
the evil of changing constantly less than that of suffering? And does
not a greatness of genius consist rather in distinguishing between those
cases in which uniformity is requisite, and those in which there is a
necessity for differences?"

Metrological reform was on the agenda of the French Revolution
from its beginning in the summoning of the Estates General and the
drafting of the *Cahiers* (1789), or lists of grievances, among which was
a demand in the *Cahier* of the Third Estate of Dourdan "That, within
a given time, weights and measures be rendered uniform throughout
the entire kingdom" (Stewart, p. 83). The Constituent Assembly in
1790 adopted Talleyrand's plan for abolition of the customary units of
length and weight, the *toise* and the *livre*, in favor of a "perfect" system
"based on a constant model, found in nature" (Langevin, p. 86). The
issue was thereby turned over to the scientists and collaboration with
England was sought. But international participation was not forthcoming immediately, despite the fact that parallel proposals were under
consideration in both England and the U.S. (Moreau, p. 5). It is
interesting that the commission of five scientists appointed by the
French Academy included two, Borda and Condorcet, whom we have
already encountered as pioneers of social measurement. Laplace was
also involved in the early work.

The idea of a decimal scale was quickly approved and in 1791 the
metre—defined as one ten-millionth of a quarter of the earth's meridian—was adopted as the fundamental unit in the new system. Financial support was provided for implementation. Further support was
authorized in 1792—at about the same time a decree made the recording of vital statistics a responsibility of the state (Stewart, pp. 322–
333)—and the geodetic survey required to determine the precise
length of the new unit was begun, despite internal disorders and external military threat. In 1793, the National Convention (successor to the
Legislative Assembly, which had superseded the National Constituent
Assembly) "convinced that uniformity of weights and measures is one
of the greatest benefits that it can offer to all French citizens," issued a
decree incorporating a new table defining the units (including a new

monetary unit, the franc), providing for dissemination of standard models and their use in constructing instruments in all municipalities, and prescribing that instructions on the new measures be given in elementary schools (Stewart, pp. 503–506). I omit details of the difficulties, both technical and political (see Langevin, pp. 88–91), that slowed the prescribed changes. In 1795 the National Convention extended the time for general adoption, but formally established the nomenclature of the *"republican* measures" and provided for the continuation of the geodesic work. By 1798 that work, carried out under most adverse conditions, seemed to be nearing completion and Talleyrand, as Minister of Foreign Affairs, called together a group of delegates from some nine countries to assist in putting the new system into its final scientific form. Crosland (1969a) indicates that this congress was the first truly international scientific conference on any subject. In addition to bestowing scientific legitimacy on the metric system, the conference delegates accomplished significant scientific work. For example, in regard to the determination of the unit of weight, they made the discovery that water has its maximum density at 4° C (reported by Thomas Bugge, as quoted in Crosland 1969b). Shortly after the conclusion of this conference in 1799 two proclamations of the Directory (successor to the Convention) "rounded out the work of the revolutionaries" (Stewart, p. 754) by inaugurating a new system of measures of volume and stating the final determination of the length of the metre. The December 1799 law included provision for a medal "to commemorate the date at which the metric system was brought to perfection," inscribed *"to all time, to all peoples"* (Stewart, p. 758).

Unfortunately, no system of human contrivance is "perfect." Subsequent scientific work has vitiated the presumption that the metric units enjoy a privileged relationship to nature:

It should be noted that the International Meter, like the Mètre des Archives from which it was copied, is about 0.2 mm. shorter than the ten-millionth part of the quadrant of the earth's meridian, original definition of the meter. The same is true of the International Kilogram, which exceeds by 0.028 g. the mass of the decimeter cube of pure water, taken at its maximum density, original definition of the kilogram. . . . [To] maintain rigorously the original definitions of the meter and the kilogram . . . would have led to new values for the standards each time the quadrant of the earth's meridian or the mass of the cubic decimeter of water is redetermined (Moreau, p. 13).

But we should note the serendipitous outcome of the attempt to devise a "natural unit":

It is to this idea that we owe the quest for ever greater precision in measures and, consequently, the very progress which has led to the discovery of its illusory character. It was because the scientists wanted an accurate measurement of what they then thought to be constant that instruments for measuring were improved and a body of skilled scientific constructors grew up in France after the Revolution. It was because temperature had to be taken into account in taking measurements, and also in determining the kilogram, that much valuable work was done on dilatation and thermometry. It was because the establishment of the unit of weight required accurate weighing that the balance was perfected. And it was because of the desire for perfection that informed the establishment of these units—which, it was hoped, would be universally adopted—that the need for precision in measurements penetrated into physics and chemistry (Langevin, p. 94).

Even more portentous, perhaps, is the fact that this metrological reform "affords the first example of scientific rationalization by society itself" (Langevin, p. 95), one enthusiastically approved by that great rationalizer and author of the neologism "sociology," Auguste Comte.

Unfortunately, neither Comte nor Herbert Spencer—Comte's near contemporary and the first British exponent of "sociology"—though he was equally emphatic in his opposition to the metric system, really helps us much in understanding the process by which the system has diffused. Writing in 1896, Spencer quoted an unnamed French correspondent as saying that the old measures had not passed out of use (although they had become illegal in 1840). Spencer argued that if the new system were "in all respects better" it would have entirely displaced the old. He observed, to the same effect, that, despite the U.S. commitment to the decimal system of coinage, prices on the New York Stock Exchange are still quoted, not in dollars, tenths, and cents, but in dollars, halves, quarters, and eighths. The argument is pursued to a consideration of the advantages of duodecimal over decimal notation, a theme that recurs in discussions by Toynbee (1957, pp. 59–60) and Boulding.

But between the French Revolution and Spencer's pamphlet there is a century eventful both scientifically (Moreau) and socially (Cox 1959a,b; Treat) for the evolution and acceptance of the metric system. A brief but poignant account of its vicissitudes in France during the first four decades of the nineteenth century is given by Moreau (p. 8), who mentions organized "resistance" and "disturbances." The period during which "the former anarchy" threatened "once more to reign" was brought to an end by the 1837 law forbidding "under the pain of severe penalties" the use of weights and measures other than metric after 1 January 1840. Curiously, the scientist who could record that "Despite the ease with which it is used, this system was not adopted immediately throughout the whole of France; its introduction was slow and difficult," took note of no difficulties in its diffusion outside of France: "Becoming gradually known and appreciated in foreign countries, the metric system made rapid progress in the world, thanks to its simplicity and its logical and rational conception" (Moreau, p. 8). The historian Cox has given us both an account of this rapid progress during the "quarter century of acceptance," 1851–1876, and some little-known details of the organized opposition to the system in the United States in the immediately subsequent period. He attributes the slow progress of metrication in Britain and the United States to their having achieved considerable uniformity within the framework of the customary units, whereas the nations of continental Europe found it advantageous, upon undergoing economic development and acceleration of international trade, to respond positively to the French attempt to disseminate their "logical and rational conception" to "all peoples."

Such an optimistic appraisal seems a little odd coming from a historian, although it is perhaps not surprising that an eminent electrical engineer, inventing his own naive method for investigating a "wonderful sociological phenomenon," should have found that "Vestiges of preexisting systems . . . are relatively rare in France and Germany" (Kennelly, 1928, pp. viii, 177). Eugen Weber, in his study of modernization in rural France, showed that "the king's foot" (Ch. 3) was by no means easy for the state's officialdom to overthrow. An official agricultural survey of 1866–67, for example, emphasized the need for renewed efforts to enforce the use of the legal measures. French peasants were similarly "backward" in relinquishing their earlier currencies. (In some areas Roman coins continued in use beyond the middle of the nineteenth century.) But the significant contribution of Weber to our topic is to embed the reform of weights, measures, and money in the broader processes of acculturation, civilization, urbanization, and nation building, with concomitant "disintegration of local cultures by modernity" (p. 486).

A most interesting chapter in the "metric controversy" in this country is recorded in the five volumes of the *Proceedings of the American Metrological Society* that cover its most active years, 1873–1885. The society was founded by F.A.P. Barnard, who was president of Columbia College (now Columbia University) from 1864 to 1889 and founder of the college for women that was given his name. A scholar of great energy and broad interests, he assembled a "number of gentlemen" who in December 1873 formed an association "to improve the system of Weights, Measures and Moneys, at present existing among men, and to bring the same, as far as practicable, into relations of simple commensurability with each other." The society's activities included consideration of scholarly papers—a number of them by Barnard himself—presentation of memorials to Congress, communications with government officials, correspondence with such groups as architects, engineers, and railway officials, and, on a limited scale, dissemination of educational materials. Although the society's endorsement of the metric system was a foregone conclusion, it looked forward only to the "gradual adoption" of that system and the enactment of laws to make its use "practical as well as legal" in certain specified contexts—foreign trade, the postal system, federal public works, coinage, and government statistics. In one recorded discussion (*Proceedings*, II:12, December 1878) Dr. Barnard stated that "the Metric System would not be likely to come into general use during our lifetime."

While carrying on its work on behalf of the metric system the society took up a number of other issues, most prominently the movement to establish a system of standard time reckoning and a set of standard meridians. The society had the satisfaction of hearing in December 1883 a report on "the recent adoption of Standard Time" and of including in its *Proceedings* (IV:25–50) a "History of the Movement by Which the Adoption of Standard Time was Consummated." A year later there was a report on the International Meridian Conference in Washington, where delegates from 26 nations resolved in favor of a single prime meridian for all nations.

Another major interest of the society was in advocating a system of international coinage and combatting bimetallism. It received periodic reports on the prices of U.S. government securities, prepared by E. B. Elliott, government actuary, and was favored with a substantial paper (II:65–84) by Dr. Barnard on "The Possibility of an Invariable Standard of Value." After reviewing evidence and mentioning causes of fluctuations in the value of money, the author arrived at a proposal for what would today be called "indexing"—the more or less continuous recomputation of the dollar values of obligations in accordance with fluctuations in the dollar's purchasing power. The measurement of those fluctuations was to be entrusted to a "permanent government commission," following a suggestion of Simon Newcomb (famed both as an astronomer and an economist). Other topics briefly noticed in the society's deliberations that bear directly upon social measurement included the census (V:49) and vital statistics; in 1880 it called for "establishment of a common, uniform and efficient system for the registration of the births, deaths, and marriages of the population" (II:138; see also III:31), a recommendation not wholly out of date a century later.

At various times the society entertained proposals concerning the replacement of the 12–hour with the 24–hour system of clock time, revision of postage rates, standards for measurements by gauge, the decimal division of angles, thermometric scales, and the use of mean sea level as a uniform base for calculating elevations. It heard reports on the bolometer (an instrument for measuring radiant energy) and a contrivance for ascertaining the date of Easter, and it published tables showing variation between states in the legal weight equivalents of the bushel of various agricultural and industrial commodities. Although I find no mention of library science in the society's *Proceedings*, it is perhaps of interest that one of its members active on the educational front was Melvil Dewey, librarian of Columbia College, who later became famous for his Dewey Decimal System of classification.

By and large, the society took little official notice of anti-metric activities (concerning which see Treat; Cox; Verman and Kaul). But a lengthy paper by Dr. Barnard, "The Metrology of the Great Pyramid" (IV:117–219), was concerned to rebut the claim of the eccentric chief engineer of the Atlantic and Great Western Railway, Charles Latimer, that the God-given customary units of the "Anglo-Saxon" system were incorporated in and certified by various dimensions and ratios of the Great Pyramid of Gizeh.

Now, all this—not just the more bizarre facets of the metric controversy, but the obligate symbiosis of sovereignty and mensuration, the bureaucratization of science consequent upon its opting for measurement standardization, the resilience of custom, the role of social upheaval in cracking custom's cake—would seem to be grist for the mill of a sociology of measurement. The closest approximation to what I have in mind is Toynbee's essay (1957, pp. 54–64) on calendars, weights and measures, and money as "imperial institutions" whose "historic mission" goes beyond "the services afforded to their beneficiaries" (p. 21). As for academic sociology, it may be that our sporadic interest in the measurement of time and the temporal framework of social organization will prove to be the entering wedge for a sociological metrology. A brilliant anticipation of the possibilities was Sorokin and Merton's "Social Time" (1937). Their heuristic premise, amply bolstered by historical and ethnographic examples, is "All time systems may be reduced to the need of providing means for synchronizing and coordinating the activities and observations of the constituents of groups" (p. 627). From this point of view, "astronomical time" itself "is a social emergent" or invention resting not less on the process of social differentiation (which gives rise to the need for coordination of activities) than on the progress of astronomical observation and mensuration. Zerubavel exploits this point of view in his 1982(a) essay explaining the evolution of the modern international system of standard time zones in terms of the exigencies of regularly scheduled mail coach and, later, railway passenger service. The other side of the coin is suggested by the prolonged inability of the Chinese to appreciate European clocks as anything more than "intricate oddities, designed for the pleasure of the senses," which could "fulfill no basic needs" (Cipolla, p. 89, quoting a late eighteenth-century Chinese text).

The hypothesis of social determination of measurement practice, in its general form, can be traced back at least to Proclus (A.D. 410–485), who took from Herodotus (484?–425? B.C.) the supposition that the ancient Egyptians invented geometry in trying to deal with consequences of the annual flood of the Nile which destroyed property boundaries, requiring plots of land to be resurveyed annually for tax purposes. "Nor is there anything surprising," Proclus thought, "in that the discovery both of this and of the other sciences should have its origin in a practical need, since everything which is in process of becoming progresses from the imperfect to the perfect. . . . Just as exact knowledge of numbers received its origin among the Phoenicians by reason of trade and contracts, even so geometry was discovered among the Egyptians for the aforesaid reason" (Thomas, p. 147).

But if practical, socially defined needs are to be invoked as an explanation for the invention or standardization of measures, we should recognize circumstances that are compatible with inconsistent measurement practices as well as those that seem to favor standardization. Maitland (1907, p. 369) had observed, with respect to problems of interpreting data of the *Domesday* survey (ordered by William the Conqueror toward the end of the eleventh century), "A general persuasion that land-measurements ought to be fixed by law and by reference to some one carefully preserved standard is much more modern than most people think." Grierson (p. 25) elaborates with respect to itinerary measures:

. . . In the middle ages, just as the term "pound" was applied to a number of weights differing from each other in size and structure, so the term "mile" was used for distances of varying lengths. Since nothing was bought or sold by a measure of such dimensions, there was little incentive to standardize it, and since the rate of travel would depend less on actual distance than on the upkeep of the roads and the nature of the countryside, there was not even much attempt to ascertain with any precision the distance from one place to another. The result was great confusion. The terms mile and league were used interchangeably in the later centuries of the middle ages, and each of them could mean several different things.

There was at least one circumstance in which these measures did become economically important. A rule in force in 1270 led a jury to make very precise measurements, with careful specification of all the units involved, to resolve a dispute over the distance between two markets, since there was supposed to be a distance of at least $6\frac{2}{3}$ leagues —one-third of a day's journey—separating them to protect established rights (Grierson, p. 27).

Here we see the social meaning of distance and its measurement emerging only via the transformation of distance into time and, implicitly, the latter into money. And indeed a major theme in the social history of horology and chronometry is the surprisingly varied and profound consequences of the dawning recognition—followed by importunate insistence—that "time is money" (see, for example, Cipolla or Wright for updating of Mumford's classic observations on the clock as "key-machine" of the industrial era; also Zerubavel 1976, p. 92).

But there are limits to rationalization, even for the French, whose "ecumenical success with their new weights and measures" contrasts with their utter defeat in their "attempt to supersede a pagan Roman calendar which had been consecrated by the Christian Church" (Toynbee 1957, pp. 59, 57). Toynbee errs in stating that the revolutionists did not decimalize the clock. The law of 1793 provided for decimal subdivisions of the mean solar day, but in 1795 "it was wisely decided to suspend this provision indefinitely," states a *savant*, Danloux-Dumesnils (pp. 64–66), who gives the post hoc explanation: "In fact, the day . . . is really an indication of a particular period in time, rather than a measure of its duration: a decimal subdivision is not necessary, and is therefore never used." Thomas Bugge, a Danish delegate to Talleyrand's conference on the metric system, reported:

According to the new metric system the day is to be divided into ten hours, the hour into a hundred minutes and the minute into a hundred seconds. Two skilled clockmakers, Berthoud and Breguet, and several others have handed a very well drafted document to the Directory on behalf of all the clockmakers in Paris, in which the many difficulties for the clock industry and the impracticability of the new division of time were indicated. The result was that the legislative authority decided to suspend the introduction of the new republican time scale for the present (Crosland 1969b, p. 203).

The same participant observer foresaw the difficulties in store for the Republican calendar—which was established by a series of decrees in 1793 (Stewart, pp. 506–512) only to be abandoned in 1806—as well as the new weights and measures in France. (He also thought there was insufficient reason for the metric system to be adopted in states that had already achieved uniformity in their systems.)

Toynbee's main thesis, supported by a comparative analysis of attempts to establish new "eras," is that "the talisman by which their success or failure has been decided is the presence or absence of a religious sanction" (1957, p. 57). Zerubavel (1977) concurs with respect to the French case that an excess of secularization—actually, a forthright attempt at de-Christianization—failed because of its underestimation of the strength of popular religious sentiments and traditional symbols. ("Happy are the units that have no history!" exclaimed Danloux-Dumesnils [p. 132] in another context.) But Zerubavel stresses the vulnerability of the revolutionists' advocacy of "nationalistic particularism at the expense of a practical and cognitive disruption

of temporal coordination on a global level" (p. 868). Replacement of
the seven-day with the ten-day week, for example, not only disrupted
the rhythm of strongly sanctioned religious observance, but also dras-
tically modified the number of and interval between rest days. And, we
might add, the new calendar and clock solved no practical problems.
(Nor were they intended to do so, but rather they were intended to
solve the political problem of reducing the legitimacy of the competing
ideology.) The urgent reform of the calendar had been accomplished
with the shift from the Julian to the Gregorian calendar in 1582
(though not until 1752 in Britain and colonial America). The "bewil-
deringly variegated tables [of weights and measures] of the Ancien
Régime" (Toynbee 1957, p. 59) were indeed a grievance of the Third
Estate, but there were no *Cahiers de doléances* complaining of difficulties in keeping time. If Louis XVI had been trying ineffectually to
manage a congeries of local and regional railway systems, the French
Revolution would have had an opportunity for notable achievement in
time standardization.

Time measurement not only illustrates how social needs and processes influence the framework and conventions of physical measurement. We can continue the discussion of time to illustrate how social
measurement—pre-scientific or scientific—in turn may employ physical dimensions. Zerubavel (1976, p. 87; also 1982b) identifies timing,
sequence, tempo, and duration as "fundamental temporal features of
social events." Let us examine cursorily some examples of scales used
to specify (1) a chronological *location* on either (a) the linear scale of
calendar time or (b) one of the circular scales (Winfree 1980) employing divisions of the day, week, month, or year; (2) a *sequence* of
events or phases; (3) a *rhythm*, or interval, frequency, or rate of recur-
rence; or (4) a *duration*. (For the physical scientist, "time" as a *dimension* or measurable physical property refers to duration, and frequency
is an aspect of duration that pertains to periodic phenomena [Danloux-
Dumesnils, pp. 56, 68].) In making any of these uses of the "time"
variable our scale may be relatively primitive (nominal or ordinal) or
more sophisticated (interval or ratio, in the terminology to be discussed
in Chapter 4). Calendar and clock, augmented by schedules and records, provide for precision measurement and control in the latter case.
Pending these elaborations of technique, or in lieu of them, people
make do or have made do with categorical representations of time.

Temporal location may be given merely as in the past, present, or future. In Chapman's translation of the *Iliad*, Book I, Homer describes the prophet Calchas: "He knew things present, past, to come." Or, on the circular scale, we may distinguish only forenoon, afternoon, and night, or among the four seasons. Historical sequence is roughly preserved by the association of events with the name of the monarch reigning when they occurred or, with greater precision, the name of the incumbent of an annual magistracy, which Toynbee (1957, p. 56) mentions as the Roman practice. Similarly, personal experiences or events in a biography or life history may be linked to one of the stages in a scheme of the life cycle; from ancient to modern times, many alternative versions of the "ages of man" have been proposed. Rowe (p. 256) states that the Inca had 12 standard age divisions or grades, not of equal or even nearly equal length in terms of solar years, which were regularly checked by the census taker. Durations or intervals may be estimated in "moons." Vico (pp. 89–90) observed that Florentine peasants would say, "We have reaped so many times" instead of giving a duration in years. Zerubavel notes (1979, p. 90) that "hospital staff often measure the passage of time in terms of number of patients, so that patients actually become units of time for them." In an outpatient clinic you may be told that your physician will see three other patients before he gets to you. Zerubavel also remarks that such a scale actually can be used with great accuracy, whereas estimates of waiting time in minutes are subject to large errors.

Replacement of an ordinal by a cardinal scale of temporal duration is nicely illustrated by certain athletic contests. For the ancient Greeks it was sufficient to know who came in first in the footrace. But now the contestants may not really be racing each other: all are racing the clock. Wright (p. 164) mentions that published athletic records date from about the middle of the nineteenth century and international records from about 1880. To be the holder of a record has a more general meaning than to be simply the most recent Olympic "champion." This is but one illustration of the Western evolution of time measurement toward greater abstraction and dissociation from nature and the rhythms of experience (Zerubavel 1981, p. 63).

Speaking of rhythm, I noted earlier the evolution in Western music from an organic to a mechanical method of establishing the musical beat. But we might observe here that the latter may have significance for other than recreational or religious functions. Work songs which help laborers to coordinate their efforts afford one obvious example. Thucydides (V. 70) reported that well-trained Spartans in joining battle "came on slowly and to the music of many flute-players in their ranks. This custom . . . is designed to make them keep in step and move forward steadily without breaking their ranks." Plutarch too, in his *Lycurgus* (xxii), called attention to the Spartan *embaterion*, or marching paean, as making both fear and excessive fury less likely in men keeping in step with its rhythm. Attic vase paintings depicting a jumper accompanied by a flute player suggest that explicit attention to rhythm was part of the jumper's drill.

Exporting Western ideas about census taking to cultures that do not compute age by the passage of years is difficult. Recently there has been interest on the part of statistical agencies in the "historical calendar method" devised by anthropologists to estimate ages indirectly. A chronology of important public events is prepared and respondents are asked which of the events they recall. An evaluation of the rather sophisticated use of this technique in a survey of the Morocco Government Central Statistical Service, 1961–63, by Scott and Sabagh, suggests that with appropriate planning and training of interviewers the method can produce more accurate age estimates than any of the available alternatives. One of the interesting checks on the method mentioned by the analysts involved a question on the number of Ramadans observed: "Ramadan is an annual period of fasting which is observed by all Moslems from the age of puberty. The culture of rural Morocco is strongly religious and it is reasonable to suppose that the first practice of Ramadan can be used to date the occurrence of puberty to within one year in nearly every case. This does not, of course, provide an exact criterion of age, both because the age of puberty varies and because the number of Ramadans so far observed may be misreported." Error from the latter source was presumably reduced by limiting this particular inquiry to males estimated by the interviewer to be between ages 15 and 20.

In ancient literature such as the *History* of Herodotus, historical intervals are commonly stated in terms of the number of generations; there may be no attempt, or at best a casual one, to convert them to years. Herodotus (Book 2) was told by the Egyptian priests that there were 341 generations from the first king of Egypt to Sethos (no Egyptian king by this name is known to modern scholars); Herodotus figured three generations per century and rounded the result to compute a total of 11,340 years. In Homer's time, genealogies tracing back to an ancient god might be only one to three generations long. Herodotus mentions that Hecataeus, another Greek historian who had visited Egypt earlier, was ridiculed by the Egyptian priests when he gave them his genealogy traced back to a god in the sixteenth generation. Although in this case Herodotus takes a generation to be equivalent to one-third of a century of calendar time, elsewhere his statements about lengths of time intervals imply that he was using a convention associated with the king-list of Sparta that would make a generation 39 or 40 years. Quite different explanations of the discrepancy are offered by Evans (p. 147) and Den Boer, but the topic of chronology in ancient historiography is much too technical to get into here. Whereas Herodotus left us no methodological reflections on that topic, Thucydides explicitly faced up to the difficulty of working with inconsistent calendars and came up with the ingenious solution that I will refer to in Chapter 4.

A well-known instance of calculation by generations is in the New Testament: "So all the generations from Abraham to David are four teen generations; and from David until the carrying away into Babylon are fourteen generations; and from the carrying away into Babylon unto Christ are fourteen generations" (Matthew 1:17). The Evangelist seems to have sometimes counted the number of men listed in his genealogy (Matthew 1:2–16), and sometimes the number of generations separating them. Only 41 persons, not $3 \times 14 = 42$, are mentioned in the text. The first is Abraham, who "begat" Isaac, who "begat" Jacob, and so on. David is the 14th man named (hence is separated by 13 generations from Abraham) and Jechonias, who was born "about the time they were carried away to Babylon," is the 28th. Joseph, husband of Mary, is listed in the 40th place, immediately preceding Jesus. However, since Mary was "with child of the Holy Ghost" and not of Joseph, the sequence of "begats" does not actually constitute a genealogy of Jesus (though it might have passed for such in the Roman census that registered the Holy Family) but only a quantification of the time elapsed since Abraham. A rather different measurement of the same kind is given in Luke 3:23–38, where the genealogy linking David to Abraham is the same as in Matthew; it is extended backward by an additional 21 generations, leading from Abraham ultimately to "Seth, which was the son of Adam, which was the son of God." Joseph, husband of Mary, and David are 41 generations apart rather than the 26 implied by Matthew's genealogy.

Contemporary research methodology concerning what are called "time-dependent questions" in Schuessler's valuable review article (1980) does, of course, make some use of "exact" calendar and clock time, as in time-series analysis and growth models. But for many purposes time is "discretized" or even dichotomized, as in the "before and after" comparisons of experiment designs or panel surveys (where the same respondents are interviewed on two or more distinct occasions). In some schemes of cohort analysis, a set of birth-year intervals may be treated as a strictly qualitative variable. And even when we record date of birth in census or other surveys, our analysis of the correlates of age is likely to be carried out with that variable represented by a set of age intervals unevenly spaced. The "generation," a notoriously variable unit of duration, is still featured in studies of occupational mobility and related phenomena, many students of which are still unwilling to face up to the conundrums thus generated that I pointed out (Duncan 1966).

Considerable conceptual precision in the measurement of durations is sought in some of the studies of time "budgets" and other investigations of the "allocation" or "expenditure" of time or of time as a "cost." About three dozen major studies and conceptual formulations are reviewed by Burch and Burch-Minakan. A strong programmatic statement on behalf of temporal quantification has been offered by Jaques, who advocates the measurement of tasks in employment work by the length of time targeted and the actual time taken for their completion. He goes so far as to suggest that "the fundamental extensive measurement of time of duration of socially established goal-directed episodes may give the same kind of starting point for measurement of objective properties in the human sciences as the fundamental extensive measurement of length and mass give to the natural sciences" (p. 173). The idea was anticipated by Herodotus who, in Book 7, reported that Xerxes spent four years mustering his troops and storing provisions for his invasion of Europe and that the invasion began with the crossing of the Hellespont, continuing for seven days and nights without interruption. In Book 2, Herodotus tells us that it took ten years of the slave labor of a hundred thousand men just to construct the causeway for hauling the stone used to erect the pyramid of Cheops (of subsequent metrological notoriety); the pyramid itself took twenty years, he said. Also to the point of Jaques's suggestion is Aristotle's description (*Constitution of Athens*, Ch. 67) of the Athenians' use of the water-clock to regulate the length of pleadings in civil litigation. In a case involving more than 5,000 drachmas, ten "gallons" were allowed for the first speech and three "gallons" for the second speech on each side. For cases relating to values of 1,000 to 5,000 drachmas, the first speech was allowed to consume seven "gallons" and the second speech two. The corresponding allocations were five and two "gallons" for cases involving less than 1,000 drachmas.

Several distinct ways in which time enters into the formulation of causal relations in social theories are discussed by Stinchcombe, who contends that clarification of the role of time in a theoretical domain is a prerequisite to effective attempts to measure concepts in that domain. The argument is too complex to summarize here, but as a minimal indication of Stinchcombe's agenda, I quote part of his "plan of the paper" (pp. 3–4):

I will treat ordinary concepts of causality (where time enters as an ordinal), concepts of an event (where time enters as a boundary which creates causal unities), concepts of rates of change (where time enters as a differential), concepts of cumulation and equilibrium (where time enters as the span of an integral), and concepts of a context or "spirit of the times" (where time enters as a summarizer of non-domain variables and concepts).

I take it that the idea of *Zeitgeist* can be carried over to the case of cohort analysis, where we entertain the hypothesis that the later behavior of members of a cohort is partially explained by the "spirit of the times" in which they were born or grew up; that is, their "time" is a summary indicator of a complex of causal influences that cannot retrospectively be disentangled, as a rule.

All measurement, we see, is social measurement. Physical measures are made for social purposes and physical dimensions may be used by social as well as biological and social scientists. But social measurement in a narrower sense deals with phenomena that are beyond the ken of physics. To extend historical metrology to include social measurement, therefore, will require some modification of thought patterns. For one thing, we shall have to overcome our tendency to think of social measurement or quantification as something external to the social system in the sense, say, that the tailor's tape measure is external to the customer's waist. On the contrary, I argue, the quantification is implicit—sometimes explicit, for an observer not blinded by methodological preconceptions—in the social process itself before any social scientist intrudes. That is the main lesson from the review, begun in the first chapter and continued in the following one, of some major innovations in social measurement.

REFERENCES

Adams, John Quincy. *Report of the Secretary of State upon Weights and Measures.* 1821. Reprint, New York: Arno Press, 1980.

American Metrological Society. *Proceedings*, Vols. 1–5, 1873–1885.

Aristotle. *See* Ross (1921).

Berriman, A. E. *Historical Metrology.* London: J. M. Dent & Sons, 1953.

Bodin, Jean. *The Six Bookes of a Commonweale.* Trans. by Richard Knolles. London: G. Bishop, 1606. Reprint, Cambridge: Harvard University Press, 1962.

Boulding, Kenneth. "Numbers Count." *Sciences* (New York Academy of Sciences) 19 (October 1979): 6–19.

Boyd, Julian P., ed. *The Papers of Thomas Jefferson*, Vol. 16. Princeton: Princeton University Press, 1961.

Bridgman, P. W. *The Logic of Modern Physics.* New York: Macmillan, 1928. Ch. 1 reprinted in Feigl and Brodbeck (1953).

Burch, William R., Jr., and Laurel Burch-Minakan. "Time-Budget Studies and Forecasting the Social Consequences of Energy Policies—A Summary and Selected Annotations." *Social Science Energy Review* 2 (Winter 1979): 1–63.

Cipolla, Carlo M. *Clocks and Culture 1300–1700.* New York: Walker & Co., 1967.

Cox, Edward Franklin. "The Metric System: A Quarter-Century of Acceptance (1851–1876)." *Osiris* 13 (1959): 358–379. (a)

Cox, Edward F. "The International Institute: First Organized Opposition to the Metric System." *Ohio Historical Quarterly* 68 (January 1959): 54–83. (b)

Crosland, Maurice. "The Congress on Definitive Metric Standards, 1798–1799: The First International Scientific Conference?" *Isis* 60 (1969): 226–231. (a)

Crosland, Maurice P., ed. *Science in France in the Revolutionary Era, Described by Thomas Bugge.* Cambridge: M.I.T. Press, 1969. (b)

Danloux-Dumesnils, Maurice. *The Metric System: A Critical Study of Its Principles and Practice.* London: Athlone Press, 1969.

Den Boer, W. "Political Propaganda in Greek Chronology." *Historia* 5 (1956): 162–177. Reprint, in H. W. Pleket, H. S. Versnel, and M. A. Wes, eds. ΣΥΓΓΡΑΜΜΑΤΑ: Studies in Graeco-Roman History, pp. 80–95. Leiden, Netherlands: E. J. Brill, 1979.

Duncan, Otis Dudley. "Methodological Issues in the Analysis of Social Mobility." In *Social Structure and Mobility in Economic Development*, edited by Neil J. Smelser and Seymour Martin Lipset: 51–97. Chicago: Aldine, 1966.

Dupree, A. Hunter. *Science in the Federal Government.* Cambridge: Harvard University Press, 1957.

Dupree, Hunter. "The Pace of Measurement from Rome to America." *Smithsonian Journal of History* 3 (Fall 1968): 19–40.

Dupree, A. Hunter. "The English System for Measuring Fields." *Agricultural History* 45 (April 1971): 121–129.

Dupree, A. Hunter. "John Quincy Adams and the Uniformity of Weights and Measures in the United States." Unpublished ms., 1977. (A version of this article serves as the introduction to the 1980 reprint of Adams's 1821 report.)

Dupree, A. Hunter. "The Social History of Measurement." Unpublished ms., 1979.

Dupree, A. Hunter. "The Significance of the Plan of St. Gall to the History of Measurement." Appendix 3 in *The Plan of St. Gall*, vol. 3, by Walter Horn and Ernest Born. Berkeley: University of California Press, 1979.

Evans, J.A.S. *Herodotus*. Boston: Twayne, 1982.

Feigl, Herbert, and May Brodbeck, eds. *Readings in the Philosophy of Science*. New York: Appleton-Century-Crofts, 1953.

Grierson, Philip. *English Linear Measures: An Essay in Origins*. The Stenton Lecture 1971. Reading, England: University of Reading, 1972.

Hallock, William, and Herbert T. Wade. *Outlines of the Evolution of Weights and Measures and the Metric System*. New York: Macmillan, 1906.

Hellman, C. Doris. "Jefferson's Efforts towards the Decimalization of United States Weights and Measures." *Isis* 16 (1931): 246–314.

Herodotus. *The Histories*. Trans. by Aubrey de Sélincourt. Rev. ed. Harmondsworth: Penguin Books, 1972.

Horn, Walter, and Ernest Born. *The Plan of St. Gall*, 3 vols. Berkeley: University of California Press, 1979.

Jaques, Elliott. *The Form of Time*. New York: Crane Russak, 1982.

Kennelly, Arthur E. *Vestiges of Pre-Metric Weights and Measures*. New York: Macmillan, 1928.

Klein, H. Arthur. *The World of Measurements*. New York: Simon & Schuster, 1974.

Langevin, Luce. "The Introduction of the Metric System." *Impact of Science on Society* 11 (August 1961): 77–95.

Lindley, Mark, and Klaus Wachsmann. "Pitch Standards Versus Chaos." In *The New Grove Dictionary of Music and Musicians*, edited by Stanley Sadie. 14: 779–781. London: Macmillan, 1980.

Maitland, Frederic William. *Domesday Book and Beyond*. Cambridge: Cambridge University Press, 1907.

Montesquieu, Baron de [Charles Secondat]. *The Spirit of the Laws*. Trans. by Thomas Nugent. New York: Hafner, 1949.

Moreau, Henri. "The Genesis of the Metric System and the Work of the International Bureau of Weights and Measures." *Journal of Chemical Education* 30 (January 1953): 3–20.

Mumford, Lewis. *Technics and Civilization*. New York: Harcourt Brace, 1934.

Neugebauer, O. "Ancient Mathematics and Astronomy." *See* Ch. 31 in Singer, Holmyard, and Hall (1954).

Ross, W. D., ed. *The Works of Aristotle*, Vol. 10. Oxford: Clarendon Press, 1921.

Rowe, John Howland. "Inca Culture at the Time of the Spanish Conquest." In *Handbook of South American Indians*, Vol. 2, edited by Julian H. Steward: 183–330. Bureau of American Ethnology Bulletin 143. Washington, D.C.: GPO, 1946.

Schuessler, Karl F. "Quantitative Methodology in Sociology: The Last 25 Years." *American Behavioral Scientist* 23 (July–August 1980): 835–860.

Scott, Christopher, and Georges Sabagh. "The Historical Calendar as a Method of Estimating Age: The Experience of the Moroccan Multi-Purpose Sample Survey of 1961–63." *Population Studies* 24 (March 1970): 93–109.

Singer, Charles, E. J. Holmyard, and A. R. Hall. *A History of Technology*, Vol. 1. New York: Oxford University Press, 1954.

Skinner, F. G. "Measures and Weights." *See* Ch. 30 in Singer, Holmyard, and Hall (1954).

Sorokin, Pitirim A., and Robert K. Merton, "Social Time: A Methodological and Functional Analysis." *American Journal of Sociology* 42 (March 1937): 615–629.

Spencer, Herbert. "Against the Metric System." In *Various Fragments*, pp. 142–170. New York: D. Appleton & Co., 1898.

Stewart, John Hall. *A Documentary Survey of the French Revolution*. New York: Macmillan, 1951.

Stinchcombe, Arthur L. "Theoretical Domains in Measurement," Parts 1 and 2. *Acta Sociologica* 16 (1972–1973): 3–12, 79–97.

Sydenham, P. H. *Measuring Instruments: Tools of Knowledge and Control*. Stevenage, U.K.: Peter Peregrinus, 1979.

Thomas, Ivor. *Selections Illustrating the History of Greek Mathematics*, Vol. 1. Cambridge: Harvard University Press, 1939.

Thucydides. *The Peloponnesian War*. Trans. by Rex Warner, with introduction by M. I. Finley. Rev. ed. Harmondsworth: Penguin Books, 1972.

Toynbee, Arnold J. *A Study of History*, Vol. 7. London: Oxford University Press, 1954.

Toynbee, Arnold J. *A Study of History*, Vols. 7–10 abridged by D. C. Somervell. New York: Oxford University Press, 1957.

Treat, Charles F. *A History of the Metric System Controversy in the United States* (U.S. Metric Study, Interim Report). NBS Spec. Pub. 345-10. Washington, D.C.: GPO, 1971.

Verman, Lal C., and Jainath Kaul, eds. *Metric Change in India*. New Delhi: Indian Standards Institution, 1970.

Vico, Giambattista. *The New Science*. Trans. from 3d Italian ed., 1744, by Thomas Goddard Bergin and Max Harold Fisch. Garden City, N.Y.: Anchor Books, 1961.

Weber, Eugen. *Peasants into Frenchmen*. Stanford: Stanford University Press, 1976.

Weber, Max. *The Rational and Social Foundations of Music*. Carbondale, Ill.: Southern Illinois University Press, 1958.

Winfree, Arthur T. *The Geometry of Biological Time*. New York: Springer-Verlag, 1980.

Wright, Lawrence. *Clockwork Man*. New York: Horizon Press, 1969.

Zerubavel, Eviatar. "Time Tables and Scheduling: On the Social Organization of Time." *Sociological Inquiry* 46 (1976): 87–94.

Zerubavel, Eviatar. "The French Republican Calendar: A Case Study in the Sociology of Time." *American Sociological Review* 42 (December 1977): 868–877.

Zerubavel, Eviatar. *Patterns of Time in Hospital Life*. Chicago: University of Chicago Press, 1979.

Zerubavel, Eviatar. *Hidden Rhythms*. Chicago: University of Chicago Press, 1981.

Zerubavel, Eviatar. "The Standardization of Time: A Sociohistorical Perspective." *American Journal of Sociology* 88 (July 1982): 1–23. (a)

Zerubavel, Eviatar. "Schedules and Social Control." In *Time and Aging*: 129–146. Edited by Ephraim H. Mizruchi, Barry Glassner, and Thomas Pastorello. Bayside, N.Y.: General Hall, 1982. (b)

Zupko, Ronald Edward. *British Weights and Measures: A History from Antiquity to the Seventeenth Century*. Madison: University of Wisconsin Press, 1977.

Zupko, Ronald Edward. *French Weights and Measures before the Revolution*. Bloomington: Indiana University Press, 1978.

3

MORE INVENTIONS

MY MAIN PURPOSE in the following notes is to suggest that social measurement should be brought within the scope of historical metrology, while that discipline learns to take advantage of sociological perspectives. I cannot hope to give even a well-rounded sketch of any part of the inquiry I am recommending, but only to document the existence of materials that could repay careful historical analysis. Nor can I demonstrate any historical thesis; but I do presume to give examples lending plausibility to heuristic principles suggested by some investigators who have opened up my subject. First, "measures" are "a key to the needs of past and present societies" (Dupree 1968, p. 39); second, successful measurement often precedes the formal theory explaining how or why it works, or, as Kendall (1956, p. 30) puts it, "Mathematics never leads thought, but only expresses it"; and, third, it often is true that "at the start of a new science an outsider and dilettante can be a true innovator and far more successful than the professionals" (Oberschall 1965, p. 95).

From classic works on the sociology of invention by Ogburn (1922) and Chapin (1928) we learned that every invention combines some element of novelty with a number of elements already existing in the culture base. The great importance of the latter factor (by comparison with "genius") is suggested by the frequent occurrence of inventions made independently, but nearly simultaneously, by two or more persons having access to the same accumulated store of past inventions

(Ogburn 1922, pp. 90ff.; also Merton; and Hacking, pp. 11–12, with special reference to the invention of probability). So-called fundamental inventions occur from time to time and precipitate modifications and other inventions, which follow rapidly (Ogburn 1922, p. 108). Therefore with adequate historical records it may be possible to isolate developments prerequisite to a given invention—as Chapin (p. 336) illustrated in a figure, "Invention of the Automobile Showing the Integration of Six Known Culture Traits into a New Pattern" and also to identify the "supplemental inventions" which elaborate on a "fundamental invention," as Chapin (pp. 339 and 358) illustrated with modifications of the commission plan of city government invented in Galveston in 1901. Ogburn and Chapin explicitly included "social" and "political" inventions within the scope of this pattern of analysis, and on one occasion Ogburn (1931) applied it to an invention in social measurement, the ammain scale proposed by Sydenstricker and King in 1918 for measuring size of families in terms of consumption requirements, weighting the members of the family, classified by age and sex, in adult male maintenance ("ammain") equivalents. Ogburn traces the antecedents of the scale in prior work on family expenditures and previous attempts to standardize between-family comparisons for variations in family composition and size. Ernst Engel, for example, had in 1883 offered the "quet," in honor of Quetelet, as the unit representing the consumption of an infant, rather than an adult male. Sydenstricker and King's "invention, then, was a step in a process," and criticism of it might roughly suggest what future inventions could be expected.

While both Ogburn and Chapin conceded that the accumulation of inventions—that is, the growth of material and scientific culture, as well as social institutions—was not necessarily continuous, with a smooth temporal pattern, they gave relatively little attention to interruptions of the process or to what might be termed aborted or premature inventions. Such discontinuities, by contrast, have been strongly emphasized in the program of research on the history of empirical sociology stimulated by P. F. Lazarsfeld (1961; also, Zeisel 1933/1971; Oberschall 1965; Lazarsfeld and Oberschall 1965; Lécuyer and Oberschall 1968; Oberschall 1972). My own observations seem consistent with an emphasis on the pulsatory character of attempts at social measurement, which necessitates, among other things, a good deal of

"reinventing the wheel." However, the reader is warned that my presentation—which a reviewer has suggested resembles beads on a
string, but I prefer to liken to nuts in a fruitcake—will exaggerate
apparent discontinuities. The antiquarian flavor results from the fact
that I am interested in the precursors rather than the contemporary
practitioners of social science and in the early versions of inventions
rather than in the latest improvements that brought them into the
forms we know today. The reader will recognize that I do not really
demonstrate that I have identified a unique set of fundamental inventions. Testing of that hypothesis will no doubt result in modifications
of my list.

Measuring the size of the group

In the modern sense of the term, census is a modern invention. The
United States has the longest continuous record of periodic national
enumerations, beginning with 1790. But various kinds of counts were
made—or at least imagined—in antiquity, and some of them are
analogous in certain ways to modern censuses or other counts bearing
upon the size, or changes in size, of social groups or units.

The famous Catalog of Ships in the *Iliad*, Book 2, appears to be in
part a rhetorical device for conveying an impression of the numerousness of the Achaean forces, in view of the vivid simile that
precedes it: ". . . as when flies in swarming myriads haunt/ The
herdsman's stalls in spring-time . . . / . . . in such vast multitudes/
Mustered the long-haired Greeks upon the plain,/ Impatient to destroy
the Trojan race" (Bryant, p. 48). The catalog itself consists of a listing
of the contingents coming from each of the regions of Greece, along
with the names of captains and the count of ships. The list begins with
the Boeotians who came in 50 ships, each carrying 120 fighters. With
one exception, there is no further indication of the actual number of
fighters. The exception is the expedition from Methonê, in seven
ships, with 50 oarsmen in every ship, all expert archers. Altogether,
some 29 contingents are named, 10 of which came in 40 ships apiece.
Most of the other numbers are similarly rounded: both 30 and 50 ships

are cited for three contingents; the numbers 12, 60, and 80 are used twice each; and the remaining counts are 3, 7, 9, 11, 22, 90, 100. The total is 1,186 ships, carrying upwards of 50,000 men, we surmise, although the text provides a total for neither ships nor men. The sum of Homer's numbers is rounded again in references, beginning in antiquity, to a "thousand" ships, as in the question of Marlowe's Dr. Faustus, upon viewing the shade of Helen, "Was this the face that launched a thousand ships?" We note poetic uses of counts to suggest that fascination with numbers and numerousness is one of the enduring themes of our culture, being present in both the Greek and the Hebrew literature on which Western social thought has drawn. But mentioning numbers is no warranty that a count was made, for the numbers may only be a way of making a description compelling. Even when an interest in the count as such may be assumed, it will often be difficult to ascertain, or even to imagine, how it was made. As Thucydides (I:10) said, "It is questionable whether we can have complete confidence in Homer's figures, which, since he was a poet, were probably exaggerated." Or, in Dr. Johnson's words, quoted by Farr, "To count is a modern practice; the ancient method was to guess; and, where numbers are guessed, they are always magnified."

It proves to be difficult to date the successful practice of accurate counting, but in some contexts we may be justified in assuming that substantial inaccuracy would have led to recognizable adverse consequences and therefore to efforts at improvement. We are told by Pareti and co-authors (p. 146) that the surviving Egyptian texts on arithmetic include problems of allocating rations of food to a group of men; figuring how many men would be needed to move an obelisk; or computing the number of bricks required to construct a building. It presumably would not be worthwhile to carry out the arithmetic if the counts were not taken as literally, if perhaps roughly, true.

The history of warfare includes a great many examples of at least three kinds of counts: numbers of troops, vessels, horses, and so on, cited as an indication of the overall size or strength of forces; tables of organization giving numbers of troops associated with the various echelons; and numbers of casualties or prisoners of war. It seems that the ancients sometimes took body counts quite as seriously as the American military statisticians did in Vietnam. Burn (p. 51) mentions records of the thirteenth century B.C. that describe how the Egyptians repelled invading groups, one of them identified by the name K-W-SH: "From a detail of how the Egyptians counted the bodies . . . by bringing in detachable portions thereof, it rather appears that the K-W-SH were circumcised; which is surprising, if they were European Achaioi."

In the *History* of Herodotus, the Persian king Xerxes is depicted as having a strong faith in numbers. His elaborate preparations for the invasion of Greece were seemingly directed toward maximizing the levy of troops from all his subject territories. Over 40 "nations" were represented in his infantry; their respective commanders, named by Herodotus, were responsible for organizing and "numbering" their troops. Someone—whether it was Xerxes, Herodotus himself, or an old soldier-informant pulling the historian's leg—devised an interesting method for getting a count, or approximation thereto:

What the exact number of the troops of each nation was I cannot say with certainty—for it is not mentioned by any one—but the whole land army together was found to amount to one million seven hundred thousand men. The manner in which the numbering took place was the following. A body of ten thousand men was brought to a certain place, and the men were made to stand as close together as possible; after which a circle was drawn around them, and the men were let go: then where the circle had been, a fence was built about the height of a man's middle: and the enclosure was filled continually with fresh troops, till the whole army had in this way been numbered. When the numbering was over, the troops were drawn up according to their several nations (Rawlinson translation, p. 377).

Herodotus also gives the total strength of the cavalry: 80,000, not counting chariots and camels. And the description of Xerxes's fleet, consisting of 1,207 triremes, exclusive of transport vessels, reads like another Catalog of Ships, with a dozen nations participating. (Other descriptions following Homer's pattern are in Herodotus's Book 6, regarding the Ionian forces opposed to Darius; in Book 8, before the engagement between Xerxes's fleet and the Greeks at Artemisium; and again in Book 8, where we have the catalog of the Greek fleet that routed the Persians at Salamis.) In at least two places in Book 7, advisers ineffectually warn Xerxes not to rely solely on the overwhelming superiority of his numbers; he listens incredulously as Demaratus explains that the Spartans will fight, no matter how badly outnumbered.

Among other notable features of Xerxes's army was the elite corps of "Immortals," consisting of 10,000 picked men, all Persians, whose strength was kept constant by immediately filling any vacancy created by death or disease—an anticipation of the demographer's concept of a stationary population.

The climactic calculation of Herodotus's description of the invading army is his estimate, naively stated to six significant digits, of the total size of Xerxes's army as 5,283,320 men, including fighting men, servants, support personnel, and so on, but omitting women and eunuchs "too numerous to count." He has already given dramatic indications of the magnitude of the invasion by depicting this army as drinking a river dry and reporting the estimate of Antipater of Thasos that it cost a Greek town 400 talents of silver to provide a meal for the Persians. Wittfogel (pp. 61–67), while concurring with critics that Herodotus's counts are exaggerated, nevertheless argues that the "hydraulic state" typically could indeed raise large armies, bringing into play, for the solution of logistical problems, the same array of organizational skills the state mobilized for civil communication and construction.

Herodotus gives a few figures on battle losses—in Book 3, where Darius deliberately sacrificed 7,000 lightly armed troops in preliminary engagements before capturing Babylon; in Book 5, where it cost the Persians 2,000 men to defeat the Carians, who lost 10,000; and in Book 6, at the Battle of Marathon, where the Athenians overcame the traditional Greek terror of the Persians, slaughtering some 6,400 while losing only 192 of their own. And much attention is given in Book 7 to the detachment of 300 Spartans at Thermopylae, all of whom—apart from two messengers sent away before the battle—perished. After Thermopylae where Xerxes lost 20,000 men, he ordered all but a thousand of the bodies buried and the burial trenches camouflaged, hoping that his sailors would not learn of the great cost of the Persian victory as they viewed the scene of battle from the sea.

Herodotus was not primarily a student of military science and tactics. It was left for such a writer as Vegetius to draw the conclusion from the Persian defeats "that the destruction of such prodigious armies is owing more to their own numbers than to the bravery of their enemies." The ancient Romans, Vegetius maintained in a disquisition offered to Valentinian II (Emperor A.D. 371–392), preferred discipline to numbers. He carefully described the organization of the Roman legion, consisting of ten cohorts, nine of which were composed of 555 foot and 66 horse each, while the Millarian Cohort at the head had 1105 foot and 132 horse cuirassiers (pp. 40–43), for a total of 6100 foot and 726 horse. Including auxiliaries, an army of 10,000 foot and 2000 horse was considered sufficient in "wars of lesser importance." This force could be doubled, or quadrupled, depending on the magnitude of the enemy's "multitudes" and their preparations, but the "ancients" were confident that excellent discipline would enable small armies to prevail against all enemies. Moreover, they insisted that the number of allies or auxiliaries in an army should not be greater than the number of Roman citizens (pp. 69–70). Vegetius's description is idealized, for his ulterior purpose was to stimulate military reform in his own time. But his editor tells us that his was the "most influential military treatise in the western world from Roman times to the 19th century" (p. 1).

Although most of the counts mentioned by Herodotus pertain to military forces, we get the impression that he would have been glad to cite demographic data had they been available. At one point in Book 4 he mentions his unsuccessful attempt to determine the population of Scythia, frustrated because reports he heard were not consistent. He was told, however, of the enumeration made by King Ariantes, who required every man in Scythia to bring him an arrowhead. Impressed by the vastness of the resulting heap of bronze, Ariantes ordered it melted down and cast into a gigantic bowl as a permanent memorial. (We never learn whether anyone first counted or weighed the arrowheads.) In Egypt, Herodotus was informed that King Amasis had instituted a system requiring each man to declare annually his means of livelihood. If he failed to do so or to show that it was an honest pursuit, he could be put to death. Herodotus indicates that Solon followed the example of Amasis, establishing the same custom at Athens. As with other ancient "census" or registration systems, we cannot know how much, if any, use was made of the counts that such a system might have produced. It is not clear whether the practice mentioned by Herodotus is the same one Breasted refers to:

An elaborate system of registration was in force. Every head of a family was enrolled as soon as he had established an independent household, with all the members belonging to it, including serfs and slaves (Breasted, 1905, p. 165).

Three distinct numberings of the children of Israel are described in the Old Testament, along with some of the attendant circumstances.

The first one came early in the period of the 40-year wandering in the wilderness of the Sinai. As we read in Exodus 30:11–16 and 38:24–31, the purpose seems to have been to levy contributions to support the construction of the tabernacle:

> When thou takest the sum of the children of Israel after their number, then shall they give every man a ransom for his soul unto the Lord, when thou numberest them; that there be no plague among them, when thou numberest them.
> This they shall give, every one that passeth among them that are numbered, half a shekel after the shekel of the sanctuary . . .
> Every one that passeth among them that are numbered, from twenty years old and above, shall give an offering unto the Lord.
> The rich shall not give more, and the poor shall not give less than half a shekel . . .

But in Numbers 1:1–3, the idea was to "take . . . the sum of . . . every male by their polls; From twenty years old and upward, all that are able to go forth to war in Israel: thou [Moses] and Aaron shall number them by their armies."

The counts by tribe, given in Numbers 1:24–46, are incredibly high, with a total of 603,550. Biblical scholars have not provided a completely convincing and consistent hypothesis as to how these counts were obtained. One attractive (but questionable) suggestion is that the term 'elef, conventionally translated "thousand," actually meant something like a "troop" of 5 to 15 soldiers. In that event, the account would imply some 598 "troops" with an aggregate of 5,550 men capable of bearing arms (Noth 1968, p. 20). Various writers indicate that counting of military manpower is known for other parts of the Near East in biblical times.

A second numbering came toward the end of the wandering and was conducted in the same way with much the same result, a total of 601,730 distributed by tribe in proportions differing slightly from those of the earlier count. But this time, anticipating that the children of Israel would overrun the land of Canaan, the Lord provided that the census would be used as a basis for distributing land to the tribes, although the formula is not described (Numbers 26:53–54):

> Unto these the land shall be divided for an inheritance according to the number of names.

To many thou shalt give the more inheritance, and to few thou shalt give the less inheritance: to every one shall his inheritance be given according to those that were numbered of him.

There are allusions to other enumerations of military manpower; see I Samuel 11:8, "And when he numbered them in Bezek, the children of Israel were three hundred thousand, and the men of Judah thirty thousand"; and I Chronicles 12:22–23, "For at that time day by day there came to David to help him, until it was a great host, like the host of God. And these are the numbers of the bands that were ready armed to the war . . . ," after which follows a total for each tribe. See also Judges 20:2; I Samuel 15:4; and II Chronicles 26:12–13; but the occasion and circumstances of these numberings are not detailed.

The third "census" for which such background is given is the one that had a disastrous consequence. According to II Samuel 24:1, "And again the anger of the Lord was kindled against Israel, and he moved David against them to say, Go, number Israel and Judah." But in I Chronicles 21:1, "And Satan stood up against Israel, and provoked David to number Israel." The narratives differ too in regard to the numerical results. II Samuel 24:9 reports "in Israel eight hundred thousand valiant men that drew the sword; and the men of Judah were five hundred thousand men." In I Chronicles 21:5 the totals are given, respectively, as 1,100,000 and 470,000. In both accounts, Joab remonstrates with David the king before carrying out the enumeration he was ordered to do. (According to II Samuel 24:8, the work was done in nine months and twenty days.) In both books, David repents immediately after the deed, but the Lord nevertheless sends a plague on Israel by way of punishment. A commentator refers to ". . . the distrust for the whole idea of a census, expressed in 2 Sam. 24:3, and widespread in the ancient world, though the reasons for this are still not known" (Coggins 1976, p. 108). The distrust has persisted to the present day, when census continues to have an intimate connection with taxation and conscription, as well as revenue sharing. A further reference to this (?) census is in I Chronicles 27:23–24, where the language again indicates that the numbering posed some kind of theological problem.

Other interesting counts or purported counts can be found with the aid of a concordance to the Bible. Jonah 4:11 gives the population of

Nineveh: "that great city, wherein are more than six score thousand persons that cannot discern between their right hand and their left hand." Ezra 2 gives the numbers, by family groups, that returned from captivity in Babylon; this is one of the few passages where we find unrounded frequencies like 2,172; 372; 775; 2,812; 1,254; and so on. (See also Nehemiah 7.) Jeremiah 52:28–30 gives a much sketchier report on the numbers taken into captivity.

One more biblical use for enumerations was in connection with a kind of corvée. When King Solomon set out to build the temple, he "raised a levy out of all Israel; and the levy was thirty thousand men. And he sent them to Lebanon, ten thousand a month by courses: a month they were in Lebanon, and two months at home" (I Kings 5: 13–14). We even have (15–16) a sort of occupational classification of this work force: 70,000 "that bare burdens," 80,000 "hewers in the mountains," and 3,300 "which ruled over the people that wrought in the work." Perhaps these frequencies are obtained by aggregating over several "courses."

Another occupational classification is found in I Chronicles 23: 3–5:

Now the Levites were numbered from the age of thirty years and upward: and their number by their polls, man by man, was thirty and eight thousand.
Of which, twenty and four thousand were to set forward the work of the house of the Lord; and six thousand were officers and judges:
Moreover four thousand were porters; and four thousand praised the Lord with the instruments which I made, said David, to praise therewith.

Our word "census" comes from Latin, and the Roman historian Livy (59 B.C.–A.D. 17) stated that the census was originated by Servius Tullius, king of Rome from 578 to 534 B.C. Livy considered Servius's use of the census to organize Roman society according to classes to be his most notable achievement. (It bears considerable likeness to the more or less contemporaneous provision of Solon's constitution, as described in Plutarch's biography of the Athenian lawgiver and in Aristotle's *Constitution of Athens*.) All Roman citizens were required to show up for registration at daybreak in the Campus Martius; it is said that 80,000 names were registered on the first occasion. Everyone was put into one of five classes based on personal wealth, or into a residual category exempted by poverty from military service. Tax contributions, assignments to various kinds of military duty, and voting rights were determined by the census assessment. However veridical Livy's account of the origin of the Roman census may be, there is no doubt that the institution evolved and experienced vicissitudes during the several centuries of its history, which is conveniently summarized by Wolfe (pp. 359–361). Suetonius records (p. 102) that Caesar Augustus "took the census of the Roman people street by street," without describing the method it replaced. Wolfe thinks that none of the Roman registrations before the first census taken by Augustus in 28 B.C. was a census in the modern sense. Suetonius implies that it was a basis for the distribution of corn to the Roman people. He also credits Augustus with reviving the office of censor, whose duties had included the interesting combination of counting the people, rating the value of their estates, and (later) inspecting their morals (p. 100, translator's note). Farr's remarks (p. 334) provide a sensible perspective on this history:

. . . In Rome . . . a group of the many functions performed by the . . . censor received the name of *census*. An enumeration of the people was only one of them. . . . They were especially directed to fiscal objects; and it does not appear that the enumeration of the people was then deemed of value as a source of statistical knowledge which might influence morals and legislation. . . . Had the enumeration been deemed of value for any such other purposes, besides the adjustment of rights and obligations . . . the notices preserved of the vast collection of statistical facts thus made would have been less scanty and meagre.

But Farr's view is that of a professional statistician notable for his innovations in the nineteenth-century General Register Office of Great Britain. To understand the evolution of the counting of people and vital events, some insight into the problems and purposes of those whose inventions comprise that evolution is needed.

Wittfogel (pp. 50–52) emphasizes that organizational requisites of the hydraulic state included counting and registering people and the preservation of the numerical results. The case of the Inca empire is especially interesting, since the Inca had no method of writing. Yet Rowe insists that they "kept accurate population statistics," although "the census totals are lost because no one committed them to paper after the Spanish Conquest" (pp. 184, 264). The officials called "curacas" were "classified according to the number of taxpayers for whom they were responsible" (Rowe, p. 263). And that classification

. . . was based on an exact head-count constantly corrected by the local officials and recorded in Cuzco for the information of the Imperial Government. It served also as the basis of taxation and service in the army, and must have been a powerful aid to Government efficiency. The system of 12 age grades . . . was used to break down the head-count in such a way that the Government had an exact report on the human resources of any province. The foremen recorded all births, deaths, and changes of age grade within their jurisdiction to their superiors, and the totals were sent up to the Governor of the province, who embodied them in an annual report presented in Cuzco. . . . The numbers were recorded by knots on colored strings, quipus. . . .

A quipu represented a series of numbers which could, perhaps, be read by any trained *Inca* accountant, but, in order that anyone but the original maker might understand what the numbers referred to, the quipu had to be explained. . . . The *Inca* had a special class of professional quipu interpreters . . . whose duty it was to memorize the statistical, historical, and liturgical material accumulated by the government and to be prepared at all times to repeat it for the benefit of officials who desired to refer to it (pp. 264, 326).

Wittfogel has brief descriptions of the evidence for systematic enumerations in China and India, some of great antiquity. His remarks suggest that a variety of methods were used and leave the impression that surviving records are fragmentary and difficult to interpret. Unlike most modern scholars who have examined the pre-modern (say, before 1650) censuses, his interest is in how the census authorities used the results, not in the value they may have today for research in historical demography. We must recognize that a document like the Domesday Book—which resulted from the survey made in England, 1083–86, at the order of William the Conqueror—may be of use to historical demographers even if William himself were interested not in numerical totals and subtotals, but only in having a record of his fiscal rights.

A transitional case seems to be the municipal census of Nuremberg in 1449, which covered its entire population and, according to Willcox, was occasioned by the threat of a siege. The authorities also took an inventory of the available food supply at that time. Wolfe states that this is the first population census for which we have records. But its interest in the present discussion is that it seems to constitute an exception to the generalization of Kendall (1972/1977, p. 36), "In the Middle Ages there were, in general, only two reasons for counting anything relating to human society; one was to find out how many men could bear arms, and the other was to ascertain how much money could be levied by way of tax."

Wolfe calls attention to the work of the German historian K. J. Beloch and various Italian scholars making use of the "remarkable list of population censuses . . . in Renaissance Italy." Beloch surmised that a need for population statistics was felt by the Italians at this time of economic growth and cultural florescence even though the main purpose still of these "descrizioni" was fiscal. I find it suggestive that this development followed what Max Weber (1950, p. 224) called the invention of "genuine bookkeeping . . . in medieval Italy" (as distinct from the merely "documentary" entries of the banking business in ancient Greece and Rome).

A beginning in the use of censuses that interested Farr—"as a source of statistical knowledge which might influence morals and legislation"—can be found in Jean Bodin's *Fourth Book of a Commonwealth*. He warns that an aristocratic state will become unstable if foreigners enter the city freely and are allowed to settle there. For example, Venice had admitted such large numbers that by the time of his writing (c. 1575) "for one Venetian gentleman there are an hundred citizens, as well noble as base descended of strangers; which may well be proved by the number of them which was there taken 20 years ago, or thereabouts" (p. 427). He summarizes the Venetian figures as showing 59,349 citizens above 20 years old, 67,557 women, 2,185 religious men, 2,082 religious women, and 1,157 Jews, for a total of 132,330 persons. Adding "a third part more" for the number under 20, he arrives at the figure of 176,440 citizens. He estimates that there were at most 3,000 or 4,000 nobility or gentlemen "not comprehended" in the foregoing figures.

And truly I cannot but marvel why the Venetians have published, yea and that more is have suffered to be put in print the number that then was taken. The Athenians long ago committed the like error, and when the city was most populous, found that upon the number taken, there were in the city twenty thousand citizens, ten thousand strangers, and four hundred thousand slaves: which open number and account the Romans would not take of their strangers, and so much less of their slaves: whom they would not either by their

countenance or attire have known from the rest of the citizens: Howbeit that
some were of opinion that the slaves ought to be known by their apparel . . . a
thing to be feared, lest the slaves entering into the number of themselves,
should make their masters their slaves, for so Seneca writeth (p. 427).

Bodin introduces several other considerations when he comes to his
systematic justification "Of Censuring or Reformation, and whether it
be expedient to enroll and number the subjects, and to force them to
make a declaration, or give a certificate of their private estates," which
is the title of Chapter 1, *Sixth Book of a Commonwealth*. He asserts
that this topic belongs with a consideration of the common interest,

> . . . which consists in the managing of the treasure, rents, and revenues, in
> taxes, imposts, coins and other charges for the maintenance of a common-
> wealth. . . . [Let] us first treat of Censuring. *Census* in proper terms is nothing
> else but a valuation of every mans goods: and . . . of all the Magistrates of a
> commonwealth, there are not many more necessary: and if the necessity be
> apparent, the profit is far greater, be it either to understand the number and
> qualities of the citizens, or the valuation of every mans goods; or else for the
> well governing and awing of the subject (p. 637).

Bodin wonders why a practice used so freely by the ancients and
esteemed by them should have been "laid aside so carelessly." Noting
the commendation of King Servius by the historians, he observes
(p. 637):

And although the people of Rome had disannulled and abolished all the
edicts and ordinances of their kings, after they had expelled them, yet this law
of censuring or surveying continued still, as the foundation of their treasure,
imposts, and public charges, &c. was continued in the Consuls persons. But
after that the Consuls were distract and drawn away for warlike employments,
they then created Censors.

The further history of the office under the Roman emperors is traced,
and Bodin then notes that modern states like Venice and Geneva have
kept the function under a different name: "at Venice in the year 1566
they made three Magistrates to reform the peoples manners, whom
they called the Magistrates for the well living of the citizens: for that
the name of Censor in a free city abounding with all kind of delights,
seemed harsh and severe" (p. 638). He proceeds to refute the theolo-
gians who think that David was punished by God for commanding that

his people be numbered, arguing that David's offense was forgetting God's commandment that every one who was numbered should also make an offering of two groats of silver. Some of the results of the biblical and Roman censuses are reviewed, along with conjectures as to how the totals may have been affected by variations in coverage, war losses, and the like. Bodin then turns to his exposition of the reasons for "censuring." I quote extensively the Jacobean English of the Knolles translation (pp. 640–642), with the spelling modernized:

The benefits which redounded to the public by this numbering of the people, were infinite: for first they knew the number, age and quality of the persons, and what numbers they could draw forth, either to go to the wars, or to remain at home, either to be sent abroad in colonies, or to be employed in public works of reparations, and fortifications: thereby they shall know what provision of victuals is necessary for every city, and especially in a time of siege, the which is impossible to prevent, if they know not the number of the people. And if there were no other benefit but the knowledge of every mans age, it cuts off a million of suits and quarrels the which are invented touching the minority and majority of persons.

. . . Moreover, to order and govern the bodies and colleges of citizens according to the estate and age of every person, as they did use in Rome and in Greece, it is more than necessary to know the number of the subjects; to gather their voices in elections the number is also requisite; to divide the people into tens, hundreds, and thousands, it is also necessary to know the number of them. But one of the greatest and most necessary fruits that can be gathered by this censuring and numbering of the subjects, is the discovery of every mans estate and faculty, and whereby he gets his living, thereby to expel all drones out of a commonwealth. . . . And as for the valuation of goods, it is no less necessary than the numbering of persons. Cassiodorus speaketh thus, The Roman territories were divided, and every private mans land laid out, that no mans possession should be uncertain, the which he had taken for the payment of a certain rent or tribute. If then a survey were taken of all the Roman empire, and the lands distributed accordingly, that it might be known what every one was to bear in regard of the goods he enjoyed, how much more necessary is it now, when as there be a thousand sorts of imposts in every commonwealth, which the ancients did never know. . . .

By this means you shall know who be miserable, who prodigal, which be bankrupts, who rich, which poor, who cozeners, which usurers, and by what gains some get so much wealth, and others are oppressed with so great want, and how to redress it: for that by the extreme poverty of some, and the exceeding wealth of others, we see so many seditions, trouble, and civil wars arise. Moreover, all edicts and decrees, and generally all judgements and sentences touching fines and amercements, should be ordered, and justice equally administered, when as every mans estate were known, seeing that the punishment may not exceed the offense. Also, all deceits in marriages, in bargains and sales, in all private and public negotiations should be discovered and known.

The chapter continues for another seven pages or so, wherein Bodin reviews the acquisition by the Roman Censor of the censuring of the lives and manners of everyone. On the whole, he approves of the development of this function and takes a good deal of space to deplore a number of "vices" (including "comedies and interludes") that subvert the morality of the commonwealth and that should be subjected to the vigilant scrutiny of such a magistrate.

If the conjunction of "censuring" and "numbering" seems odd today, still we can recognize in Bodin's exposition many functions that, *mutatis mutandis*, are performed by our modern censuses. For the most part, we have gotten away from the idea of a census as a collection of records of individuals that will be used in transactions between the citizen and the state. But not entirely—census documents are still used for proof of age, for example, when a birth certificate does not exist. And we suspect that the tax authorities are willing to countenance the confidentiality of census schedules only because they can readily turn to other kinds of records. Bodin was talking about what a government needs to know to rule effectively and not about the division of labor between units of the bureaucracy in a modern state.

During the last quarter century a remarkable florescence of historical demography not only has enriched our understanding of population dynamics but also has shed much light on the statistical properties of data compiled from archival sources. As instances in point, Tomasson presents an analysis of the statistics produced by "the first modern national census," the "general census of the whole population of Iceland . . . taken in 1703"; Cipolla evaluates the Italian "Bills of Mortality," which go back to 1385 (in Florence) and the reasons for which "varied from genuine demographic interest to preoccupations about adequate provisioning of the city"; and Hajnal analyses data on marital status for the adult population of Zurich in 1357, 1467, and 1637, making use of lists of inhabitants periodically drawn up by the clergy. All this material speaks to the generalization that learning to enumerate is a slow and painful process which is accelerated by the learning of clever and significant uses of the counts. It is hard to say how early in history a connection was established between the uses of counts in normative or positive social theory and the practice of accurate registration and enumeration. Plato was a great believer in the idea of population registration as well as the standardization of physical weights and measures; he had an elaborate numerical—if not numerological—scheme for organizing his ideal *polis*. In Book V of the *Laws* he (or his "Athenian stranger") envisages a community with 5,040 households. Now, 5,040 = 7! and is, therefore, divisible by each of the first ten integers, by 12, and by 48 larger divisors, so that exact partitionings of the group on a variety of scales for different administrative purposes are available. I do not know of any influence that Plato's idea had on subsequent practice of counting, although I suspect there is some continuity with modern ideas about optimum city size. Plato, incidentally, appreciated that it would be difficult to hold a community to its exact optimum size, but recommended that strong efforts be made to do so.

Valuing goods and services

I was tempted to designate this invention simply "money." A more basic idea is that of obligations or debts that can be fulfilled by an act of payment of valuable goods or services, or tokens thereof. Some of the social forms or contexts of valuing (in this sense) include payments for labor or services (wages), gifts, prizes, fines, restitution, alimony, ransom, taxation and tribute, dowry and bridewealth, barter, trade, and, of course, commercialized exchange of the kind we associate with organized markets. All of these occurred historically before there were coins and currency, although the latter inventions surely facilitated the process. Frankfort (1956, pp. 73, 115) notes that the absence of money in ancient Mesopotamia and Egypt helps to explain certain crudities in the temple economy of the former and the tax collection practices of the latter. How wage payments might be effected in this kind of economy is suggested in the report on the Egyptian system given by Herodotus (pp. 83–84 of the Macaulay translation):

The warriors are called Calasirians and Hermotybians . . . and they . . . had
certain advantages in turn and not the same men twice; . . . a thousand of the
Calasirians and a thousand of the Hermotybians acted as bodyguard to the
king during each year; and these had besides their yokes of land an allowance
given them for each day of five pounds weight of bread to each man, and two
pounds of beef, and four half-pints of wine.

The detailed descriptions of gifts in the *Odyssey* and explicit remarks
by Homer's characters leave no doubt that even in a society without
our kind of money a rather fine calculation may underlie the bestowal
of gifts upon persons one is obliged to favor in this way. It would
appear that in ancient Peloponnesus as well as modern Middletown
(not to mention the institutions, *kula* and potlatch, beloved of anthropologists), "Most gifts are scaled to the formal relationship between
giver and receiver" (Caplow, p. 383). In the world of Odysseus, "There
were rather strict lines of giving, and grades and ranks of objects. . . .
the gift and the relationship between giver and recipient were insepar-
able" (Finley, p. 98).

Herodotus in his Book 6 indicates that the customary ransom in
Peloponnesia was two minae (or 200 drachmas). The same figure is
mentioned in Book 5 in connection with Boeotian and Chalcidian
prisoners of war taken by the Athenians. The first historian took much
interest in the schedules of tribute paid by the satrapies to the central
Persian authority and indicates in Book 6 that one of the satraps had
his provincial territory "surveyed and measured in parasangs" to settle
the tax each state should pay, although the method of calculating the
assessment is not given. Still another kind of payment is described in
connection with an "ingenious custom" in Babylonia, the annual
village auction of brides. The auctioneers took the most beautiful girls
first and their price was bid up by the rich men, while the plain or even
misshapen ones went to the poor men at low prices. But the proceeds
from the sale of the beauties were used to create dowries for their less
attractive sisters. (No data are given on the actual prices or method of
payment.)

A fascinating comparison of ancient economies that differed markedly with regard to use of money is given by Polanyi (1960). He depicts
classical Athens as a polis in which a retail marketplace dependent on
currency had developed. The social and political structure was not,
however, conducive to the emergence of a full "market economy,"

nineteenth-century (Adam Smith) style. Mycenaean Greece of the thirteenth century B.C. provides an instance of a palace economy that flourished in "the complete absence of money." The palace accounts, written in Linear B, were kept separately for each of the major staples, wheat or barley, oil, olives, figs, and so on. "One kind of goods can never be equated with, or substituted for, an amount of goods of a different kind" (p. 342). Yet a composite tax could be imposed on a locality by stating ratios, in physical units, of the amounts of the several staples to be paid. It appears that Linear B incorporated a new system of fractional notation that facilitated this kind of "submonetary device." An intermediate case is that of Alalakh, a small North Syrian kingdom, archeological data for which pertain to the eighteenth century B.C. Polanyi suggests that there was a "prestige sphere" within which silver was widely used for payments and provided the established standard of account. But in the subsistence sphere of the common people, grain served as a "potential currency." Palace accounts of deliveries and rations were "in kind," with no schedule of equivalencies for various staples being known.

Measured weights of precious metals were in use as "money" long before coinage proper was invented. Some writers indicate that the practice of putting an identifying design on a piece of metal of standard weight began during the seventh century B.C. in Ionian Greece. Even after coinage was widespread, differences in the systems used by the several city-states led to the use of weighing in preference to reliance on the face values of the coins. Hence, it has been noted, many of the Greek coins that have been preserved have escaped "clipping."

Among the obvious advantages of the metal coin is that it may carry an image of the ruler, reminding the bearer to "Render, therefore, unto Caesar the things which are Caesar's" (Matthew 22:17). But many items other than lumps of metal have served as means of payment and, perhaps, also as a medium of exchange, a standard of value, a store of wealth, a means of expressing debt, or as a unit of account, to mention the uses of monies analyzed by Neale (1976). Incidentally, that author's sharp warning against the fallacy of confusing logical with historical relationships among the functions of money (as in the speculative "history" usually found in the first chapter of a text on money and banking) is one that should be broadened to the whole topic of social measurement. According to Pareti, Brezzi, and Petech (p. 139):

The first extant Greek coins probably go back to the first half of the sixth century B.C. Yet Aristotle's generation of Greeks still thought of coined money as a genuine article of exchange whose value had to be equivalent to that of the goods it bought. Only in later periods (fourth century) shall we find some development of the conception of forced currency and fiduciary money.

But another passage in the same work (p. 403) indicates that after Darius I issued Persian coins as a "world currency," because it was of lesser intrinsic value than the face value fixed by the government, it drove Greek silver coins competing with it out of circulation. It is also stated that Athens resorted to debasing of the currency during the war against Sparta, to pay the army (p. 404). Whatever the actual sequence of these events, it seems likely that "fiduciary money" and "fiat money" are inventions that follow hard on the heels of coinage itself. Complaints about the practice seem to be at least as frequent as grievances relating to false weights and divers measures. Writing at the end of the sixteenth century, Bodin (p. 687) was emphatic:

. . . [There] is nothing that doth more trouble and afflict the poor people, than to falsify the Coins, and to alter the course thereof: for both rich, and poor, every one in particular, and all in general, receive an infinite loss and prejudice, the which cannot precisely in every point be described, it breeds so many inconveniences. The Coin may not be corrupted, no not altered, without great prejudice to the Commonwealth: for if money (which must rule the price of all things) be mutable and uncertain, no man can make a true estate of what he hath, contracts and bargains shall be uncertain, charges, taxes, wages, pensions, rents, interests, and vacations shall be doubtful, fines also and amercements limited by the laws and customs shall be changeable and uncertain: to conclude, the estate of the treasury and of many affairs both public and private shall be in suspense.

This process was described by Montesquieu—in the middle of the eighteenth century as he reviewed several examples of the monetary practices of nations, ancient and recent—as a substitution of "ideal money" for "real money." He was led to exclaim (p. 377), "Nothing ought to be so exempt from variation as that which is the common measure of all," thereby pre-echoing the thought of F.A.P. Barnard, which we noted in the preceding chapter.

For the invention and properties of other "monies"—such as paper currency, bank notes, credit, negotiable instruments, and all the wonderful apparatus of modern banking and finance—reference is made to Neale (1976) and the literature he cites. "Modern money is different," he states (p. 65), in regard to the variety of goods and services that can be bought, purchase of which requires only the participation and agreement of a buyer and seller; and with respect to the way in which money is "created" when demand deposits are accepted by banks. From the standpoint of social measurement, the implication is that in a social system with modern money a great many valuations are more or less automatically measured, whether or not the measurements are recorded. We should also note that developing *pari passu* with money are the accounting systems that make it work, as Max Weber was at pains to point out. Indeed, the modern system may not be far from the situation in which there is little or no "money" at all, in the historical sense of tokens that pass from hand to hand. All the money is "in" the system of accounts, entries in which are made electronically with the permission of plastic cards and secret codes. There will remain, of course, the problem of extracting from the accounts the measurements desired for purposes of social control and scientific analysis.

Defining social rank

The inventions mentioned so far, in their most highly developed form—counting votes, enumerating the population, and valuing goods and services in monetary units—lead to measurement on scales with well-defined, equivalent units. I know of no system of social rank—apart from ones defined solely in terms of economic wealth or income—that could be said to yield measures with such strong properties. Indeed, even the highly contrived indexes of socioeconomic status, occupational prestige, and social class used in contemporary sociology are regarded as having meaningful units largely as a matter of fiat, convenience, or professional courtesy. Nevertheless, I suspect (here is a piece of speculative history) that social rank is one of the oldest kinds of measurement and that society's contentment with ordinal scales of rank (or even rather ambiguous approximations thereto) over the millennia is due to a lack of need for refinement. In situations where rank matters—that is to say, in almost all situations except informal interaction of formally equal persons—it is enough to know who precedes whom, who gives and who receives deference, who gives and who takes orders. Only where rank determines relative shares in a distribution of goods or money do we see a principle of ratio calibration. A bureaucracy will usually have an explicit pay scale corresponding to the grades or levels of the functionaries. Even so, the pay scale may provide for intervals for each rank, oftentimes wide enough to overlap the pay intervals set for adjacent ranks.

The principle of rank, as realized in formal hierarchies and tables of organization, can be traced back to early times for military and ecclesiastical organizations. Vegetius's account of the Roman legion is interesting in that he reported a ranking of the ten cohorts as well as a system of ranks of officers and soldiers within cohorts. Hence:

A soldier, as he advances in rank, proceeds as it were by rotation through the different degrees of the several cohorts in such a manner that one who is promoted passes from the first cohort to the tenth, and returns again regularly through all the others to the first with a continual increase of rank and pay. Thus the centurion of the primiple, after having commanded in the different ranks of every cohort, attains to that great dignity in the first with infinite advantages from his service in the whole legion (pp. 55–56).

Herodotus's observations on military rank are not very specific, but he gives some attention to the nature of the Persian hierarchy in Book 7, and in Book 8 we learn that when Xerxes visited his commanders to secure their advice, they were seated in the order of precedence he had assigned them. In civil life, according to Book 1, Persians meeting in the streets took ritual note of rank: equals kissed upon the mouth; if there was a slight difference of rank, the superior was kissed on the cheek, and a considerably inferior man prostrated himself. Persians ranked their own nation highest and their respect for other nations diminished with their distance from Persia. The Medes incorporated this principle into the governing of the empire, reserving supreme authority for themselves and requiring each subject territory to rule in turn over the next most distant neighboring state.

Among other customs he describes, Herodotus notes (Book 4) that Scythian warriors were esteemed according to the number of enemy scalps they displayed, that among the Gindanes of Libya the women who wore the largest number of leather bands on their ankles—one for each lover taken—enjoyed the greatest reputation, and (Book 5) that among the polygynous Thracians there was competition among wives of a dead husband to decide which of them he loved the most—the reward to the winner being the privilege of burial with him. Herodotus's story of the origin of dual royalty in Sparta (Book 6) includes a methodological lesson in what Webb and co-authors call "unobtrusive measurement." King Aristodemus died shortly after his wife Argeia gave birth to twins. Since she refused to identify the first born, the Spartans took the advice of the Delphic oracle and made both of them king, but were perplexed by the oracle's further advice, which was to give greater honor to the elder. An early behavioral scientist, one Panites from Messenia, advised them to watch Argeia to see which son she washed and fed first, arguing that if the order was consistent it would betray her knowledge, inasmuch as the one preferred would "of course" be the son of higher rank.

At one point in Book 2 Herodotus verges on proposing a society-wide system of rank. The Egyptians, he states, "are divided into seven distinct classes: priests, warriors, cowherds, swineherds, tradesmen, interpreters, and pilots of boats." Warriors and priests were said to have certain exclusive special privileges, and warriors, in particular, were forbidden to take up any craft or trade. A prejudice against trade and handicrafts, Herodotus notes, is found not only among Greeks (though less so in Corinth) but also Thracians, Scythians, Persians, and Lydians, as well as other barbarians.

Martindale (pp. 124–125) quotes a Chinese document of the third century B.C. that is more explicit concerning the principle of rank:

As the days have their divisions in periods of ten each, so men have their ten ranks. It is by these that inferiors serve their superiors, and that superiors perform their duties to the spirits. Therefore the king has the ruler (of each feudal state) as his subject; the rulers have the great prefects as their subjects; the prefects have their officers; the officers have their subalterns; the subalterns have their multitude of petty officers; the petty officers have their assistants; the assistants have their employees; the employees have their menials. For the menials there are helpers, for the horses there are grooms, and for the cattle there are cowherds. And thus there is provision for all things.

Early in the sixth century B.C., Solon's new constitution for Athens (as described in documents such as Aristotle's *Constitution of Athens* from the fourth century or later) provided for four "census classes": the *pentakosiomedimnoi*, or "five hundred bushel men," with annual incomes of 500 or more *medimnoi* of corn, or equivalent in other produce; the *hippeis*, knights or horsemen, with incomes in the 300–500 *medimnoi* interval; the *zeugitai*, named after the yoke of oxen, who produced the equivalent of 200–300 *medimnoi*; and the *thetes*, the lowest class of citizens, who could not afford the armor required to serve in the infantry. Civic rights and eligibility for various offices were governed by this classification.

Plato (*Laws* 744), sketching a constitution for his ideal *polis*, took over the idea of four classes graded by amount of property and enunciated the principle that "for the sake of equalising chances in public life" (Bury translation) honors and offices, as well as contributions, should be proportional to wealth. He felt, however, that extremes of both wealth and poverty should be eliminated by action of the authorities. Fines for certain offenses are graduated by class. A man convicted of throwing away his weapon in battle will be fined, according to class, proportionately to 10, 5, 3, or 1. Note that neither equal differences nor equal ratios are maintained (945a,b; Pangle, p. 346). Even the fine for malicious litigation has a schedule by class—here the fines are proportional to 12, 8, 6, and 2 (948a,b; Pangle, pp. 349–350).

But class stratification is not the only form of rank in Plato's community. No less than seven bases for "title to rule" are recognized, and it is of special interest that one of them explicitly involves the aleatory element. First, it is "correct" for "parents to have title to rule over their descendants." Second, the well born over the not well born. Third, the elderly over the younger. Fourth, slaves are ruled by masters. Fifth, the stronger rule and the weaker are ruled. Sixth, the "greatest title" is that of the prudent to lead and the ignorant to follow. Finally, the seventh has to do with being "dear to the gods" or "lucky"— "where we bring forward someone for a drawing of lots and assert that it is very just for the one who draws a winning lot to rule and for the one who draws a losing lot to give way and be ruled" (609a–c; Pangle, p. 74). We can almost hear the round of applause from Jencks and co-workers, who noted in regard to *Inequality* (1972) in America that "Income also depends on luck; . . . Those who are lucky tend, of course, to impute their success to skill. . . . In general, we think luck

has far more influence on income than successful people admit"
(p. 227).

Servius Tullius, sixth king of Rome and roughly contemporary with
Solon, is credited by some historians with a "census" that is variously
described. The version of his "fixed scale of rank" in Livy's Book 1 is
classic. The divisions, in terms of the capital value of property, were at
100,000, 75,000, 50,000, 25,000, and 11,000 *asses* (plural of *as*, a
Roman coin). Both the offensive weapons and the protective armor of
the five classes admitted to military service differed by rank. The First
Class carried the sword and spear and had the full panoply of bronze
helmet, round shield, greaves, and breastplate; whereas the Third
Class, for example, wore only the breastplate and had a long shield.
Fourth Class offensive equipment was spear and javelin only, while
the Fifth Class used slings and stones. In addition to the infantry
equipped in this manner and organized into "centuries," there was
also the cavalry. The centuries of these "Knights" were enrolled from
the citizens of greatest wealth and prominence. Muirhead (p. 676)
speaks of the Servian reforms as "an advance towards equality between
patricians and plebeians," since the intent was "to admit the plebeians
to some at least of the privileges of citizenship, imposing on them at
the same time a proportionate share of its duties and burdens." Livy
himself noted that the greater financial burden assumed by the wealthy
was compensated by political privilege because Servius abolished the
traditional manhood suffrage and substituted for it a sliding scale, such
that all power was actually held by Knights and First Class. Only in the
event that their votes disagreed was the Second Class called upon to
vote.

We have taken note of still another census system that was intimately linked to social rank. The Inca officials were classified "according to the number of taxpayers for whom they were responsible"
(Rowe, p. 263): the Chief of 10,000, followed by the Chiefs of 5,000,
1,000, 500, and 100, below whom were "two ranks of foremen . . .
responsible for 50 and 10 taxpayers respectively." The office of Chief,
but not that of foreman, was hereditary. Plato might have approved,
although he would have preferred a more flexible arithmetic than this
rudimentary decimal system.

In France under the *ancien régime* the observer trying to formulate a
scale of rank was confronted by an embarrassment of opportunities. In

addition to the church and military hierarchies but intersecting them
in a complex fashion there was, on the one hand, the unsteady set of
relationships pertaining to monarch and nobility, a status at least
symbolically descended from that of the feudal lord; and, on the other
hand, there was the increasing differentiation by occupation and ac-
quired wealth of the increasing mass of urban citizenry. Jean Bodin
solved his problem by describing several hierarchies. An ostensibly
straightforward one appears in Book 3, Chapter 6:

> In every well ordered Commonwealth there be three degrees of Magis-
> trates: The highest, which is of them which may be called sovereign magis-
> trates, and know none greater than themselves, but the sovereign Majesty
> only: The middle sort which obey their superiors, and yet command others:
> And the lowest degree of all, which is of them which have no command at all
> over any other magistrates, but only over particular men subject to their
> jurisdiction.

There follows a long and legalistic discussion of the sphere of authority
of the several magistrates and their powers with respect to each other.
    Earlier in his work (Book 1, Ch. 9), the central theme of which is
the nature of sovereignty and political authority, Bodin has essayed a
classification by "degrees of subjection." There are no less than "nine
degrees of inferiors" below the monarch, who acknowledges no
superior but "almighty God." The first four are themselves "princes"
or "kings," their ranks distinguished by various kinds of feudal obligations. The fifth "sort" are not kings, but "mere vassals," and the sixth
are "liege vassals."

> The seventh sort are they whom we call subjects, whether they be vassals or
> tenants, or such as hold no land at all, who are bound to fight for the honor
> and defence of their prince as well as for themselves, and to have the same
> enemies and the same friends that he hath. The eighth sort is of them, which
> in former time delivered from slavery, yet retain a certain kind of servitude, as
> do they which are tied unto the soil, and are of us called Mort-maines. The
> last sort are the right slaves.

In Book 3, Chapter 8, some of these distinctions are recapitulated,
with modifications. Distinctions among kinds of slaves and former
slaves are brought out:

Next unto slaves are they whom they call State-free men, and after them the Libertines, or as we may term them the manumitted men, who were everywhere of divers sorts and condition, as there were also divers sorts of slaves (p. 388).

We now have a category of "citizens" (instead of the earlier "subjects") who are to be carefully distinguished from the nobility (p. 389):

The rest of the citizens are divided according to the variety of their conditions and estates, and diversity of their manners and customs. Yet that is common almost to all people, that noble men should in order and dignity be divided from the vulgar and common people.

There follows a comparative analysis of the criteria of nobility among the Romans, Greeks, Jews, and Egyptians, emphasizing the variety of criteria—ancestry, virtue, appointment, wealth—that have sometimes served to define this estate. But the upshot is clear (p. 396): "[What] can be more absurd or pernicious, than to measure reputation by gain, degree by money, and nobility by wealth?"

The discussion eases into the classification of citizens by way of a consideration of ways in which nobility may be lost—Herodotus and others are cited in regard to the proposition that handicrafts are "base trades"; in Rome "Artificers and men of occupation" were either slaves, strangers, or "men of most base and low estate and condition"; there was disagreement among the "Lawyers and ancient writers" concerning the "trade of merchandise," but this trade is "not only honest, but also necessary"; the "order and vocation of Husbandmen and Graziers" was in ancient times "also right commendable"; and so on. This survey of the literature forces the recognition of cultural diversity: "For necessity itself (yea oft times against reason) enforceth the dignity of degrees and vocations of men to be disposed of according to the laws and customs of every city and country" (p. 401).

At this point in Book 3, Chapter 8, Bodin presents in relatively brief compass what must be one of the earliest occupational prestige scales. (Treiman, pp. 116–128, examines data on "occupational wealth and prestige levels" in eight data sets for "past societies," including caste rank for Nepal, 1395, and guild rank for Florence, 1427; the other data sets refer to wealth or income levels of occupations, ranging from

Florence, 1427, to London, c. 1890.) Quoting again from the Knolles translation (pp. 402–403, 405):

Wherefore in what order citizens are to be placed, is to be referred unto the judgement and discretion of the masters of the ceremonies of every city, for the unlikeness of their laws and customs almost infinite. Yet I suppose, that citizens in a monarchy might in this order not unaptly be placed. That next unto the king himself, who out of the number of the citizens, going far before the rest, should follow the holy order of the clergy: next unto the sacred order of the clergy, the Senate: after the Senate should follow the martial men, and amongst them, first the general of the army, or great constable, & then the dukes, counts, marquesses, governors of provinces, landgraves, burgraves, captains of castles, vassals, and other soldiers, with such others, as upon whom the charge of the wars, by the custom of our ancestors lieth. After them should follow the order of gown men, which should contain the colleges of magistrates, and companies of judges, properly divided into their places, with orators, lawyers, pleaders, advocates, attorneys, proctors, scribes, registers, notaries, sergeants, apparitors, garders, cryers, trumpeters, jailors, and all the company belonging to the law. Next unto whom should follow the order of physicians, surgeons, and apothecaries. And after them school men, such as professed to instruct the youth, or are themselves instructed; the professors (I say) of divinity, law, and physic, natural philosophers, mathematicians, logicians, rhetoricians, historiographers, poets, and grammarians. After the order of gown men, I suppose are to be placed merchants, agents, farmers of the common custom, bankers, money changers, brokers, and especially they which have the charge for the bringing in of corn into the city, and of such other things as are most necessary for the feeding of the citizens, such as are the cornmongers, butchers, fishmongers, fishers, bakers, puddingmakers, cooks, unto whom we will join husbandmen and graziers; and unto these all kind and sort of handicraftsmen; which for that they seem almost innumerable, of them, they which are the most profitable, ought to have the first place, carpenters (I say), armorers, masons, metal men, coiners, gold beaters, goldsmiths, metal melters, glassmakers, smiths, bakers, potters, horners, chandlers, weavers also, and such as deal in spinning of silk, wool, beasts hair, hemp, cotton wool, and such other like, whereof we see cloth, ropes, garments, hangings, sails, and paper to be made. Next unto whom follow curriers, skinners, fullers, dyers, tailors, shoemakers: unto which occupations although printing be not for antiquity to be compared, yet seemeth it for the excellence thereof, before all the rest worthily to be preferred. For as for painters, image makers, carvers, makers and sellers of womens paintings, minstrels, players, dancers, fencers, tumblers, jesters, and bawds, are in mine opinion either to be quite driven out of cities, or else to be placed in the lowest place of all: so that even bath keepers, barbers, sailors, hucksters, hostlers, coachmen, grave makers, sargeants, and hangmen, are to be placed before them: For that these are indeed necessary for the carrying out of filth, and the cleansing of the citizens and cities: whereas the other with their most base trades, the ministers of foul and vain pleasures, not only corrupt the citizens manners, but utterly overthrow even the cities themselves. But we have so described the orders of citizens, not so much that the dignity, as the condition of every one of them might so the better be understood. . . . Now as for the order and degree of women, I meddle not with it; only I think it meet them to be kept far off from all magistracies, places of command, judgements, public assemblies, and councils: so to be intentive only unto their womanly and domestical business.

A few decades later, Bodin's exercise was repeated by Charles Loyseau, whose *Traité des ordres et simple dignitez* was first published in 1610. His ideas are summarized in their historical context by Sewell (1980, pp. 23, 24, 35, 64, 125), to whom I am indebted for access to an unpublished translation (by Sheldon Mossberg and William Sewell) of excerpts from Loyseau's text. His discussion lacks the comparative scope of Bodin's, being focused on France and concerned, in particular, to clarify the concept underlying the institution of the Estates General (clergy, nobility, and Third Estate) and the "subalternate orders" of these three orders. There are elaborate analyses of rank within the first two orders, which I shall not abstract. (For a careful exegesis, see Sewell 1974.) Then the "orders or degrees of the Third Estate" are given as men of letters, financiers, practitioners (men of affairs, apart from lawyers and judges, who do work related to the business and legal transactions of others, for example, notaries and appraisers), merchants (the last group "who carry the quality of honor"), plowmen (who till for others, as tenants), and artisans and laborers (Masters, Journeymen, and Apprentices). The last category is further differentiated: certain trades involve a combination of manufacture and commerce and, therefore, are honorable rather than "vile": but "most vile" of all the common people are porters and laborers who have no vocation, but who—since they earn a living— are more highly esteemed than beggars living in idleness.

As Loyseau noted, two of the prerogatives of orders are title and rank, the latter being defined as the "prerogative of seating or of marching." Both seating and marching are mentioned in the banquet scene (III: iv) of Shakespeare's *Macbeth*, where the protagonist greets his guests, "You know your own degrees; sit down./ At first and last, the hearty welcome." The bulk of the action concerns Macbeth's horror and disorientation at the appearance of the ghost of Banquo, whom he has just caused to be murdered, and Lady Macbeth's attempt to reassure the assembled company that Macbeth is just experiencing a "momentary fit." Finally she must ask the guests to leave quickly: "at once, good night,/ Stand not upon the order of your going./ But go at once." Both prerogatives, as they were understood in Victorian England, were prescribed in meticulous detail in articles by Drummond on "Titles of Honour" and "Precedence" in the 1894/1895 edition of *Encyclopaedia Britannica*. The latter term "means priority of place, or superiority of rank . . . on occasions of public ceremony and in the intercourse of private life" (p. 660). The author indicates that formal "tables of precedence" date from the end of the fourteenth century. His own table of "General Precedence of Men" lists, following "The sovereign," no less than 63 ranks, from the Prince of Wales (1) through treasurer of the household (32) to gentlemen (63). For women, there are a mere 50, following the queen. A set of ten detailed "canons or rules" for determining precedence is provided. And there are ten "tables of special precedence," such as ecclesiastical, legal, military, naval, colonial, and academical. The last named includes nineteen distinct ranks.

One of the few sociological studies of tables of precedence (Burrage and Corry) makes use of some 40 lists of "companies" in London issued by city authorities over the period 1328–1604. The report also includes information from "the order of precedence compiled for the Royal Commission on Municipal Corporations in 1837," which is said to be "essentially the same as the order of precedence at the present time" (p. 382). The various lists include as few as 14 and up to as many as 89 orders. The authors stress the evidence of status mobility provided by the shifts in rank position on the lists and by anecdotes on status disputes, sometimes violent, between companies. One such dispute was resolved when the lord mayor and aldermen decreed that the Merchant Taylors' Company and the Skinners' Company should take sixth and seventh positions in the procession to Westminster in alternate years. This is the origin of the expression, "at sixes and sevens" (p. 385).

Appraising competence or performance

In these days of grade inflation and other apparent threats to a tradition of academic excellence, one is bemused by the observation that only in the athletic department is frank and open competition still the norm on the American campus. That would be a nice irony, if it is true that our present ideas about formal assessments of personal competence are derived in significant measure from procedures first developed in athletics. The Olympic Games, whose tradition we still honor quadrennially, were just one of several such organized competitions for the Greeks. And for the competitors in the Greek Olympics, the games organized by Achilles in the *Iliad* were a vital part of the cultural tradition.

One might have thought that the practices described by Homer would have evolved within the ancient period toward something more closely resembling the quantification and measurement that infuse our sports today. If so, the evidence has been lost. For example, Harris (1972, pp. 34–35) notes, with respect to the pentathlon:

> There has been endless discussion about the method of deciding the winner of the event. First places alone counted; the Greeks set great store by victory and generally were little concerned even with second or third places. Any system of reckoning points for places is unthinkable. . . .
>
> The most likely interpretation of the evidence is this. The pentathlon was conducted like a five-set tennis match; as soon as one competitor had won three events, the contest ended. The three events peculiar to the pentathlon—the jump and the two throws—were held first. If a competitor won all three, he was "victor in the first triad," as the Greeks put it. Otherwise, when this stage was completed, there were either three competitors, A, B and C, with one win each, or one, A, with two wins and another, B, with one. In the latter case, these two ran a 200-yard race. If A won, he now had three wins and was the victor. If B won the race, A and B now had two each and they wrestled to decide the champion. If after the triad there were three athletes with one win each, these three ran the race. One of them, A, now had two wins, while B and C still had one each. B and C now wrestled in a semi-final; in virtue of his two wins, A was given a bye and sat by as *ephedros*. He then wrestled with the winner of the semi-final, who now also had two wins, and the winner of this bout was the victor in the whole event.

Harris's premise that only first places counted may be too strong. An alternative theory of how the pentathlon was decided (Gardiner, Ch.

XIII) allows for the possibility that a competitor might be second in each of the first four events but finally be declared victor by winning the final one (wrestling). But the point of this example is not to establish the formula actually used at Olympia—the scraps of evidence may forever remain consistent with a variety of alternative formulas—but to realize that the Greeks themselves must have explicitly considered the problems of designing the competition and of aggregating the results according to some rule or decision function. We are entitled to wonder, as well, that as early as 708 B.C. it was thought desirable to attempt such an aggregation, rather than to retain as separate events the footrace, the jump, the diskos, the javelin, and wrestling. Gardiner suggests (p. 177) that "the pentathlon began not as a separate competition but as a sort of athletic championship, a means of deciding who was the best all-round athlete among the victors at a meeting." But "all-round" athletic ability is, in modern parlance, a latent or unobserved variable, indicators of which are the performances in five contests. We may suspect that the Greeks had some sense of the fallibility of indicators if they required three falls for a victory in wrestling (Gardiner, p. 185). And it appears that some competitions among ball teams were conducted according to a kind of tournament system (p. 231). No doubt the theory behind such practices was largely implicit.

On the matter of the alleged focus on first places, it is worth noting that at the Athens games second prize was worth about one-tenth of the first prize (Young 1983, 1984), and there is other evidence suggesting an interest in the ranking of leading contestants. Herodotus, Book 6, refers to the distinction of Callias, not only in defending his country's freedom but also in the Olympic games, where he took the first prize in the horse race and was second in the four-horse chariot race. Thucydides (VI:16) quotes the boast of Alcibiades that he had taken the first, second, and fourth places in the Olympic chariot race, having entered no fewer than seven of his chariots in the contest. There is also the suggestive incident in the *Iliad* where Menelaus argues that he should be awarded second rather than third place, since another competitor had fouled him. These items may only show that the chariot race was regarded differently from the other contests Harris had in mind. Even so, they do indicate that there was a concept of a rank ordering of outcomes and not merely that of a single winner. But I have found no evidence that Harris erred in surmising that the Greeks lacked the idea of point scoring for individuals or teams. The team competition, via the aggregation of results for individual contests, strongly emphasized in modern Olympics, was not a feature of the original games. (Hacking cites a work by Luca Pacioli, 1494, that describes a ball game in which a team gets 10 points for each goal and needs 60 points to win. I suppose such scoring systems may have a longer history, but I have not found it.)

Another ostensible failure to quantify may be noted in connection with javelin-throwing (Harris, p. 37):

> There is no record of the distance of any throw in antiquity, so we have no means of knowing what the Greeks achieved in this event. One of the most remarkable differences between ancient and modern athletics is the carelessness of the Greeks about the measurement of throws and jumps compared with our feverish concern with records and record-breaking. In running the absence of standards was inevitable; fortunately for themselves, the Greeks had no stop-watches or electrical timing devices. But even where measurement would have been easy for them—they had widely accepted standard weights and measures—they seem to have been little concerned to apply them to athletic performances. The best Greek athletes were content to defeat those who were in immediate competition with them, and did not care what others had done at other times and places.

The last statement requires qualification. Pindar's numerous odes to the victors in the various games are full of references to the number and locations of their previous victories. Apparently it was the practice to keep a careful record of the number of contests won. Nevertheless, Harris's observations warn us to beware of anachronisms in searching for precursors of our social measurements. The Greek tendency to practice forms of measurement that did not lead to actual quantification has been noted as an attribute of their technology and natural science as well (Sydenham 1979, p. 146).

In poetry as in games the Greeks took much interest in competition and prizes. The system at the festival of Dionysus, where the great tragedies of Aeschylus, Sophocles, and Euripides (as well as many lesser works) were produced, was roughly as follows (Walton 1980, pp. 75–76):

> After all the preliminaries, sacrifices, processions, and various performances during the festival itself, the prizewinners were chosen. . . . Before a

festival began, each tribe put forward a number of names of potential judges. From among these names, one representative of each of the ten tribes was then selected. . . . After the performances each representative made his selection, wrote it down, and deposited it in the voting urn. The *archon* then selected, at random, five votes, and prizes were awarded accordingly. Whether each judge attempted to place all plays or chose a single winner we do not know, nor do we know what happened if equal votes were cast for two sets of plays.

The account implies that the prizes were not monopolized by first place winners. *Oedipus the King* was one of a group of plays that placed only second (it was the whole group that was judged, not a single play).

That the poetry prizes may sometimes have been controversial is consistent with the burlesque in *The Frogs* of Aristophanes (405 B.C.). Dionysus is called upon to judge a poetry contest in Hell where Euripides, recently arrived, has challenged the incumbent, Aeschylus, for the Chair of poetry. Xanthias, the slave of Dionysus, asks, "Can tragedies be weighed?" to which Pluto's servant replies, "Of course they can. More than that: there'll be compasses and rulers and T-squares. . . . Also wedges, and instruments to calculate diameters." Each poet is to read from his own work and criticize the work of the other. When Aeschylus remarks, "The one thing left is to weigh my verse against his in the scales, That will decide," Dionysus calls for "the cheese-scales: they're the only thing for weighing poetry." Each poet is instructed to hold one of the pans of the scale and to recite a line. At the signal, "Cuckoo," from Dionysus, both poets release their pans. Aeschylus wins when his pan drops, and the judge, Dionysus, gives far-fetched explanations about why Aeschylus's lines are found weightier (Fitts 1962, scenes v, ix, x).

No doubt Aristophanes succeeded in getting laughs with his absurdities concerning the weighing of poetry. Yet the metaphor does not die: a current item relates to "weighing the quality of doctoral programs in American universities" (Leeper 1982).

That the Greeks had tests of academic as well as athletic skills is implied by Doyle's survey of their educational practices, and Toynbee (1957, p. 70) mentions that "At the Inca Emperor's court at Cuzco there was a regular course of education, with tests at successive stages." DuBois claims (pp. 29–30), however, that the Chinese "invented the psychological test," inasmuch as a "rudimentary form of proficiency testing" was used as a basis for promoting the emperor's officials as early as 2200 B.C. and that a system of formal examinations was in place by 1115 B.C., to continue in some form until the beginning of the twentieth century.

According to Cressey (1929), the celebration of success in the Chinese literary examination was quite as exuberant as the enjoyment of victory by the Olympic champions. As he describes the system, there were three levels or degrees. Examinations for the first degree were given twice every three years in a number of prefectural cities. They lasted a week and called for writing of poetry and essays. There were only 60 or 70 successful candidates for every 4,000 or 5,000 who competed, and they achieved only the privilege of taking the second degree examination. It was given every three years in provincial capitals. The candidates were sequestered in enclosures with individual cells and had three separate trials lasting two days. They wrote formal dissertations on topics from the classical literature. Perhaps one percent of the 6,000 to 8,000 candidates were successful. The examination for the third degree was given the following spring in Peking, and was conducted in a similar fashion, although standards were higher. In Cressey's estimate, the examination system was successful in assuring a supply of intellectually competent candidates for bureaucratic offices, although it was a conservative influence in Chinese society in view of the examinations' extreme emphasis on reproduction of ideas from classic texts and discouragement of original thinking.

Additional sociological observations on this system are due to Max Weber (1951, pp. 115–119), who was primarily interested in whether it succeeded in establishing the merit principle for appointment to bureaucratic offices. Although the "first traces of the examination system *seem* to emerge about the time of Confucius" (551–478 B.C.), the "bestowal of offices according to merit was raised to the level of a principle" during the Han dynasty (206 B.C.–A.D. 220) and "regulations [were] set up for the highest degree" in 690 A.D., after which the "examination system has been fully carried through" (p. 116). Unfortunately, Weber gives no details on the methods of examining and evaluating candidates, although he makes it clear that there were multiple examinations: "These examinations consisted of three major degrees, which were considerably augmented by intermediary, repetitive, and preliminary examinations as well as by numerous special conditions. For the first degree alone there were ten types of examinations" (p. 115). Despite pressures on the system throughout its long history, Weber gives it credit for preventing the formation of a "feudal office nobility," since "admission to the ranks of aspirants was open to everybody who was proved educationally qualified" (p. 119).

The account of Wittfogel (1957, pp. 347–354) is somewhat less sanguine. He cites statistical studies of the social origins of officials in support of his assessment:

Many details of the Chinese examination system still need clarification, but this much seems certain: if the Sui and T'ang emperors established the examination system, in part at least, in order to alter the social composition of the ranking officialdom, then it must be said that the system failed to achieve this purpose. The examinations provided the ambitious core of the ruling class with a most intensive intellectual and doctrinal training; and they added a varying amount of "fresh blood" to the ranking officialdom. But they did not destroy the trend toward sociopolitical self-perpetuation which dominated the thoughts and actions of this group.

If such variance of scholarly opinion is disconcerting, it is well to reflect that there is much disagreement as to the extent of meritocracy in contemporary Britain and the United States, notwithstanding the availability of data many times more voluminous than what we have for imperial China.

Of the scholars I have cited, only DuBois is a psychometrician. It is of special interest, therefore, that he finds no evidence that the Chinese anticipated such elements of modern testing as the use of multiple-choice questions or the carrying out of item analyses. But he contends that the problems of achieving objectivity and uniformity in testing were recognized and that tests were sometimes evaluated independently by more than one examiner. Moreover, he feels that until China began its modernization the tests had sufficient validity for their use to contribute in a positive way to the quality of the civil service.

We may conjecture that proficiency examinations of some kind, however informal, are as old as the educational process itself, which is to say, as old as human society. But we are looking for the use of explicit, standardized procedures yielding quantified results. Such procedures evidently were introduced gradually into the continuing process by which teachers assess the performance of students and masters evaluate the work of apprentices. In medieval English universities, acceptance as a Bachelor or Master

depended on whether a candidate had attended a certain prescribed course of lectures. Secondly, he had to have participated in some disputations (e.g., "Sophomes," "Inceptions," "Determinations," and "Quadragesimals"); and thirdly, he needed to have answered certain questions orally (e.g., "Priorums" and "Postiorums" in logic at Oxford). Fourthly, there might be set pieces, such as "Clerums" and other sermons (Montgomery 1965, p. 4).

According to Montgomery written questions were introduced into the mathematics tripos at Cambridge just after the middle of the eighteenth century, although vestiges of the old system "founded on scholastic debate and similar exercises of an earlier age" (p. 6) continued in use. In 1800 Oxford provided for the appointment of public examiners, and honors lists were published. Reforms continued throughout the century, in good part in response to public pressure, and the examination methods of the universities came to serve as prototypes for many other systems in Britain. Montgomery's account of the growing use and influence of formal examinations is quite detailed; unfortunately he gives little specific information on the psychometric specifications and properties of the examinations as such. Some clues are provided by the Reverend Henry Latham, whose article in the *Encyclopaedia Britannica* of 1895 seems to have been written in 1878. He notes that examinations have "lately" come into wide use, particularly as "tests or instruments for selection," as distinguished from their function as "appliances for education." The use of the tripos examinations at Cambridge for awarding fellowships is credited with maintaining their focus on a single subject, one "which admits of questions being set of every shade of difficulty, and for which there is a definite right and wrong," to the exclusion of the "ethical element," which was prominent in the Oxford examinations. A long discussion of the benefits and drawbacks of an emphasis on examinations (which I must pass over, while saluting its valuable insights) is followed by a distinction between the competitive examinations used by the army and civil service, where the intention is "to get rid of patronage" and "to secure the ablest men," and the "pass examinations," designed to demonstrate that candidates have reached "a certain standard" in their education. Finally, a brief statement on "practical methods of examining" considers *viva voce* examinations (requiring two "skilled examiners" sitting at least 15 minutes with each candidate), the essay, and the written examination of one question (the "German system") or a dozen questions ("as in England"). To "mark" a paper "the examiner distributes his marks to the questions according to the difficulty or the time they take to answer." But perhaps "one quarter of the marks" should be used to record the impression of the paper as a whole, and negative marks are used when ignorance is revealed by "parrot-work." At the end, "It is a good plan to add to the marks got the excess above half the full value assigned to the paper, and then deduct one quarter of the full value," so that (for example) a candidate who obtains 400 when the "full value" is 500 will receive the score of $425 = 400 + 150 - 125$. No rationale for this linear transformation of total "marks" into a "score" is suggested. The author finds (on evidence not described) that of 1,000 young men entering a university, roughly 250 "will take creditable honours," 200 may "get a place in an honour school or tripos," the next 150 "will be the more vigorous pass men," and "200 more will pass without failure," while 100 "will meet with failures more or less frequently" and "100 will never pass any university examination at all."

In a monograph on practices in five American universities, up to 1900, Smallwood notes rather few innovations before the latter part of the eighteenth century. But the ensuing decades witnessed more or less continuous experimentation, stimulated—as Smallwood analyzes the evidence—by changes in institutional needs occasioned by broadening of curricula, introduction of ability classification, attempts to raise standards of scholarship, and dissatisfaction with earlier methods: "One method after another was tried, each change was motivated by some external social, political, or economic variation in the world. This in turn had its effect on the kind and growth of legislation within the walls of the universities" (p. 115). Some of the developments recorded in this study are noted below.

The earliest examinations in these universities were oral and were used only to establish that the student was qualified for a degree. Written examinations were introduced at Yale in 1830, to be administered at the end of the sophomore and senior years. Harvard had written examinations from 1833, and used them for entrance qualifications beginning in 1851. The first documented formal marking system is from a 1785 diary of the president of Yale, recording results for 58 students present at an examination: 20 *Optimi*, 16 second *Optimi*, 12 *Inferiores* (*Boni*), and 10 *Pejores*. Point scoring on a scale of 4 was introduced at Yale in 1813, and "the average result of the examination of every student in each class" was recorded (p. 43). In that year, averages ranged from 1.3 to 3.7. Harvard introduced a point system based on 20 in 1830, but some professors were using 100 as the basis in 1837. Grade letters, A to E, with specified percentage equivalents, were adopted at Mount Holyoke College in 1896.

Scoring of examinations was legislated by the faculty of William and Mary in 1851: "A list of questions shall be prepared by the instructor of the class, to each of which he shall attach a numerical value—such that the sum of all the values shall equal the number denoting the highest grade of scholarship. . . . he shall assign values to the answers. The sum of the values of the answers given by any student shall be the number obtained by him at the examination" (pp. 77–78). In 1843 the Harvard faculty voted "that the aggregate scale be made up by adding the marks actually received both in the required and elective studies" (p. 92). The several departments received different weights in the aggregate; this was accomplished by specifying different maximum values for the departments.

Smallwood reports little discussion of what might be termed the operating characteristics of the various scales that were tried. But it is clear that faculties then, as now, were quite capable of forming opinions on the advantages and disadvantages of alternative systems without benefit of psychometric theory or controlled experiment. The University of Michigan even toyed with what we now call the pass-fail system in the middle of the century, but the plan was abandoned shortly thereafter.

From a psychometric standpoint, even more interesting innovations are those recorded in the following account, quoted indirectly (unsigned 1913) from an 1864 article on "Statistics of Educational Results," by E. Chadwick, which described the practice of a Rev. George Fisher at Greenwich Hospital School:

A book, called the "Scale-Book," has been established, which contains the numbers assigned to each degree of proficiency in the various subjects of examination: . . . to determine the numerical equivalent corresponding to any specimen of "writing," a comparison is made with various standard specimens, which are arranged in this book in order of merit; the highest being represented by the number 1, and the lowest by 5, and the intermediate values by affixing to these numbers the fractions $\frac{1}{4}$, $\frac{1}{2}$, or $\frac{3}{4}$. So long as these standard specimens are preserved in the institution, so long will instant numerical values for proficiency in "writing" be maintained. And since facsimiles can be multiplied without limit, the same principle might be generally adopted.

The numerical values for "spelling" follow the same order, and are made to depend upon the percentage of mistakes in writing from dictation sentences from works selected for the purpose, examples of which are contained in the "Scale-Book," in order to preserve the same standard of difficulty.

By a similar process values are assigned for proficiency in mathematics, navigation, Scripture knowledge, grammar and composition, French, general history, drawing, and practical science, respectively. Questions in each of these subjects are contained in the "Scale-Book," to serve as types, not only of the difficulty, but of the nature of the questions, for the sake of future reference; . . .

In respect to the numerical values of "reading," as regards accuracy, taste or judgment, it is obvious that no other standard of measurement can be applied, beyond the interpretation of the terms "good," "bad," "indifferent," etc., existing at the period of examination. And the same observation will apply to the estimation of numbers of "characters" and "natural abilities," as determined by the united testimony of the respective masters.

. . . the advantage derived from this numerical mode of valuation, as applied to educational subjects, is not confined to its being a concise method of registration, combined with a useful approximation to a *fixed standard* of estimation, applicable to each boy; but it affords also a means of determining the *sum total*, and therefrom the means or average condition or value, of any given number of results.

According to Ayres (1918), Rev. Fisher's innovations were not adopted elsewhere, so that the twentieth-century mental testing movement had to reinvent some of them. And it is only quite recently that psychometrics has seriously returned to the procedure of item banking, as it is now called, after a long period during which reliance was placed on calibration of one test to another rather than on standards established in terms of individual items.

In the United States, a remarkable study was carried out in the Boston public schools in 1845. The system at that time was one in which the school committee made annual formal inspections of the schools; these evidently included some oral questioning of pupils, although the procedure had become quite perfunctory with the growth of the school system. For reasons that are now obscure, the Grammar School Committee decided to administer written questions in several subjects, preprinted and carefully administered to forestall cheating. The committee members wrote explicit rules for scoring the papers, a task they apparently carried out themselves. The examination questions and specimen responses of the pupils were published and detailed tables were provided showing, for each school, the number answering each question correctly as well as the percentages of answers correct in the whole test for each subject. Some of these details are preserved in a report of a partial replication of the study carried out in 1919 (Caldwell and Courtis 1924). That project itself was remarkable for its time, involving the testing of some 12,000 pupils located in most of the 48 states. Some of the results were reported on a question-by-question basis in the fashion recently adopted by the National Assessment of Educational Progress, whose reports began to be issued in 1970.

The Boston experiment apparently provided useful ammunition for advocates of written examinations. The last step of moving to the so-called objective or new-type examination belongs entirely to the twentieth century. In 1930, Cubberley (pp. vii–viii) wrote:

The significance of this new testing movement has been large, and its scientific purpose has been to create a series of standardized testing and measuring devices, known as standard tests and scales, which would provide us with units and norms of accomplishment applicable to the measurement of school work anywhere. . . . These newer types of testing procedures have been created in numerous forms, such as the true-false test, the multiple-choice test, the recall test, the matching test, and combinations of two or more of these forms. Their advantage lies in the far wider sampling of pupil knowledge made possible in the use of hundreds of test questions or choices instead of five or ten, and, at the same time, in the ability to score the results quite rapidly with the entire elimination of the subjective judgment of the teacher in the scoring.

We are interested in examinations and grading systems, not only as fundamental inventions of measurement methods which have been elaborated in modern psychometrics, but also as historical records of student quality and performance (however crude) that might be useful as input to quantitative sociological analysis. A pioneer in this as in many other aspects of psychological measurement, Francis Galton (1869, pp. 14ff. in 1914 edition) reported data on "numbers of marks obtained by those who gain mathematical honours at Cambridge." Some 400 to 450 men took degrees each year, of whom about 100 gained "honours in mathematics, and are ranged by the examiners in strict order of merit." About the first 40 "are distinguished by the title of wranglers" and "senior wrangler . . . is . . . the highest distinction." (Galton notes that at Oxford candidates were grouped in classes and listed alphabetically within classes.) The examination lasted five and one-half hours per day and continued for eight days. "All the answers are carefully marked by the examiners, who add up the marks at the end and range the candidates in strict order of merit. . . . Unfortunately . . . the marks . . . are not . . . assigned on a uniform system, since each examiner is permitted to employ his own scale of marks; but whatever scale he uses, the results as to proportional merit are the same." (Galton does not attempt to justify this large claim or, indeed, to explain exactly what it might mean.) Numerical results are shown in the form of a frequency distribution of "number of marks obtained by [200] candidates" in 16 intervals, from under 500 to 7,500 to 8,000, of the marks of "a Cambridge examiner to two examinations." Galton's main purpose in commenting on these results is to establish the fact of "enormous intellectual differences." He observes that "in the more remarkable of these two years" the senior wrangler obtained 7,634 marks, "more than thirty-two times as many" as the 237 marks of the lowest man in the list of honors. He figures that there are some 300 "poll men" below the lowest man with honors. While some of these men are lazy, there are, say, "100 who, even if they worked hard, could not get them." Further discussion leads into "the very curious theoretical law of 'deviation from an average,' " in which the work of Quetelet is drawn upon. Galton does not return to the analysis of the Cambridge mathematics examination marks, but turns to other material, such as examination marks for candidates for the Royal Military College, in an attempt to establish a scale of "grades of natural ability," which serves as a tool in the remainder of his inquiry on inheritance of ability, where he is restricted to qualitative data.

Another investigator who glimpsed the potential scientific value of institutional records of intellectual performance was Adolph Wagner

(1864). I draw upon the account of Oberschall (1965), who states (pp. 46–47):

For a number of years the high schools of Bavaria had kept a complete record of each student's marks in all subjects including discipline and diligence, his rank order in his class, as well as information about his family such as religion, occupation of father, and social status. [Wagner] described how in some topics, such as Greek and Latin, the teachers were in the habit of grading according to the number of orthographic, grammatical and stylistic errors, so that "the subjective judgement of the teachers is on the whole limited" and the grades therefore comparable. In order to analyze this data, Wagner proposed that all school subjects could be reduced to four basic mental abilities: numerical ability (mathematics), linguistic abilities (all languages), memory (geography and history) and lastly general talent (German composition), and that the interrelation of these four mental abilities be studied in great detail, as well as the influence of religion, family status, and age on each type of ability separately. Furthermore the problem of the early versus the late bloomers might also be studied quantitatively through this data and even the hotly debated question whether or not the rank order of standing in the school was related to a subsequent rank order of success and achievement in later life.

Oberschall attributes Wagner's failure to follow up on these possibilities to a lack of resources. Wagner was one of several German social scientists who perceived the need for statistical bureaus or research institutes to organize work on the scale required to obtain worthwhile results. But decades elapsed before research units of this kind actually came into being. In the meantime, at least in the United States, a "demand for testing" developed as a consequence of research on school failure, such as L. P. Ayres's report on *Laggards in Our Schools* (1909) to the Russell Sage Foundation (cited by Resnick). By this time, scientific innovations in psychometrics were in the picture, and I mention them in a later discussion.

Rewards and punishments

I have noted the Greeks' interest in contests yielding prizes and honors, specifically for athletic performance and poetry. Unfortunately, we do not know the form and value of the prizes at the festival of Dionysus. While they may have been monetary, Knox points out that even the greatest of the tragedians, Aeschylus, Sophocles, and Euripides, did not depend on proceeds of their writings for livelihood. He thinks that the "glory and admiration of one's fellow-citizens" was the real reward. In Book 8 of Herodotus's *History*, the Persians with Xerxes were astonished to learn that the Greeks were holding the Olympic games during the war and were competing for the olive wreath and not for money. In Book 1, Herodotus tells of the Games of the Triopian Apollo, where bronze tripods were awarded to the victors. But the prize winners were supposed to leave their awards at the temple, dedicated to the god. When this custom was defied by Agasicles, his home city was henceforth excluded from privileges of the temple.

Actually, there was considerable hypocrisy in the pretense that the only reward for athletic victory was honor. True, at the four Panhellenic festivals—the Pythian, the Isthmian, and the Nemean, in addition to the Olympian—the prizes as such were symbolic. But at local games, such as those at Athens, prizes of material value were awarded. And at least as early as Solon, who offered 500 drachmas to any Athenian achieving a victory at Olympia, statesmen began to subsidize the training and participation of their athletes in the Panhellenic games (Gardiner, p. 37). Both Gardiner and Young have noted the consequent professionalization of Greek athletics, a development deplored by Euripides and Socrates, among others.

There are explicit descriptions of schedules of prizes in the earliest surviving Greek literature, the *Iliad* (Book XXIII), where Achilles directs the games that followed the funeral of Patroclus. The first event was a race of horse-drawn chariots.

> Then for the swiftest steeds
> A princely prize he offered first,—a maid
> Of peerless form, and skilled in household arts,
> And a two-handled tripod of a size
> For two-and-twenty measures. He gave out
> The second prize,—a mare unbroken yet,
> Of six years old, and pregnant with a mule.
> For the third winner in the race he staked
> A caldron that had never felt the fire,
> Holding four measures, beautiful, and yet

> Untarnished. For the fourth, he offered gold,
> Two talents. For the fifth, and last, remained
> A double vessel never touched by fire.

Following the race, in which the reputed "ablest horseman" came in last because his yoke was broken by Athena, Achilles proposed to give him the second prize, "as is just." But the man who would have been displaced by that action protested, so Achilles came up with a different consolation prize for Eumelus,

> The brazen corselet which my arm in war
> Took from Asteropaeus, edged around
> With shining tin,—a gift of no mean price.

The prizes for two boxers were advertised in this way:

> To the middle space
> He led a mule, and bound him, six years old
> And strong for toil, unbroken and most hard
> To break, while to the vanquished he assigned
> A goblet.

(I note in passing that Achilles was not, despite the Greek emphasis on victory, of the same mind as the late Vince Lombardi, coach of the Green Bay Packers: "Winning isn't everything, but losing isn't anything.")

> Then, third in order, for the wrestling-match
> The son of Peleus brought and showed the Greeks
> Yet other prizes. To the conqueror
> A tripod for the hearth, of ample size,
> He offered; twice six oxen, as the Greeks
> Esteemed, were its price. And next he placed
> In view a damsel for the vanquished, trained
> In household arts; four beeves were deemed her price.

This third event illustrates how Achilles's problem actually was two-fold. First, he had to estimate what first, second, and lower (if any) places in a contest were worth on a subjective but socially acceptable scale—a kind of ratio judgment as to the relative merit and not merely the order of the places—and then he had to pick prizes from his store such that the ratios of their values reflected his scale of merit. In the case of the wrestling bout we see that the award to the winner was three times as valuable, in the coin of oxen or beeves, as the award to the loser. Whether the same ratio held in the boxing contest we cannot tell, for lack of a numéraire (a commodity that might serve as "money") of the kind mentioned in connection with the wrestling prizes. However that may be, there was evidently some kind of calculation of the relative values of the events, as well as the places for each event. Homer's view that the chariot race was by far the most important event can be inferred from the fact that his description of it is so protracted. (Herodotus, Book 5, makes explicit such a comparison among the Thracians, for whom the single combat had the most valuable prize.) But Achilles's scale for events can be partially inferred if you compare the awards for the charioteers with those for contestants in the footrace. Three prizes were put up for that event. First was "a wrought silver cup/ That held six measures, and in beauty far/ Excelled all others known." Second prize was "A noble fatling ox; and for the last,/ Gold, half a talent." We see that third and last place in the footrace was worth only a quarter as much as fourth prize in the chariot race. (As it happened, however, Achilles was so pleased by the graceful speech made by Antilochus after the race that he doubled the third-place prize.)

The spoils of war are a classic form of reward which, no doubt, usually goes disproportionately to those of the victors most adept at looting. After the Greek victory at Plataea, according to Herodotus, Book 9, Pausanias ordered that everything of value left by the defeated Persians be collected by the helots. Herodotus suspected that, contrary to instructions, the helots declared to their superiors only objects too large to conceal. But the booty they did turn in was divided by rule: a tenth for the god at Delphi and ten of everything—women, camels, and so on—for Pausanias himself, with the rest divided among the soldiers each "according to his deserts" or each "receiving his due" (depending on which translation you read). Although there was no record of special awards for valor in the battle, Herodotus "imagined" that such awards would have been made.

Concerning honorific awards for distinction in warfare, Herodotus (Book 4) mentions the Scythian custom of an annual celebration where each warrior who has killed one of the enemy is allowed to drink from the wine bowl—two cups if he killed many—while those with no claim to this recognition are segregated in disgrace. Suetonius reported (p. 102) that Caesar Augustus was "unsparing in the reward of military merit," having granted 30 special honors himself and persuaded the Roman senate to vote triumphal decorations for even more generals.

I began this discussion with rewards, rather than punishments, taking note of Bodin's observation: whereas a Commonwealth will flourish only if the good are rewarded and the bad punished, "It is not so necessary to discourse of punishments, as of rewards, for that all laws and books of lawyers are full of them, but I find not any one that hath written of rewards" (p. 584). He distinguishes between rewards that are honorable, or profitable, or both, and observes that "the more profit rewards have in them, the less honorable are they." Honors include "triumphs, statues, honorable charges, estates, and offices" (p. 585). A great danger is the depreciation of the value of honors caused by bestowing them too freely or selling them: "In old time there was more difficulty to create a simple Knight, than is now to make a General" (p. 588). (It seems that inflation is a generic problem in social measurement and not one confined to money.) Bodin's criterion is a seemingly straightforward one: "Rewards are to be distributed to good men, according to every mans merit" (p. 596). In Bodin's scheme of things merit often turns out to be strongly correlated with rank: "If a Consul be allowed a triumph, it is reason that captains and lieutenants should have the estates and offices, the horsemen the crowns and horses, and the private soldiers also should have part of the arms and spoils" (p. 588). Curiously, in his chapter on reward and punishment Bodin does not refer to Plato, although he is explicit elsewhere that he is building on the work of the Greek philosophers. Plato was much concerned with distributive justice but recognized the incompatibility of two distinct principles. Whereas the "truest and best equality . . . gives due measure to each according to their nature," hence "greater honors always to those who are greater as regards virtue," the city must sometimes blur the differences among men in merit, "if it is to avoid partaking of civil war." Here the "equality of the lot" comes into play, although the type of equality "that depends on chance" should be employed "as rarely as possible" (Laws, 757b–58a, Pangle translation).

When Bodin wrote it was still natural to think of outstanding military service as the paradigmatic action meriting a special award, although the pope had begun to confer decorations for other kinds of achievement some centuries earlier. The French Legion of Honor, which dates from the beginning of the nineteenth century, is regarded as the prototype for the orders of merit and special awards that have since been established, many under nongovernmental auspices. The *World Dictionary of Awards and Prizes* covers some 62 countries and classifies awards into 155 subjects, including Acoustics, Audiology, Children's Literature, Drama, Folklore, History of Art, Navigation, Philology, Religion, and Tropical Medicine. Among the fields in this classification with the largest numbers of different awards are Chemistry, Literature, and Science. Behind each of the prizes is some mechanism for weighing, evaluating, assessing, and comparing achievements and some procedure for aggregating or reconciling divergent judgments. A comprehensive comparative study of this social apparatus with systematic attention to the concept(s) of measurement (implicitly) incorporated therein would be a worthwhile complement to Goode's functional analysis of prestige processes. Goode, incidentally, points to a dearth of "quantitative data" and "operational indexes" of the kind needed for research in this area (p. viii). I would rather argue that we need to find out what kind of quantification the reward system already is using rather than to develop merely "operational" indexes that would facilitate the social scientist's statistical analysis.

Bodin's advice to the prince was to "refer the punishment of offenses to the Magistrate, as it is expedient, and reserve rewards unto himself, giving by little and little according to every ones merit, that the thanks may be the more durable" (p. 593). Yet, as we have just noted, the making of awards is no longer the exclusive prerogative of princes, whereas the trend of government is to monopolize the administration of punishment. Muirhead speaks of a time before this trend had run its course (p. 676):

That there must have been other wrongful acts that were regarded in early Rome as deserving of punishment or penalty of some sort, besides those visited with death, sacration, or forfeiture of estate, total or partial, cannot be doubted; no community has ever been so happy as to know nothing of thefts, robberies, and assaults. The XII Tables contained numerous provisions in reference to them; but it is extremely probable that, down at least to the time of Servius Tullius, the manner of dealing with them rested on custom, and was in the main self-redress, restrained by the intervention of the king when it appeared to him that the injured party was going beyond the bounds of fair reprisal, and frequently bought off with a composition. When the offence was strictly within the family, the *gens*, and perhaps the guild, it was for those who exercised jurisdiction over those corporations to judge of the wrong and prescribe and enforce the penalty.

When the king comes to insist on defining "fair reprisal" in all cases, an institution somehow resembling the provision of standards for weights and measures comes into being. I take the simile from Toynbee (1954, p. 309, note):

It will be seen that the invention of coinage is analogous, in the field of commerce, to the epoch-making change that takes place in the field of criminal law when a government takes to treating crimes as political offences against itself instead of regarding them merely as personal injuries to be avenged by the private self-help of the victim or his surviving kinsmen, in regard to which the government's own responsibility, at its widest, is limited to promulgating a tariff of *wergelds*.

A "tariff of wergelds," designed on an obvious principle, seems to be precisely what is involved in the following bit of historical metrology, from Grierson (p. 3):

The literature on English weights and measures opens in a dramatic, indeed in a sinister, fashion. It is in the laws of King Ethelbert of Kent, which date from the first decade of the seventh century, that we meet with our earliest units, one of length and two of weight. Those of weight, which are used to define the quantities of gold required in compensations for injuries and offenses, are the *sceatta*, . . . a grain (barleycorn) of gold . . . , and its multiple the shilling (*scilling*) of twenty sceattas. The unit of length is the inch (*ynce*). Inch and shilling come together in clause 67, §1, which deals with the depth of wounds in the thigh: "if over an inch, one shilling; two inches, two shillings; over three, three shillings."

This rule takes no account of who is wounded. But Landtman (p. 297) observes that the seriousness of a violent crime is likely to depend on the victim's status: "It is very usual for the wergeld in the case of homicide to vary according to the rank of the person killed, and the higher his dignity, the higher the amount will be." However the gravity of the offense is calculated, adjustment of the penalty to it, Kelsen

argues, derives from the ancient principle of retribution. The issue for
social measurement is then the following (pp. 252–253):

> Only when the evil of wrong and the evil of punishment are quantitatively
> determinable substances can they be counterbalanced in retribution. . . .
> Neither wrong nor punishment are objectively measurable quantities. Never-
> theless, something like equivalence of wrong and punishment seems to be
> imaginable. The more harmful a fact, qualified as wrong, is regarded, the
> more must be feared the evil threatened to prevent it and the more "severe"
> must be the punishment. The problematical character of this proportion is
> borne out by the fact that the measurements of the two elements have no
> objective character but represent merely subjective evaluation.

Subjectivity notwithstanding, criminal codes, ancient and modern,
have provided explicit schedules of deprivations and sanctions for
specific classes of offenses. And Sorokin (Vol. 2, Ch. 15) demonstrated the possibility of documenting historical variation in these
schedules over countries and time periods. Work of this kind immediately brings to light a conceptual complexity: punishments differ
not only in degree, but also in kind. Sorokin considered that there are
six "main types" of punishment: capital punishment and bodily punishments; banishment and hard labor; imprisonment aggravated by loss
of rights or bodily punishment; imprisonment in pure form; depriva-
tion of honors and rights; and economic punishments. Within each
type he distinguished four to six grades of severity of punishment. An
attempt to equate punishments across types is justified by the remark
(p. 583), "The lawmakers themselves, in several codes . . . indicate
how one kind of punishment may be replaced by another under certain circumstances. Since such a procedure is given in the codes, a
more systematic application of it is not a subjective procedure." Nevertheless, we shall not here examine the particular "scale of values"
Sorokin developed on this rationale. It suffices to note that the invention of graduated punishments should be credited to the various
sociolegal systems, and not to the social scientists who have sought to
rationalize the provisions of these systems. Hall's research (1952, Ch.
3), moreover, cautions us that the actual penalties administered in a
system of criminal justice may differ widely from those stipulated in
the code. From the early eighteenth century a variety of practices
virtually nullified the capital penalty for a great many offenses until the

English Parliament, over the period 1820–1860, abolished it for more than 190 offenses.

Indeed, we have to presume that no single rationale controls the development of schedules of punishment. Sorokin's working hypothesis was that the "gradation of the punishments is a fairly good indicator of the comparative gravity of the wrongfulness of the specified class of prohibited action, as it appears to the respective societies and culture mentalities. The greater the crime, the greater, usually, the punishment" (p. 528, italicized in original). But "gravity" or seriousness itself may be a composite rather than a unidimensional quantity. As Hobbes maintained (*Leviathan*, 1960 edition, p. 198):

The degrees of crime are taken on divers scales, and measured, first, by the malignity of the source, or cause; secondly, by the contagion of the example; thirdly, by the mischief of the effect; and fourthly, by the concurrence of times, places, and persons.

(Unfortunately, Hobbes did not follow up the possibility of deriving actual measures of seriousness on any of these "scales.") As I shall note later, contemporary research has investigated the scalability of seriousness as a subjective phenomenon, but as far as I know, it has not been suggested that a quantification of seriousness other than that implied in the prescribed or actual punishments meted out can be inferred from records or operating characteristics of systems of criminal justice.

A further complication is that punishments are not always motivated solely by the principle of retribution. Kelsen claimed (p. 253) that "if the ideology of retribution is abandoned and, in place of retribution, prevention as the purpose of punishment is accepted, then the equivalence of wrong and punishment loses its sense." (But the passage quoted earlier had already introduced "prevention.") Not only retribution and deterrence, but also rehabilitation are prominent features of some systems of penology, as in the modern practice of indeterminate sentence. In the *Laws* we can see Plato, fascinated as he is with the details of schedules of punishment, vacillating among these principles, as well as that of restitution. In 867b he calls for harsher penalties for those who kill deliberately than for those killing impulsively. An "ultimate deterrent" was called for, in 880e–881b, for whoever assaults his parent; but death is not the ultimate punishment and what is needed is to inflict on the living offender what he might expect in Hades. In 862c,d, the focus is not on calibrating the retribution to the magnitude of the offense, but in teaching the offender not to commit it again. For involuntary offenses, restitution suffices (879b): it is up to the judge to assess the value of the injury. But some offenses, such as encroaching on a neighbor's land, should be discouraged by requiring payment of twice the cost of the damage (843c,d). I noted earlier that fines for certain offenses, although not exactly proportional to the offender's status or wealth, were directly related thereto. But a negative correlation with status is incorporated in the following rule (845b, Bury translation):

The law shall forbid our foreigners to share in the so-called "coarse" fruit, and the like; and should either a master or a slave touch these, in ignorance, the slave shall be punished with stripes, and the free man shall be sent off with a reproof and be instructed to touch only the other crop, which is unfitted for storing to make raisins for wine or dried figs.

We should note at least one more principle sometimes incorporated in rules for arriving at appropriate punishments. Herodotus (Book 1), speaking from his "personal knowledge" of Persian customs, stated that in the case of an offense that could be punished by death, their way was to balance the misdeeds of the offender against his services and to proceed with the punishment only if the former outweighed the latter.

All this talk of "The right division of rewards and punishments," as Bodin observed in the last chapter of his *Sixth Book*, belongs to a consideration of Justice. He maintained that "it is needful for us to borrow the principles of the Mathematicians" to arrive at a correct general solution to the problem of justice. Bodin's "mathematics" need not detain us long. But we note his claim to improve upon the formulations of the Greek philosophers by introducing a third principle of justice unknown to them. In Aristotle's version (Bodin seems to be referring to Book 5 of the *Nicomachean Ethics*), *distributive* justice takes account of merit and expresses a proportion between the shares in a division and the degrees of merit—however the latter may be measured. *Corrective* justice is that which restores equality (such as may have existed before one party inflicted an injury on another) or assures that in a voluntary exchange the values received by the two parties are equal. (Aristotle observes that the need to compare products of different kinds, such as shoes and houses, is what led to the invention of money.) Corrective justice does not take account of the needs or merits of the parties to a transaction, but only the transaction itself.

Now, Bodin proposes a third principle, that of "Harmonical Justice . . . whereof no man hath as yet spoken" (p. 755). It is the one best suited to a "Royal Estate," the "most excellent" estate of a Commonwealth, in combining the "Geometrical proportion" of distributive justice with the "Arithmetical proportion" of commutative (i.e., corrective) justice. The mathematics of this combination I find opaque, but the general idea seems to be to find an optimum combination of government by law, or inflexible rule, and government by discretion, taking account of equity and "that the variety of persons, of facts, of time, and place, is infinite and incomprehensible; and such as should always present unto the judges, cases still much unlike one of them unto another" (p. 771). The formulation would almost seem to rule out the possibility of measurement against any kind of fixed standard—which is to say, rule out the possibility of measurement. Hence the flexibility Bodin would leave to the magistrate is unacceptable to a utilitarian, such as the influential reformer Beccaria, whose tract of 1764 called for punishment proportionate to the crime as dictated by the law, which should not be open to interpretation by judges. But Beccaria did allow (p. 44) that the "scale of punishments should be relative to the state of the nation itself," in that greater severity is needed to make a strong impression on the "callous spirits" of a people recently in a state of savagery, while a socialized populace has increased sensibility, so that "the force of punishment must diminish if the relation between object and sensory impression is to be kept constant." Indeed a nice problem in calibration—especially when linked to the requirement that the "true measure of crimes" be the "harm done to society" (p. 64).

Probability: measuring chance

There are several reasons why a discussion of social measurement should be concerned with the idea of probability, and some of those reasons apply to my later notes. Here, I want to focus on the notion of the objective probability of well-defined events, such as the number of spots showing when two dice are thrown, or the occurrence of a death within a specific period of time. A splendid analysis of the emergence of this notion from a pattern of earlier ideas in which "probability" meant something like plausible opinion (as opposed to demonstrable truth) has been given by Hacking. I do not draw extensively upon his account, as most of the following discussion was written before I saw it. But let me refer to his statement (p. 14)—"The propensity to give heads is as much a property of the coin as its mass, and the stable long run [relative?] frequency found on repeated trials is an objective fact of nature independent of anyone's knowledge of it, or evidence of it"—as a philosopher's blessing on the idea of probability I am using. (I will also allow a reference to Hacking to serve in lieu of the discussion of "subjective probability" that some readers might expect to find here.)

As Sumner observed in *Folkways* (1906, p. 7), "The element of luck is always present in the struggle for existence. . . . The aleatory element has always been the connecting link between the struggle for existence and religion." The uncertainty as to what will come of a marriage, for example, has led to widespread practices intended to assure that the marriage will be lucky or to divine what may be in store for it. So a preoccupation with chance is far older than history. Probability, as a concept, involves at least a beginning of the demystification or disenchantment (Max Weber: *Entzauberung*) of chance. There is no measurement or basis for measurement as long as chance is *only* the whim of the gods. I have noticed, however—as have others before me—that devotees of the game of craps are not only deeply superstitious but also observant as to the habits of dice. So their long-run strategies of play are at least roughly calibrated to the objective odds (as a probabilist might compute them) on the various outcomes, although from time to time they will accept a wager assuming longer odds if they feel the dice are "hot."

Now, the standard history of probability theory begins with an inquiry of a gambler, the Chevalier de Méré, to a mathematician, Pascal, concerning a purported "fallacy in the theory of numbers." Neyman (1950, p. 4) writes as though Méré had discovered by "empirical trials" that the probability of at least one double six in 24 throws of a pair of dice is less than $\frac{1}{2}$; and David suggests that he was able to "distinguish empirically" between the former probability, 0.4914, and 0.5. This seems to be conjecture, and I don't know where it originated. But Ore rejects it with what I take to be a decisive argument (see also Hacking, pp. 59–60). Most of the history of probability follows the incident, of course. But there have also been efforts to uncover the earlier history or prehistory of the idea of probability. This inquiry has shown that some respectable mathematical work preceded the Pascal-Fermat correspondence (a translation of which is given by David, Appendix 4). Galileo, for example, wrote a cogent memorandum on the probabilities in a game with three dice (reproduced by David, Appendix 2). David recounts the even earlier stirrings of formal mathematical ideas in the Italian Renaissance. And she, as well as Kendall (1956), looked closely at the small amount of historical and archeological evidence we have concerning the games of chance played in antiquity and the Middle Ages. The details are fascinating, but the general outcome of the investigation is negative, in a sense, as I can indicate most briefly with excerpts from Kendall (1956):

. . . Playing with dice . . . continued from Roman times to the Renaissance without interruption (p. 20).

It might have been supposed that during the several thousand years of dice playing preceding, say, the year A.D. 1400, some idea of the permanence of statistical ratios and the rudiments of a frequency theory of probability would have appeared. I know of no evidence to suggest that this was so (p. 21).

In my opinion relative chances were all reached on the basis of intuition or trial and error in the games played up to the middle of the seventeenth century (p. 29).

. . . Before the Reformation the feeling that every event, however trivial, happened under Divine providence may have been a severe obstacle to the development of a calculus of chances (p. 32).

The last remark may overlook the role of magic, as distinct from religion. As Small (p. 269) observed, "We are content to predict only when we do not dare to think of control." The gambler uses his favorite magic in the attempt to control the fall of the dice and, curiously enough, is intermittently successful. Modern psychology shows that intermittent reinforcement may be favorable for learning, and the relevance of this relationship for habitual gambling has been noted (Pliskoff and Ferster, p. 140). As long as magic "works," there may be insufficient motive for careful experiment and calculation.

Both David and Kendall give some attention to divination as well as games of chance, but strangely enough hardly any attention to the casting of lots or, in particular, to the use of randomization in selecting officials and jury members. Perhaps these topics were left to the other scholars whose contributions appear in two anthologies of papers on the history of statistics and probability, of which Kendall was co-editor. Hasofer (1967; reprinted in Pearson and Kendall 1970) has shown that, although gambling with dice was forbidden to the Jews, lots were drawn from an urn for both religious and civil purposes. He indicates "that the only methods of drawing lots which were in use had strictly equiprobable outcomes." (See also Lichtenstein and Rabinowitz 1971–72.) Rabinovitch (1973; see also his two papers reprinted in Kendall and Plackett 1977) presents a painstaking analysis of ancient and medieval Jewish texts that supposedly "demonstrate that probabilistic reasoning has a very long history" (p. 172). The careful review of this work by Zabell concurs "that over 18 centuries ago Jewish scholars in Babylon and Israel used probabilistic reasoning in their legal decision-making at a remarkable level of complexity" (p. 996), but also complains "of the author's projection of modern conceptions of probability and statistics onto the subject matter." Among the interesting examples given by Rabinovitch are those concerning rules proposed for deciding how many deaths in a short time constitute evidence that a "plague" is occurring (pp. 86–88) and how many cures must be attributed to an amulet before it can be approved for prescription rather than rejected as sorcery (pp. 89–90). As I read Rabinovitch, he is not claiming that the Jewish writings directly influenced the Italian and French mathematicians who, by general consent, invented the mathematical calculus of probability. Perhaps we can conclude, though, that it was only a "historical accident" that games of chance rather than, say, the inheritance problem much studied by Arab and Jewish scholars (Rabinovitch, pp. 161–166) afforded the immediate stimulus to the fundamental mathematical work.

On the other hand, one scholar's sifting of the scientific and philosophical ideas of the Greeks fails to suggest that they were on the point of discovering regularities in chance or of giving a mathematical formulation of its laws. Sambursky (1956, reprinted in Kendall and

Plackett 1977), to whom we are indebted for a summary of Greek thought most closely related to this topic, found it "surprising" that there were no probability calculations in ancient Greece, inasmuch as "the great popularity of games of dice in all strata of society had created favorable conditions for the accumulation of observations which could have led to quantitative results" (p. 12).

What the Greeks failed to discover was demonstrated in the research of an eighteenth-century English physician, John Arbuthnott, "the first man to set up a formal test of a statistical hypothesis," according to Kendall (1977, p. 35). Arbuthnott examined the number of christenings by sex for 82 years (1629–1710) in London, during which period the annual total varied between 6,000 and 17,000. He found that in every year, "82 times running," male births were more numerous than female and calculated the probability of such a run on what we would now call the null hypothesis, $p_0 = 0.5$, "by the Table of logarithms" as $(\frac{1}{2})^{82} = 1/(4.836 \times 10^{24})$ or 2.0678×10^{-25}. Noting that "Males" are more subject to "external Accidents" than "the other Sex," he surmised, "To repair that Loss, provident Nature, by the Disposal of its wise Creator, brings forth more Males than Females; and that it is almost a constant proportion" (Arbuthnott 1710, reprinted in Kendall and Plackett 1977). He neither calculated that proportion nor demonstrated its constancy, other than showing it consistently exceeded 0.5. But the idea of "constant proportion" is just what we mean by an objective probability, the estimation of which is a species of social measurement.

Arbuthnott did not originate the idea of estimating such proportions. David (p. 103) states that John Graunt "was the first Englishman to calculate empirical probabilities on any scale" in his *Natural and Political Observations Made Upon the Bills of Mortality* (1662). The subsequent history of "political arithmetic," which Graunt's work initiated, has been summarized in various places (e.g., Lécuyer and Oberschall 1968; Lazarsfeld 1961) and I shall not recapitulate that history, which tends to stress the increasing interest in quantitative economic and demographic data. What I think is most interesting for the present account is David's remark, "Graunt's importance both as a statistician and an empirical probabilist lies possibly in his attempts to enumerate . . . the population at risk to the several diseases such as are given in the Bills of Mortality" (p. 106). In fact Graunt had no firm figure for the population at risk and, as David recounts, went to considerable lengths to make the crudest estimate of it. The immediate problem he struggled with was not solved in a fully satisfactory way until periodic population censuses were instituted in the nineteenth century.

Concomitantly, but perhaps not coincidentally, the idea of population took on a more general significance in natural science:

> Beginning with the nineteenth century, and increasing in the twentieth, science brought about "pluralistic" subjects of study, categories of entities satisfying certain definitions but varying in their individual properties. Technically such categories are called "populations." A "population" studied may be a population of humans . . . , a population of galaxies . . . , or a population of molecules of a quantity of gas in a container, all moving in different directions and with different velocities. With reference to this latter example, the subject of a pluralistic study would not be the happenings to any individual molecule (this would be an "individualistic" question) but rather the properties of the quantity of gas, as a whole, perhaps its temperature or pressure, which depend on how frequently the molecules move rapidly or slowly (Neyman 1974, p. 417).

With respect to Neyman's third example, we note that Gillispie (1963; 1972) gives reasons for believing that in 1859 James Clerk Maxwell borrowed from social science the statistical approach used in his kinetic theory of gases, his immediate source being a laudatory review by the astronomer John Herschel of Adolphe Quetelet's applications of probability theory to the analysis of social (or "moral") statistics. (For more on Quetelet, see Lazarsfeld 1961.) That Maxwell was aware of Quetelet is a fair inference from his reference to "an imaginary being called the Mean Man"—Quetelet's *homme moyen*, I presume—in an essay of 1873 (first printed in the appendix to the biography by Campbell and Garnett). He was also aware of the ideas of Laplace and Buckle about the "statistical method of investigating social questions." He found these ideas compatible with the "recent developments of Molecular Science," which he hoped would "remove that prejudice in favour of determinism" that arose from the physical science of the past.

Gillispie provides a quotation from Herschel (1850, pp. 40–41) that epitomizes the optimism generated by the discovery that human traits and acts are distributed according to laws of probability:

Whether statistics be an art or a science . . . or a scientific art, we concern ourselves little. . .it is the basis of social and political dynamics, and affords the only secure ground on which the truth or falsehood of the theories and hypotheses of that complicated science can be brought to the test. It is not unadvisedly that we use the term Dynamics as applied to the mechanism and movements of the social body; nor is it by any loose metaphor or strained analogy that much of the language of mechanical philosophy finds a parallel meaning in the discussion of such subjects. Both involve the consideration of momentary changes proportional to acting powers—of corresponding momentary displacements of the incidence of power—of impulse given and propagated onward—of resistance overcome—and of mutual reaction. Both involve the consideration of time as an essential element or independent variable; not simply delaying the final attainment of a state of equilibrium and repose—the final adjustment of interest and relations, and, in effect, rendering any such final state unattainable. . . .

Number, weight, and measure are the foundations of all exact science; neither can any branch of human knowledge be held advanced beyond its infancy which does not, in some way or other, frame its theories or correct its practice by reference to these elements. What astronomical records or meteorological registers are to a rational explanation of the movements of the planets or of the atmosphere, statistical returns are to social and political philosophy. They assign, at determinate intervals, the numerical values of the variables which form the subject matter of its reasonings, or at least of such "functions" of them as are accessible to direct observation; which it is the business of sound theory so to analyse or to combine as to educe from them those deeper-seated elements which enter into the expression of general laws.

As it turned out, the further development of probabilistic reasoning in the social sciences did not follow quite the direction suggested by Herschel's first paragraph, but was deflected toward the biometric approach of Francis Galton and, later, Karl Pearson. Galton too was immensely indebted to Quetelet, but his most important innovations in statistical method derived from his interest in inheritance of anatomical and especially intellectual traits. So we owe to Galton the basic ideas for methods of correlation and regression analysis. And social research has been so preoccupied with elaborating these methods that it has rather lost sight of the more basic problem of measuring or, more precisely, estimating the probabilities that govern the characteristics of human populations or events occurring in them. In Coleman's (1964) mathematical sociology and similar kinds of work of the past two or three decades, a part of sociology has come back to

Herschel's "Dynamics . . . the consideration of momentary changes proportional to acting powers, etc.," although I am not aware of any direct dependence of the recent work on his statement.

In the meantime, the population sciences established, in partnership with probability theory and statistics, the new paradigm suited to "pluralistic" objects of investigation, to use Neyman's term quoted earlier. The decisive developments were the theories of Darwin and Mendel. Lewontin (p. 170) has shown that "Darwin's revolution lay in turning his attention away from the type of the species and concentrating on the actual individuals that made it up. . . . he took the actual variation between individuals to be the proper object of study." (Note that "concentrating on the individual" is quite consistent with the idea of population science, because the "variation between individuals" is a property of the population, not of the individuals as such.) As is well known, Darwin's understanding of inheritance was faulty, and it is one of the great ironies of history that he never knew the work of his contemporary Mendel, which was, in effect, the missing element of the theory of evolution of biological populations. Mendel too focused on differences between individuals, and the critical aspect of his experimental method, according to Lewontin (p. 174) was that "he kept separate records on the outcome of breeding of separate individuals. Whether or not two plants looked the same, *their offspring were separately collected and separately analyzed.*" Only in this way was Mendel able to demonstrate gene segregation and thus discredit the blending theory of inheritance in which Darwin believed, an error Galton and Pearson were unable to rectify. It remained for R. A. Fisher (see the biography by Box) to rescue the "biometric school" from the fatal consequences of this error when he, along with Sewall Wright and J.B.S. Haldane, provided the mathematical and statistical foundations for the modern or "synthetic" theory of evolution (Provine).

In nineteenth-century social science, the population concept was enriched theoretically by economists arguing about the issues concerning population growth and resources bequeathed to their discipline by the Reverend T. R. Malthus (whom Darwin explicitly acknowledged as a catalytic agent for his own thinking) and on the observational side by government statisticians developing methods for census and registration of vital events (Lorimer). Of strategic importance for our topic of measuring chance, it seems to me, was the work of the epidemiologists, as described by Susser. In 1842 Edwin Chadwick compared death rates over three decades in two communities, one of which was drained of water during the period. It showed a substantial decrease in death rate while the control community actually showed a small rise. On the basis of such evidence concerning causes of change in probability of dying, Chadwick introduced a method of sanitation which "probably saved more human lives than any other single health measure up to the post-World War II era" (Susser, p. 51). Comparable outstanding work was done by John Snow in demonstrating the elevation of cholera death rates by contaminated water supplies.

The somewhat parallel work in social or moral statistics in Germany, France, and England has been well described in studies by Lazarsfeld and associates that I cited earlier. For sociologists by far the most significant research related to this tradition appeared at the very end of the century. By general consent, Durkheim's *Suicide* (1897; translation 1951) eclipsed its predecessors by virtue of its theoretical coherence (Oberschall 1965, p. 46) and the author's systematic method of exhaustively sifting the evidence bearing on key hypotheses (Selvin 1958). *Suicide* is a *tour de force*. Durkheim considers an act which might seem to be essentially, profoundly individualistic—not to say solipsistic—but by counting such acts and relating the aggregate number to the population at risk (work done for the investigator by anonymous statisticians), he derives rates (that is, estimates of objective probabilities) that show striking patterns of variation according to sociological categories and striking uniformities across time within such sociologically defined sub-populations. The perspective from which the data are studied provides the argument for the conclusion that suicides are produced by social forces (Durkheim 1951, pp. 309–310):

Collective tendencies have an existence of their own; they are forces as real as cosmic forces, though of another sort; they, likewise, affect the individual from without, though through other channels. The proof that the reality of collective tendencies is no less than that of cosmic forces is that this reality is demonstrated in the same way, by the uniformity of effects. When we find that the number of deaths varies little from year to year, we explain this regularity by saying that mortality depends on the climate, the temperature, the nature of the soil, in brief on a certain number of material forces which remain constant through changing generations because independent of individuals. Since, therefore, moral acts such as suicide are reproduced not merely with an equal but with a greater uniformity, we must likewise admit that they depend on forces external to individuals. Only, since these forces must be of a moral order and since, except for individual men, there is no other moral order of existence in the world but society, they must be social. . . . So truly are they things *sui generis* and not mere verbal entities that they may be measured, their relative sizes compared, as is done with the intensity of electric currents or luminous foci.

Thus did a masterly exercise in social measurement serve to provide a foundation for sociology itself as a nomothetic discipline.

Randomization and representation

We have seen that lots were used extensively by the ancient Hebrews. The Old Testament not only describes many uses of randomization but also provides a rationale for it: "The lot is cast into the lap; but the whole disposing thereof is of the Lord" (Proverbs 16:33). But in some contexts it may be that randomization was simply a means of insuring fairness or the appearance of fairness and not, specifically, a way of discerning the divine will: "The lot causeth contentions to cease, and parteth between the mighty" (Proverbs 18:18). When the children of Israel took over the land of Canaan, they were instructed by the Lord to divide the land according to lots (it is not stated how this procedure was to be reconciled with the principle of allocation according to population). At one point, "there remained among the children of Israel seven tribes, which had not received their inheritance" (Joshua 18:2), so three men were sent from each tribe to make a survey: "Ye shall therefore describe the land into seven parts, and bring the description hither to me, that I may cast lots for you here before the Lord our God" (18:6).

Judges 20 describes a war declared to avenge a Levite whose concubine was abused and killed by men of Gibeah, with the punitive expedition to be manned by conscription: "But now this shall be the thing which we will do to Gibeah; we will go up by lot against it; And we will take ten men of an hundred throughout all the tribes of Israel, and an hundred of a thousand, and a thousand out of ten thousand, to fetch victual for the people" (Judges 20:9–10). Just as the Greek precedent in regard to jury selection is followed in our legal system, the Jewish precedent concerning conscription was followed in World Wars I and II in the United States, as well as the more recent draft lotteries. (The actual prototype for the World War I lottery may have been the draft procedure used in Austria-Hungary between 1889 and the war, Fienberg suggests.) The 1970 and 1971 lotteries have been subjected to careful statistical analysis (Fienberg 1971), which indicates that the procedures of the former were seriously flawed, while remedial steps were taken successfully for the latter.

Sambursky, although he might well have done so, did not comment on the extensive use of chance mechanisms by the Greeks in their conduct of public affairs. Along with elections by vote there were also many carried out by lot. In his *Politics*, Aristotle produced a three-dimensional classification of appointments to offices, distinguished according to (1) who appoints (all the citizens or only some); (2) from whom (magistrates are chosen out of all or only out of those qualified by property, birth, or merit); and (3) how (by vote or by lot). In Aristotle's account of the Athenian system, magistrates involved in routine administration were elected by lot but military officers by vote.

A particularly detailed description of the selection by lot of the juries for law courts is given in *Constitution of Athens*, Chapters 63–67, and some aspects of Aristotle's account have been clarified by modern research (Dow 1939). Given the Athenian penchant for litigation, hundreds or sometimes thousands of jurors were required each day. The pivotal feature of the selection process was a curious device, the *kleroterion*. As each *dikast* (citizen over age 30, eligible for duty) arrived he placed a ticket bearing his name and a letter identifying the section of the tribe to which he belonged in a chest designated for that tribe and section. The *archon* drew a ticket at random from each chest to pick ticket-inserters, who then drew the remaining tickets from the chest in random order, inserting them in slots on the face of the *kleroterion*. That device contained a tube into which counters had been placed in random order. As the *archon* drew one counter at a time from this tube, its color determined for the corresponding row of tickets whether their bearers would serve on that day.

I am not sure that we have either an explicit rationalization for the

practice just described or any cogent analysis of its latent social functions. It is true that jurors were paid for their services, so, to maintain a
sense of fairness, it may have seemed important to shift responsibility
for their selection out of the hands of the officials administering the
system. Staveley (1972, pp. 54–57) argues that use of the lot by the
Athenians in appointing councilors and many of the magistrates was a
derivative of the principle of rotation, itself a device to prevent the
emergence of a governing class. Be that as it may, the elaborate business of the *kleroterion* surely testifies to "their fascination with luck . . .
and their penchant for intricate machine-like institutions" (Dow 1939,
p. 1).

On the strength of Larsen's analysis of "representative government"
in Greece and comments by Staveley (pp. 29, 35) on the selection of
public officials in Athens, I am prepared to argue that the Greeks
actually invented stratified random sampling in their effort to achieve
representativeness—although this is surely one of the spectacular cases
of technology preceding science. In the fifth century B.C. the *boule*
(council) of Athens was made up of 500 men, selected by lot, 50 from
each of ten tribes. The "tribes" themselves, following the reforms of
Cleisthenes at the end of the preceding century, were no longer actual
kinship groups, but artificial entities comprising small geographic units
called *demes* (roughly, "wards"). Each tribe included a group of demes
located in the city proper, another group of demes in outlying areas of
inland Attica, and a third group of demes located along the coast. The
three *trittyes* (thirds) usually were not geographically contiguous, as
one can see from the map shown by Green (p. 95). The tribes were
originally intended to be of about equal population size. The demes
differed in size and were, accordingly, assigned quotas to make up the
tribal quota of 50. Larsen (pp. 5–10) concedes that there may have
been deviations in practice from the principle of "representation in
proportion to population," but insists that representativeness in this
sense was the intention of the system. He argues, further (p. 9), that
"Representation of demes in proportion to population meant virtually
the representation of most elements of the citizen body in proportion
to their numbers. This was a natural result of the fact that the members
of one deme consisted largely of farmers; of another, of handicraftsmen
and workers, and so on." One could well believe that Cleisthenes
understood that under random sampling the expected proportion of

group A in a sample is just the proportion of A's in the population, and that sampling randomly with probability proportional to size, within strata defined by a characteristic (such as geographic location) correlated with group membership, will reduce the sampling variance of the proportion.

My thesis on the invention of sampling by the Greeks is not, of course, as firmly grounded as the observation that modern census taking, most notably in the United States, is likewise constitutionally anchored in a notion of political representation. But in the American theory there is no presumption that representatives (legislators or members of Congress) are a "sample viewed as a miniature, or perhaps a mirror, of the population," which is one of the meanings of "representative sampling" discussed by Kruskal and Mosteller (1979, p. 250). On the contrary, the American electorate is presumed to choose as representatives persons who are outstandingly well qualified. The Athenians fully understood this idea, and when they selected their military officers they used the method of voting rather than sortition (Aristotle, *Constitution of Athens*, Ch. 42). But to man the council which acted in lieu of the entire assembly of voters, their aim was "representative" sampling. The modern theory of "proportional representation" harks back to the Greek idea in aiming at "a legislative body reflecting with more or less mathematical exactness the strength of groups in the electorate" (Gosnell 1934, p. 541). Modifications of *electoral* systems, such as the Hare plan, intended to secure greater "representativeness" are all complex and at best only partially successful. In any event, as Kruskal and Mosteller point out, no miniature (or scale model) can resemble the population in every particular. Who is to specify the "groups" to be represented, and what tolerances shall be allowed with respect to their proportions in the legislature, or sample? Critical analysis of the very concept of "representation" in both political theory and statistical theory brings to light distressing conundrums. In 1934, although Gosnell reported that enthusiasm for proportional representation had "waned" in the light of experience, he managed to convey the notion that the movement for electoral systems incorporating this principle was still viable. But authorities on "Representation" writing in the 1968 *International Encyclopedia of the Social Sciences* seemed to be saying, at some length, that the concept is not clear and the empirical determination of "representativeness" is difficult at best. (There was news, however, of some progress in measuring "representative behavior," as inferred from the similarity of the congressman's and his constituents' views. This is, of course, quite a different notion from that behind the older advocacy of representativeness in terms of group memberships and is, accordingly, beyond the scope of this discussion.)

The political scientists' recognition of difficulties in the idea of "representation" parallels to some extent the change in view of statisticians, who began to understand in the 1930s that purposive sample selection—the attempt to match sample characteristics to population characteristics—however carefully controlled, could not be relied upon to produce either "representativeness" in general or a rational basis for statistical inference (Kruskal and Mosteller 1980). For the last half century professional statisticians have been nearly unanimous in recommending random or "probability" sampling (which may incorporate purposive features, provided only that the final selection of the unit of observation is made by a chance mechanism).

Kruskal and Mosteller note (1980, p. 175) that the possibility of drawing a sample by lot turned up in the statistics literature as early as 1897, but made slow headway. A number of ways of selecting cases for statistical analysis other than random sampling were used in different fields. In studies of public opinion a rather vigorous, if brief, career was enjoyed by the straw vote or straw poll (Robinson 1932; 1934). Several major U.S. newspapers and magazines carried out these simulated elections by one of three main kinds of methods: printed ballots which readers were asked to remove from the publication and send in; personal interviews at haphazardly chosen places where many participants could be recruited; and ballots sent in the mail to selected persons, such as automobile owners or telephone subscribers. For the most part, the resulting data were used in election forecasts, but the *Literary Digest* took polls on such questions as the soldiers' bonus and prohibition that received considerable attention. In the mid-1930s the straw vote with volunteer respondents (sometimes numbering in the millions) was superseded by the household interview survey of a relatively small national sample. Through the 1940s these surveys were usually done with so-called quota samples, in which the final selection of the respondent was up to the interviewer, whose quota was stated in terms of age, sex, and economic level. Although quota sampling continues to be used, probability sampling was widely adopted by the polling industry in the 1950s and later.

Robinson (1934) notes the similarity of the straw poll to advisory (non-binding) initiatives and referenda in some states of the U.S. The initiative and referendum proper, as methods of direct legislation, were used extensively in the early years of this century and seem to have enjoyed a recent resurgence of popularity. In one sense they circumvent the representation problem, in that the electorate itself, rather than the legislature, makes the decision. But low and differential rates of voter turnout tend to weaken the force of that argument on their behalf. An interesting brief discussion of "Quantitative Methods in Politics" (Rice 1938; not to be confused with his 1928 book of that title) compared two "methods of measurement" in studies of public opinion: the method of election, "a voluntary self-recording of opinion by some members of the electorate upon a greatly simplified statistical schedule"; and "the method of census" in which complete coverage of the universe is attempted and questions may be somewhat elaborated— "Trained enumerators may elicit more accurate formulations of opinion from some individuals than these would be able to construct for themselves independently." The straw poll, Rice noted, may be obtained by either method, but the "sample census" as employed by the Gallup Poll seems less subject to "bias" than the voluntary response method of the *Literary Digest*. Hence such poll findings might actually summarize "American attitudes and opinions more accurately than do elections," even though elections are more "democratic" in the sense that they are voluntary. The discussion was premised on "the extent that [Gallup] is able to master the problems of sampling." It did not anticipate the problem of non-response to household interview surveys which was obscured by the quota selection method.

I conclude with a reference to a supposed precursor of modern opinion surveys (Fang 1954, p. xiv):

It is said that there were Court Anthologists in the early days of the Chou Dynasty (1134 B.C.–247 B.C.) whose function was to collect songs through the length and breadth of the land for the sake of supplying the king with data for gauging the mores (*feng*) of his realm; in other words, the Odes served as straw votes. This Gallup-poll theory has some plausibility; since ancient Chinese were noted for their love of the arts and for their obsession with politics, to the extent of making a fine art of playing politics, it is not hard to believe that they managed to combine politics with poetry.

Not only did the Chou anthologists anticipate Gallup. Their technique also adumbrated that of the contemporary school of "unobtrusive measures" (Webb and others 1966).

Recent inventions by social scientists

The fundamental inventions I have identified—or, at any rate, most of them—have this in common. They came into being as "crescive" rather than "enacted" institutions, to use an old sociological distinction, and their origins seem to represent attempts to meet everyday human and social needs, not merely experiments undertaken to satisfy scientific curiosity. The same contrast, I suspect, can be drawn in the history of physics: the measurement of length or distance, area, volume, weight, and time was achieved by ancient peoples in the course of solving practical, social problems; and physical science was built on the foundation of those achievements. Later, scientists themselves invented ways to measure temperature and electrical quantities, and their instruments and measurements turned out to have practical applications. The "scientific era" of social measurement, characterized by a self-conscious attempt on the part of persons defining themselves as at least amateur social scientists, is now more than three centuries old: Clark (1972, p. 21) speaks of "pantometry," the "belief that all things can be measured," which he traces to the "pansophism" of Bacon's time and to the drift of science toward mathematics after Descartes.

    It would take a little nerve to suggest a short but comprehensive list of *fundamental* inventions in the domain of social measurement during the scientific era. E. G. Boring, a prodigious scholar in the history of psychology, has done such a thing for his discipline. He finds (1961, p. 108) "a pretty clear history of the entry of measurement into psychology," rather neatly divisible into four histories: (1) psychophysics, conventionally dated to 1860 with the publication of Fechner's treatise, but with antecedents in inquiries made during the preceding century; (2) measurement of reaction time, described as an ultimately unproductive "mental chronometry"; (3) quantification of learning or memory, followed by experiments on conditioning; and (4) measurement of individual differences, pioneered by Galton and by James McKeen Cattell, who proposed the term "mental test" in 1890. We will find that at least the first and the last of these have had important applications in social measurement. I have already tried to suggest that psychometrics, in the sense of tests of intellectual performance, had a lengthy pre-scientific history.

Kendall (1972/1977) begins his overview of social measurement with some of the achievements we have already noted. The two additional inventions he emphasizes are Le Play's "quantified case studies" of family budgets (see also Lazarsfeld 1961) and the social survey, as practiced most notably by Charles Booth in the nineteenth century (see also Pfautz 1967) and extended by A. L. Bowley in the twentieth century. (I would suggest that the budget of family expenditures is an invention that presupposes the invention of money and accounts, and that the social survey is an elaboration of the fundamental invention of counting or census. But there is no need to press these points.) Bowley is credited, in particular, with insisting on quantifiable concepts with operational meaning and with introducing probability sampling into the method of social survey.

Elsewhere, Kendall (1969/1977) summarizes the early history of price indexes, the first crude version of which he attributes to a Bishop Fleetwood who, in 1707, calculated price increases for four commodities since the mid-fifteenth century but was "relieved of the necessity of averaging his four price-relatives, or of considering their weights" by the fact that all four commodities showed about the same decrease in the purchasing power of the pound. A little later, Dutot computed a rudimentary aggregated price index. The principle of aggregating heterogeneous quantities by formula or fiat is, of course, widely (if not always wisely) used and for some writers seems to represent a summum bonum of measurement technique. Whether the price index was the actual ancestor of all such indexes I cannot say.

Perhaps a prior question is how the idea of averaging as such arose. In a 1971 address (unfortunately still unpublished), Churchill Eisenhart traced from antiquity the idea of the arithmetic mean as the indication of the value that a set of discordant measurements were intended to express. From his collection of examples, it would appear that the midrange (average of the largest and smallest values in an array) was the predecessor of the arithmetic mean proper. According to Plackett, although ancient astronomers grappled with the problem of reconciling discrepant observations, "The technique of repeating and combining observations made on the same quantity appears to have been introduced into scientific method by Tycho Brahe towards the end of the sixteenth century."

But the averaging of prices really addresses a different problem— that of somehow reconciling intrinsically disparate quantities, or choosing a single representative or typical value to summarize a collection of such variable values. The popularization of this method of treating statistical data on human behavior was the achievement of Quetelet, who clearly distinguished the two situations. Jevons (p. 363) suggested that scientists should use "the word *mean* only in the former sense when it denotes approximation to a definite existing quantity; and *average*, when the mean is only a fictitious quantity, used for convenience of thought and expression." A parallel distinction between "observations" and "statistics" was made by F. Y. Edgeworth in 1885 (as quoted by Stigler, pp. 295–296): "Observations and statistics agree in being quantities grouped about a Mean: they differ in that the Mean of the observations is a cause, as it were the source from which diverging errors emanate. The mean of statistics is a description, a representative quantity put for a whole group. . . . Different measurements of the same man are observations; but measurements of different men, grouped around *l'homme moyen*, are . . . statistics." Apparently, Edgeworth was the first to recognize the applicability of the theory of errors, originally proposed for "observations," to the variation of means derived from "statistics" and "to estimate the probability that . . . differences in . . . averages . . . are not accidental" (quoted by Stigler from an 1884 review by Edgeworth of a monograph by Jevons). Going beyond such investigators as Quetelet, Galton, Jevons, and Lexis, who used probability descriptively, Edgeworth took the theory of errors as a point of departure in developing a rigorous method of statistical inference suited to social data.

Jevons's suggestion as to terminology—to reserve "mean" for "observations" and to use "average" in connection with "statistics"—has not prevailed; and the distinction itself is often lost in modern presentations of statistical methods. This may reflect, in part, the fact that "averages," like "statistics" itself, have heterogeneous origins. Jevons (p. 360) mentions that "the old arithmeticians recognized ten kinds" of means, as stated by Boethius (c. 475–524). Aristotle explained that "corrective justice must be the [arithmetic] mean between loss and gain" and the judge, who is the incarnation of justice, may for this reason be known as the "mediator." He restores equality by taking from the greater half of its excess over the lesser and adding it to the latter. "That is to say, we must add to the party who has too little the amount by which the mean exceeds what he has, and take away from the party who has too much the amount by which the mean is exceeded by what he has" (*Nicomachean Ethics*, Thomson translation, pp. 129–130). The English "average" is derived from the Old Italian *avaria*, damage to a ship or cargo, at first sight an implausible etymology. The article on "Average" in the 1894 *Encyclopaedia Britannica* explains that it is

a term used in maritime commerce to signify damages or expenses resulting from the accidents of navigation. . . . General average arises when sacrifices have been made, or expenditures incurred, for the preservation of the ship, cargo, and freight, from some peril of the sea, or from its effects. It implies a subsequent contribution, from all the parties concerned, rateably to the values of their respective interests, to make good the loss thus occasioned.

Both Aristotle's mean and the maritime average have to do with a total (of, say, expenditures) that may be equally or unequally divided among two or more parties. The mean is then the total divided by the number of parties. But when we come to the nineteenth-century Harvard practice of averaging grades over departments, it is difficult to conceive of the total of all grades as a meaningful aggregate, although it is obtained as a step in the calculation of an average whose motivation seems transparent enough. From there it is a relatively short step to procedures intended to aggregate heterogeneous quantities in an overall "figure of merit" for purposes of selecting among alternative courses of action. The resulting composite score will be compounded of somewhat arbitrarily weighted strategic elements, each of them having been evaluated on a somewhat arbitrary scale, such as might be used to assess "figure, poise, and personality" in a beauty contest. This method of "weighted statistical logic," it is claimed (Epstein, p. 306), supplies a sophisticated, if less than "completely intelligent," procedure whose "objective is creation of a system maintaining a constant proportionality of relative values throughout the course of a single decision and throughout a series of strategic decisions." Epstein does not, however, represent his "figure of merit" as a measurement. His proposal appears to be an updating of the score card method widely used in animal husbandry since, at the latest, the beginning of this century. Rommel (1904, 1905) exhibits over a hundred different score cards in use in agricultural colleges for various animals. He and other authorities (e.g., Barrows, Barrows and Davis, Thompson, Bedell) seem to regard the score card as a device for training livestock judges, who are not expected, however, to make formal use of it in the show ring.

Among the fundamental "scientific" inventions is one that didn't quite get made. The gist of the story is "that at one time economists held that utility is measurable, although no one could devise a hedonimeter" (Georgescu-Roegen 1968, p. 264). I would have let it go at that, but I noted an excerpt from Plato's *Protagoras* quoted as the epigraph to *Foundations of Measurement* (Krantz and others 1971). It has to do with "weighing" pleasures and pains, a striking anticipation of the utilitarian calculus. (Jeremy Bentham was later to mention the possibility of a "moral thermometer.") A passage immediately following reports a Socratic lecture on the use of measurement (by unspecified techniques) to correct sense impressions (*Protagoras* 356c–357b; Taylor 1976):

> Now . . . answer me this. Do the same magnitudes look bigger when you see them from near at hand, and smaller at a distance, or not? . . . And similarly with thicknesses and numbers? And the same sounds are louder near at hand and softer at a distance? . . . So if our well-being had depended on taking steps to get large quantities, and avoid small ones, what should we have judged to be the thing that saves our lives? The art of measurement or the power of appearances? . . . since we have seen that the preservation of our life depends on a correct choice of pleasure and pain, be it more or less, larger or smaller or further or nearer, doesn't it seem that the thing that saves our lives is some technique of measurement?

Like Plato, students of the "foundations" of measurement have been taken with the idea of measuring utility; see, for example, the treatises of Pfanzagl (1971, Ch. 12), Krantz and others (1971, Ch. 8), and Roberts (1979, Chs. 6–8). I do not want to suggest an evaluation of work that is far beyond my ken though obviously ingenious and rigorous mathematically. I merely note that working hedonimeters are not yet part of the standard equipment of the social research laboratory. That situation could change.

I will add just two more categories of fundamental inventions in social measurement. (1) One is the collection of statistical methods for measuring distributions, association, dependence, and influence of variables. (2) The other is the corpus of mathematical ideas, particularly from geometry, topology, and matrix theory, for quantifying patterns and abstract properties of collections of items, events, relationships, and so on. To give just one example—not necessarily the earliest or most fundamental—for each category: (1) Pearson's correlation is often used to measure the degree of assortative marriage with respect to anatomical, psychological, and social characteristics of spouses. Spuhler (1962) cites studies giving sample correlations of $r = .28$ for the correlation between stature of husband and stature of wife and $r = .47$ for intelligence of spouses. United States data on large samples suggest a value around $r = .6$ for number of years of school completed (Warren 1966). Note that the phenomenon "measured" here is a property of the bivariate population, husband's characteristic by wife's characteristic, and not a property of that characteristic or its univariate distribution. We are comparing the "assortativeness" of marriage with respect to three different characteristics in the findings just reported. (2) A rather common kind of social data is the matrix of relationships among the persons in a group. The matrix might show, for example, for each pair of persons, i and j, in the group whether i chooses j as a friend $(x_{ij} = 1)$ or does not $(x_{ij} = 0)$. The matrix $\mathbf{X} = (x_{ij})$ can then be analyzed in various ways. Holland and Leinhardt (1978), for example, show that there are 16 possible types of triads in the group if each dyad making up the triad is classified as having a mutual, asymmetric, or null relationship. The triad census is the number of triads of each type. The investigators define indexes constructed from these counts, using various weighting systems, which may be used to test the hypothesis that the matrix is "structured," rather than "random," both terms having been given explicit mathematical definitions. Again, note that the "measurement" in question here is at some stages removed from the actual observations, which are made on the binary scale (1, 0) in recording the presence or absence of a friendship relationship of i to j. Some writers might wish to maintain that the term measurement should be restricted to the making of a quantitative observation (whether on a binary, a categorical, or a numerical scale). In that case, we could use the term quantification or index construction to refer to numbers derived from the elementary observations. In the present state of the art, such a distinction is probably premature and certainly unenforceable.

In summary, I suggest that the fundamental inventions—or perhaps I should say, the main kinds of fundamental invention—in social measurement are, for short, (1) voting, (2) enumerating, (3) money, (4) defining social rank, (5) appraising competence or performance, (6) graduating rewards and punishments, (7) probability, (8) random sampling of populations, (9) psychophysical scaling, (10) index numbers, (11) utility (?), (12) measures of univariate, bivariate, and multivariate distributions, and (13) measures of properties of social networks. I make no strong claims for the list. It is a beginning of a historical and logical structuring of "The World of Social Measurements" (cf. *The World of Measurements*, Klein 1974). Many subsequent inventions amount to elaborations on, or combinations of, several of these. For example, the modern social-psychological household interview survey involves a probability sample of a well-defined human population; the respondents may be invited to select from or to rank two or more alternative views on a social issue—in short, to "vote"; the respondents are counted within categories of a variety of social classifications; the survey questionnaire may include psychometric tests or analogous instruments; it may involve tasks involving judgments after the fashion of a psychophysical experiment; and so on. Someone writing a history of social measurement might try to ascertain the circumstances under which the more consequential combinations or elaborations of the fundamental inventions occurred.

A good critical history of social measurement, taking this long view, though badly needed, is not yet a sociology of measurement. A friendly critic suggests that my essay falls short of providing a treatise on this topic because I think it is not worth the effort. On the contrary, it is worth a great deal more effort than I can mobilize, and I fully agree with the critic that a serious research project intended to produce a theory of the interactions of society with measurements of society could increase our understanding of social history and of social science a great deal. (I do not take a stand on the question raised by some other critics of how all this may relate to attempts to improve social policies.) It goes without saying (at any greater length) that the project will have to get much deeper than I did into what is "fundamental" about the "fundamental inventions" in social measurement. The loosely chronological and blatantly anecdotal approach I have taken is probably not the best way to attack this question.

In the remainder of the essay, in shifting into the role of critic without entirely abandoning the attempt to achieve historical perspective, I shall be raising some issues about our current conceptions and practice of social measurement. The issues are ones that I have had occasion to reflect on, and I make no stronger claim to cover the domain spanned by my entire set of fundamental inventions.

REFERENCES

Arbuthnott, John. "An Argument for Divine Providence, Taken from the Constant Regularity Observ'd in the Births of Both Sexes." *Phil. Trans.* 27 (1710): 186–190. Reprint, in Kendall and Plackett (1977, Ch. 5).

Aristotle. *Constitution of Athens. See* Ross (1921).

Aristotle. *Nicomachean Ethics. See* Thomson (1953).

Aristotle, *Politics. See* Ross (1921).

Ayres, L. P. "History and Present Status of Educational Measurement." *Seventeenth Yearbook of the National Society for the Study of Education* (1918), Part 2, Ch. 1.

Barrows, H. P. *Judging Horses as a Subject of Instruction in Secondary Schools.* U.S. Department of Agriculture Bulletin 487. Washington, D.C.: GPO, 1917.

Barrows, H. P., and H. P. Davis. *Judging the Dairy Cow as a Subject of Instruction in Secondary Schools.* U.S. Department of Agriculture Bulletin 434. Washington, D.C.: GPO, 1916.

Beccaria, Cesare. *On Crimes and Punishments,* 1764. Trans. by Henry Paolucci. Indianapolis: Bobbs-Merrill, 1963.

Bedell, G. H. *Judging Sheep.* U.S. Department of Agriculture Farmers Bulletin 1199. Washington, D.C.: GPO, 1921.

Bodin, Jean. *The Six Bookes of a Commonweale.* Trans. by Richard Knolles. London: G. Bishop, 1606. Reprint, Cambridge: Harvard University Press, 1962.

Boring, Edwin G. "The Beginning and Growth of Measurement in Psychology." In *Quantification: A History of the Meaning of Measurement in the Natural and Social Sciences,* edited by Harry Woolf. Indianapolis: Bobbs-Merrill, 1961.

Box, Joan Fisher. *R. A. Fisher: The Life of a Scientist.* New York: Wiley, 1978.

Breasted, James Henry. *A History of Egypt.* New York: Scribner's, 1905.

Bryant, William Cullen, trans. *The Iliad of Homer.* Boston: Houghton Mifflin, 1870.

Burn, A. R. *The Pelican History of Greece.* Rev. ed. Harmondsworth: Penguin, 1978.

Burrage, Michael C., and David Corry. "At Sixes and Sevens: Occupational Status in the City of London from the Fourteenth to the Seventeenth Century." *American Sociological Review* 46 (August 1981): 375–393.

Caldwell, Otis W., and Stuart A. Courtis. *Then & Now in Education 1845:1923*. Yonkers-on-Hudson, N.Y.: World Book Co., 1924.

Campbell, Lewis, and William Garnett. *The Life of James Clerk Maxwell*. London, 1882. Reprint, New York: Johnson Reprint Corp., 1969.

Caplow, Theodore. "Christmas Gifts and Kin Networks." *American Sociological Review* 47 (June 1982): 383–392.

Chapin, F. Stuart. *Cultural Change*. New York: Century, 1928.

Cipolla, C. M. "The 'Bills of Mortality' of Florence." *Population Studies* 32 (November 1978): 543–548.

Clark, G. N. "Social Science in the Age of Newton." In *The Establishment of Empirical Sociology*, edited by Anthony Oberschall. New York: Harper & Row, 1972: 15–30.

Coggins, R. J. *The First and Second Books of the Chronicles*. Cambridge: Cambridge University Press, 1976.

Coleman, James S. *Introduction to Mathematical Sociology*. New York: Free Press, 1964.

Cressey, Paul F. "The Influence of the Literary Examination System on the Development of Chinese Civilization." *American Journal of Sociology* 35 (September 1929): 250–262.

Cubberley, Ellwood P. "Editor's Introduction." In *Modern Methods in Written Examinations*, by Albert R. Lang. Boston: Houghton Mifflin, 1930.

David, F. N. *Games, Gods and Gambling*. New York: Hafner, 1962.

Dow, Sterling. "Aristotle, the Kleroteria, and the Courts." *Harvard Studies in Classical Philology* 50 (1939): 1–34.

Doyle, Kenneth O. "Theory and Practice of Ability Testing in Ancient Greece." *Journal of the History of the Behavioral Sciences* 10 (April 1974): 202–212.

Drummond, Frederick. "Precedence." *Encyclopaedia Britannica*, 9th ed. 19: 660–668. Chicago: Werner, 1894.

Drummond, Frederick. "Titles of Honour." *Encyclopaedia Britannica*, 9th ed. 23: 417–418. Chicago: Werner, 1895.

DuBois, Philip H. "A Test-Dominated Society: China, 1115 B.C.–1905 A.D." In *Testing Problems in Perspective*, edited by Anne Anastasi. Washington, D.C.: American Council on Education, 1966: 29–36.

Dupree, Hunter. "The Pace of Measurement from Rome to America." *Smithsonian Journal of History* 3 (Fall 1968): 19–40.

Durkheim, Emile. *Suicide: A Study in Sociology*, 1897. Trans. by John A. Spaulding and George Simpson. Glencoe, Ill.: Free Press, 1951.

Epstein, Richard A. *The Theory of Gambling and Statistical Logic*. New York: Academic Press, 1967.

Fang, Achilles. "Introduction." In *Shih-ching: The Classic Anthology Defined by Confucius*, by Ezra Pound. Cambridge: Harvard University Press, 1954.

Farr, William. "Census." *Encyclopaedia Britannica*, 9th ed. 9: 334–340. Chicago: Werner, 1894.

Fienberg, Stephen E. "Randomization and Social Affairs: The 1970 Draft Lottery." *Science* 171 (22 January 1971): 255–261.

Finley, M. I. *The World of Odysseus*. 2d ed. Harmondsworth: Penguin, 1979.

Fitts, Dudley. *Aristophanes: Four Comedies*. New York: Harcourt Brace Jovanovich, 1962.

Frankfort, Henri. *The Birth of Civilization in the Near East*. Garden City, N.Y.: Doubleday, 1956.

Galton, Francis. *Hereditary Genius*, 1869. 2d ed., reprint. London: Macmillan, 1914.

Gardiner, E. Norman. *Athletics of the Ancient World*. Oxford: Clarendon Press, 1955.

Georgescu-Roegen, Nicholas. "Utility." *International Encyclopedia of the Social Sciences* 16: 236–267. New York: Macmillan, 1968.

Gillispie, C. C. "Intellectual Factors in the Background of Analysis by Probabilities." In *Scientific Change*, edited by A. C. Crombie, Ch. 14. New York: Basic Books, 1963.

Gillispie, Charles Coulston. "Probability and Politics: Laplace, Condorcet, and Turgot." *Proceedings of the American Philosophical Society* 116 (February 1972): 1–20.

Goode, William J. *The Celebration of Heroes*. Berkeley: University of California Press, 1978.

Gosnell, Harold F. "Proportional Representation." *Encyclopaedia of the Social Sciences* 12: 541–545. New York: Macmillan, 1934.

Green, Peter. *Ancient Greece: An Illustrated History*. London: Thames and Hudson, 1973.

Grierson, Philip. *English Linear Measures: An Essay in Origins*. The Stenton Lecture 1971. Reading: University of Reading, 1972.

Hacking, Ian. *The Emergence of Probability: A Philosophical Study of Early Ideas About Probability, Induction and Statistical Inference*. Cambridge: Cambridge University Press, 1975.

Hajnal, J. "European Marriage Patterns in Perspective." In *Population in History*, edited by D. V. Glass and D.E.C. Eversley, Ch. 6. Chicago: Aldine, 1965.

Hall, Jerome. *Theft, Law, and Society*. 2d ed. Indianapolis: Bobbs-Merrill, 1952.

Harris, H. A. *Sport in Greece and Rome*. Ithaca, N.Y.: Cornell University Press, 1972.

Hasofer, A. M. "Random Mechanisms in Talmudic Literature." 1967. Reprint, in Pearson and Kendall (1970), Ch. 5.

Herodotus. *The Histories*. Trans. by Aubrey de Sélincourt. Rev. ed. Harmondsworth: Penguin Books, 1972.

Herodotus. *The History*. Trans. by George Rawlinson. New York: Tudor, 1956.

Herodotus. *Second Book of the Histories*. Trans. by G. C. Macaulay. New York: Collier, 1910.

Herschel, John [Unsigned]. "Art. I" [Review of publications on probabilities by A. Quetelet]. *Edinburgh Review* 92 (July 1850): 1–57.

Hobbes, Thomas. *Leviathan*, 1651. Reprint, Oxford: Basil Blackwell, 1960.

Holland, Paul W., and Samuel Leinhardt. "An Omnibus Test for Social Structure Using Triads." *Sociological Methods and Research* 7 (November 1978): 227–256.

Jencks, Christopher, and others. *Inequality*. New York: Basic Books, 1972.

Jevons, W. Stanley. *The Principles of Science*. London: Macmillan, 1892.

Kelsen, Hans. *Society and Nature*. London: Kegan Paul, Trench, Trubner, 1946.

Kendall, M. G. "The Beginnings of a Probability Calculus," 1956. Reprint, in Pearson and Kendall (1970), Ch. 2.

Kendall, M. G. "The Early History of Index Numbers," 1969. Reprint, in Kendall and Plackett (1977), Ch. 7.

Kendall, M. G. "Measurement in the Study of Society," 1972. Reprint, in Kendall and Plackett (1977), Ch. 6.

Kendall, M. G., and R. L. Plackett. *Studies in the History of Statistics and Probability*. Vol. 2. New York: Macmillan, 1977.

Klein, H. Arthur. *The World of Measurements*. New York: Simon and Schuster, 1974.

Knox, Bernard. "Greece and the Theater." In *The Three Theban Plays*, Sophocles, trans. by Robert Fagles. New York: Viking, 1982.

Krantz, David H., R. Duncan Luce, Patrick Suppes, and Amos Tversky. *Foundations of Measurement*, Vol. 1. New York: Academic Press, 1971.

Kruskal, William, and Frederick Mosteller. "Representative Sampling, I: Non-scientific Literature." *International Statistical Review* 47 (1979): 13–24.

Kruskal, William, and Frederick Mosteller. "Representative Sampling, II: Scientific Literature, Excluding Statistics." *International Statistical Review* 47 (1979): 111–127.

Kruskal, William, and Frederick Mosteller. "Representative Sampling, III: The Current Statistical Literature." *International Statistical Review* 47 (1979): 245–265.

Kruskal, William, and Frederick Mosteller. "Representative Sampling, IV: The History of the Concept in Statistics, 1895–1939." *International Statistical Review* 48 (1980): 169–195.

Landtman, Gunnar. *The Origin of the Inequality of the Social Classes.* Chicago: University of Chicago Press, 1938.

Larsen, J.A.O. *Representative Government in Greek and Roman History.* Berkeley and Los Angeles: University of California Press, 1955.

Latham, Henry. "Examinations." *Encyclopaedia Britannica.* 9th ed. 8: 777–783.

Lazarsfeld, Paul F. "Notes on the History of Quantification in Sociology—Trends, Sources and Problems." In *Quantification*, edited by Harry Woolf. Indianapolis: Bobbs-Merrill, 1961.

Lazarsfeld, Paul F., and Anthony R. Oberschall. "Max Weber and Empirical Social Research." *American Sociological Review* 30 (April 1965): 185–199.

Lécuyer, Bernard, and Anthony R. Oberschall. "Sociology: The Early History of Social Research." *International Encyclopedia of the Social Sciences* 15: 36–53.

Leeper, E. M. "Weighing the Quality of Doctoral Programs." In National Research Council *Issues and Studies: 1981–1982.* Washington: National Academy Press, 1982.

Lewontin, R. C. "Darwin and Mendel—The Materialist Revolution." In *The Heritage of Copernicus*, edited by Jerzy Neyman. Ch. 7. Cambridge: MIT Press, 1974.

Lichtenstein, Murray, and Louis Isaac Rabinowitz. "Lots." *Encyclopaedia Judaica*, pp. 510–514. New York: Macmillan, 1971–1972.

Livy. *The Early History of Rome.* Trans. by Aubrey de Sélincourt. Harmondsworth: Penguin, 1960.

Lorimer, Frank. "The Development of Demography." In *The Study of Population*, edited by Philip M. Hauser and Otis Dudley Duncan. Ch. 6. Chicago: University of Chicago Press, 1959.

Loyseau, Charles. *Traité des ordres et simple dignitez.* In *Les Oeuvres.* Paris: 1666.

Martindale, Don. *Social Life and Cultural Change.* Princeton: D. Van Nostrand, 1962.

Merton, Robert K. "Singletons and Multiples in Scientific Discovery." *Proceedings of the American Philosophical Society* 105 (1961): 470–486.

Montesquieu, Baron de [Charles Secondat]. *The Spirit of the Laws.* Trans. by Thomas Nugent. New York: Hafner, 1949.

Montgomery, R. J. *Examinations: An Account of Their Evolution as Administrative Devices in England.* Pittsburgh: University of Pittsburgh Press, 1965.

Muirhead, James. "Roman Law." *Encyclopaedia Britannica*, 9th ed. 20: 669–715. Chicago: Werner, 1894.

Neale, Walter C. *Monies in Societies.* San Francisco: Chandler and Sharp, 1976.

Neyman, Jerzy. *First Course in Probability and Statistics.* New York: Holt, 1950.

Neyman, Jerzy, ed. *The Heritage of Copernicus.* Cambridge: MIT Press, 1974.

Noth, Martin. *Numbers: A Commentary.* Philadelphia: Westminster Press, 1968.

Oberschall, Anthony. *Empirical Social Research in Germany 1848–1914.* Paris: Mouton, 1965.

Oberschall, Anthony, ed. *The Establishment of Empirical Sociology.* New York: Harper and Row, 1972.

Ogburn, William Fielding. *Social Change*, 1922. New ed. New York: Viking Press, 1950.

Ogburn, William F. "A Device for Measuring the Size of Families, Invented by Edgar Sydenstricker and W. I. King." In *Methods in Social Science*, edited by Stuart A. Rice. Ch. 12. Chicago: University of Chicago Press, 1931.

Ore, Oystein. "Pascal and the Invention of Probability Theory." *American Mathematical Monthly* 67 (May 1960): 409–419.

Pareti, Luigi, Paolo Brezzi, and Luciano Petech. *The Ancient World: 1200 B.C. to A.D. 500* (UNESCO History of Mankind, Vol. 2). New York: Harper, 1965.

Pearson, E. S., and M. G. Kendall, eds. *Studies in the History of Statistics and Probability.* London: Griffin, 1970.

Pfanzagl, Johann. *Theory of Measurement.* Würzburg: Physica-Verlag, 1971.

Pfautz, Harold W., ed. *Charles Booth on the City.* Chicago: University of Chicago Press, 1967.

Plackett, R. L. "The Principle of the Arithmetic Mean," 1958. Reprint, in Pearson and Kendall (1970), Ch. 8.

Plato. *Laws*, 2 vols. Trans. by R. G. Bury. London: Heinemann, 1926.

Plato. *Laws*. Trans. by Thomas L. Pangle. New York: Basic Books, 1980.

Plato. *Protagoras*. Trans. by C.C.W. Taylor. Oxford: Clarendon Press, 1976.

Pliskoff, Stanley S., and Charles B. Ferster. "Learning: Reinforcement." *International Encyclopedia of the Social Sciences* 9: 135–143.

Polanyi, Karl. "On the Comparative Treatment of Economic Institutions in Antiquity, with Illustrations from Athens, Mycenae, and Alalakh." In *City Invincible*, edited by Carl H. Kraeling and Robert M. Adams. Background Paper 5. Chicago: University of Chicago Press, 1960.

Provine, William B. *The Origins of Theoretical Population Genetics*. Chicago: University of Chicago Press, 1971.

Rabinovitch, Nachum L. *Probability and Statistical Inference in Ancient and Medieval Jewish Literature*. Toronto: University of Toronto Press, 1973.

Resnick, Daniel. "History of Educational Testing." In Committee on Ability Testing, National Research Council. *Ability Testing: Uses, Consequences, and Controversies*, Part 2, pp. 173–194. Washington, D.C.: National Academy Press, 1982.

Rice, Stuart A. "Quantitative Methods in Politics." *Journal of the American Statistical Association* 33 (March 1938): 126–130.

Roberts, Fred S. *Measurement Theory*. Reading, Mass.: Addison-Wesley, 1979.

Robinson, Claude E. *Straw Votes*. New York: Columbia University Press, 1932.

Robinson, Claude E. "Straw Vote." *Encyclopaedia of the Social Sciences* 14: 417–419. New York: Macmillan, 1934.

Rommel, George M. *The Score Card in Stock Judging at Agricultural Colleges*. U.S. Department of Agriculture, Bureau of Animal Industry, Bulletin 61. Washington, D.C.: GPO, 1904.

Rommel, George M. *The Score Card in Stock Breeding*. U.S. Department of Agriculture, Bureau of Animal Industry, Bulletin 76. Washington, D.C.: GPO, 1905.

Ross, W. D., ed. *The Works of Aristotle*, Vol. 10. Oxford: Clarendon Press, 1921.

Rowe, John Howland, "Inca Culture at the Time of the Spanish Conquest." In *Handbook of South American Indians*, Vol. 2, edited by Julian H. Steward, pp. 183–330. Washington, D.C.: GPO, 1946.

Sambursky, S. "On the Possible and Probable in Ancient Greece." 1956. Reprint, in Kendall and Plackett (1977), Ch. 1.

Selvin, Hanan C. "Durkheim's *Suicide* and Problems of Empirical Research." *American Journal of Sociology* 63 (May 1958): 607–619.

Sewell, William H., Jr. "Etat, Corps, and Ordre: Some Notes on the Social Vocabulary of the French Old Regime." In *Sozialgeschichte Heute*, edited by Hans-Ulrich Wehler, pp. 49–68. Göttingen: Vandenhoeck & Ruprecht, 1974.

Sewell, William H., Jr. *Work and Revolution in France*. Cambridge: Cambridge University Press, 1980.

Small, Albion W. "Fifty Years of Sociology in the United States (1865–1915)," 1916. Reprint, *American Journal of Sociology*, Index to Volumes 1–52, 1947.

Smallwood, Mary Lovett. *An Historical Study of Examinations and Grading Systems in Early American Universities*. Cambridge: Harvard University Press, 1935.

Sorokin, Pitirim A. *Social and Cultural Dynamics*. Vol. 2, *Fluctuation of Systems of Truth, Ethics, and Law*. New York: American Book Co., 1937.

Spuhler, J. N. "Empirical Studies on Quantitative Human Genetics." In *The Use of Vital and Health Statistics for Genetic and Radiation Studies*, Proceedings of the Seminar sponsored by the United Nations and the World Health Organization, Geneva, 1960. New York: United Nations, 1962.

Staveley, E. S. *Greek and Roman Voting and Elections*. Ithaca: Cornell University Press, 1972.

Stigler, Stephen M. "Francis Ysidro Edgeworth, Statistician." *Journal of the Royal Statistical Society*, Ser. A, Vol. 141 (Part 3, 1978): 287–313.

Suetonius. *Lives of the Caesars*. Trans. by Alexander Thomson, revised by T. Forester. London: George Bell & Sons, 1906.

Sumner, William Graham. *Folkways*. Boston: Ginn and Co., 1906.

Susser, Mervyn. *Causal Thinking in the Health Sciences*. New York: Oxford University Press, 1973.

Sydenham, P. H. *Measuring Instruments: Tools of Knowledge and Control*. Stevenage, Eng.: Peter Peregrinus, 1979.

Thompson, E. H. *Judging Beef Cattle*. U.S. Department of Agriculture, Farmers Bulletin 1068. Washington, D.C.: GPO, 1919.

Thomson, J.A.K., trans. *The Ethics of Aristotle*. London: George Allen & Unwin, 1953.

Thucydides. *History of the Peloponnesian War*. Trans. by Rex Warner. Harmondsworth: Penguin, 1972.

Tomasson, Richard F. "A Millennium of Misery: The Demography of the Icelanders." *Population Studies* 31 (November 1977): 405–427.

Toynbee, Arnold J. *A Study of History*. Vol. 7. London: Oxford University Press, 1954.

Toynbee, Arnold J. *A Study of History*. Vols. 7–10 abridged by D. C. Somervell. New York: Oxford University Press, 1957.

Treiman, Donald J. *Occupational Prestige in Comparative Perspective*. New York: Academic Press, 1977.

Unsigned. "Educational Measurements of Fifty Years Ago." *Journal of Educational Psychology* 4 (October 1913): 551–552.

Unsigned. *World Dictionary of Awards and Prizes*. London: Europa Publications Limited, 1979.

Vegetius. *The Military Institutions of the Romans*. Trans. by Lt. John Clark, edited by Brig. Gen. Thomas R. Phillips, U.S.A. Harrisburg, Pa: Military Service Pub. Co., 1944.

Wagner, Adolph. *Die Gesetzmässigkeit in den Scheinbar Willkürlichen Menschlichen Handlungen vom Standpunkte der Statistik*. Hamburg: Geisler, 1864.

Walton, J. Michael. *Greek Theatre Practice*. Westport, Ct.: Greenwood Press, 1980.

Warren, Bruce L. "A Multiple Variable Approach to the Assortative Mating Phenomenon." *Eugenics Quarterly* 13 (December 1966): 285–290.

Webb, Eugene L., Donald T. Campbell, Richard D. Schwartz, and Lee Sechrest. *Unobtrusive Measures: Nonreactive Research in the Social Sciences*. Chicago: Rand McNally, 1966.

Weber, Max. *General Economic History*. Trans. by Frank H. Knight. Glencoe, Ill.: Free Press, 1950.

Weber, Max. *The Religion of China*. Glencoe, Ill.: Free Press, 1951.

Willcox, Walter F. "Census." *Encyclopaedia of the Social Sciences* 3:295–300. New York: Macmillan, 1930.

Wittfogel, Karl A. *Oriental Despotism*. New Haven: Yale University Press, 1957.

Wolfe, A. B. "Population Censuses Before 1790." *Journal of the American Statistical Association* 27 (December 1932): 357–370.

Young, David C. "Professionalism in Archaic and Classical Greek Athletics." *Ancient World* 7 (Spring 1983): 45–51.

Young, David C. *The Olympic Myth of Greek Amateur Athletics*. Chicago: Ares Publishers, 1984.

Zabell, Sandy. "Review of Rabinovitch (1973)." *Journal of the American Statistical Association* 71 (December 1976): 996–998.

Zeisel, Hans. "Afterword: Toward a History of Sociography." In *Marienthal: The Sociography of an Unemployed Community*, by Marie Jahoda, Paul F. Lazarsfeld, and Hans Zeisel. Chicago: Aldine, 1971.

4

ON SCALES
OF MEASUREMENT

MEASUREMENT is one of many human achievements and practices that grew up and came to be taken for granted before anyone thought to ask how and why they work. There is a striking analogy— perhaps something more—in the history of mathematics. What we now take to be the "foundations" of that subject only began to be investigated in the nineteenth century. According to Nagel and Newman (p. 5), "Until modern times geometry was the only branch of mathematics that had what most students considered a sound axiomatic basis." But what a marvelous superstructure had already been erected on the nonexistent foundations! In regard to our topic, Sydenham (1979) remarks, "In many instances of the late 19th century and continuing well into this century, where discussion of measurement was a key subject," as in certain physics texts, "it is as though the writers believed that their readers were already totally familiar with the fundamental nature and characteristics of a measurement." He also observes that present-day concern with philosophy of measurement is found especially in "academic studies" that "generally go under such general descriptors as the soft sciences, the empirical sciences, the inexact sciences or the fringe sciences," whereas "practising engineers or physical scientists . . . generally have been content with the fact that they have been able to devise what ever hardware they needed to measure the variables that have arisen" (pp. 452–453).

The situation Sydenham describes, in which it is the "empirical sciences" that are working the hardest on philosophy of measurement, is somewhat recent. Early studies on the formal logic of measurement by Helmholtz in 1887, Hölder in 1901, and Campbell (1920) set the pattern of looking to operations used in physics in trying to establish "foundations" of measurement. The work by Campbell was regarded as authoritative in some quarters for many years. Subsequently a literature on this subject developed in the philosophy of science, with important essays being contributed by such writers as Nagel, Hempel, and Carnap. For the most part these authors, like Ellis (1966) in his more extensive treatise, were content to explicate the procedures followed in physics to produce so-called fundamental measurement (not to be confused with my term "fundamental inventions" pertaining to social measurement, although some of them do involve fundamental measurement). This is not astonishing inasmuch as philosophy of science has historically given most of its attention to physics, with only side glances at the biological and social sciences. The main reason to be concerned about that bias is our tendency to interpret statements in the philosophy of science as being prescriptive (what one must do to obtain scientific results) rather than descriptive (what science has done successfully in the past). As a matter of fact, even as description much of the philosophy of science is potentially misleading, for it usually gives a neat ex post facto rationalization for what in actuality was a messy, trial-and-error process. To see this one has only to compare the schematic outlines of the development of temperature scales in Ellis (1966, Ch. 6) or Carnap (1966, Ch. 6) with the history of thermometry presented in some detail by Middleton (1966) or Barnett (1956).

In the era to which Sydenham's observation applies, we have two mainstreams of literature on measurement theory. One is closely linked to ideas and methods of psychological scaling. The other is a primarily mathematical discourse on "foundations" of measurement. I shall have little to say about the latter, since its technical level is quite beyond me, or beyond anyone lacking thorough preparation in some specialized areas of mathematics. Indeed, one of the "foundations" texts, Roberts (1979), is in a series entitled "Encyclopedia of Mathematics and Its Applications." The works of Pfanzagl (1971) and Krantz and others (1971) are similarly mathematically formidable. The earlier remark on a certain deficiency of realism in philosophical discussions of measurement could be applied here as well. The idealization of the measurement process is carried even further in this fully mathematical approach, in which it proves to be quite difficult, for example, to acknowledge the facts that all measurement in the real world is subject to error and that there is no empirical means for demonstrating that two objects have exactly equal values on any continuous quantitative dimension (see Adams 1965; Bunge 1973; Leaning and Finkelstein 1980). In the present discussion I focus on the idea of scale types and the way in which this notion has both facilitated and impeded our understanding of problems of social measurement. In Chapter 6 I shall look at specific applications of scaling procedures that have proved to be useful or hold promise of being useful in the social sciences.

The acknowledged founder of the theory of scale types is the psychologist S. S. Stevens, whose brief article published in 1946 has been widely cited, discussed (sometimes in polemical vein), and reprinted (for example, in 1960; 1970). In an autobiographical section of his posthumously published text, Stevens (1975, p. 38) tells us that his "new outlook on the problem of measurement . . . began to crystallize in the 1940's" as a "direct response to the challenge raised by the problem of measuring sensation," and specifically that the "challenge had taken explicit form" in the work of a committee of physicists and psychologists appointed in 1932 by the British Association for the Advancement of Science to "assess the possibility of 'quantitative estimates of sensory events.' " In its final report of 1940 there was a diversity of positions taken by members of the committee on the question of whether sensation can be measured. The committee had given special attention to the Sone scale of loudness proposed by Stevens and Davis in 1938, and one member had formulated the view "that any law purporting to express a quantitative relation between sensation intensity and stimulus intensity is not merely false but is in fact meaningless unless and until a meaning can be given to the concept of addition as applied to sensation" (quoted by Stevens 1946). Stevens's response to this challenge included the following elements: a classification of scales of measurement (to which we shall turn in a moment), a number of remarks on "the statistical manipulations that can legitimately be applied to empirical data" (which we shall largely ignore in the present discussion), and a brief argument intended to show that the additivity criterion is overly restrictive: A "procedure . . . too long to describe . . . is mentioned . . . to suggest that physical addition . . . though . . . sometimes possible, is not necessarily the basis of all measurement." Further, the work on the Sone scale is summarized to show that within "limits imposed by error and variability" it is possible for "human observers" to "judge the loudness ratios of pairs of tones." Hence, "within these limits the Sone scale ought properly to be classed as a ratio scale."

My reading of the subsequent literature is that Stevens's counter-challenge to the British committee and, in particular, to the intellectual legacy of N. R. Campbell (1920) was successful in the sense that recent theorists agree that physical addition (as of one rod to another in measuring length) is not the only operation that can provide a logically consistent resolution of what the "foundations" literature calls the "representation problem," the "problem of finding axioms under which measurement is possible" (Roberts, p. 4). To that extent, Stevens surely attained his goal of "freedom" for the "ever wider generalization of rules and principles" which he saw as a salient feature of the development of mathematics (1975, p. 46) and which he thought we should seek in the development of measurement.

Although the example of the Sone scale served to illustrate the possibility of an approach to measurement not requiring the additivity condition, Stevens later turned to scaling techniques other than the one he first used. Therefore we need not be concerned here with the persuasiveness of the particular example he presented in 1946.

In later articles as well as his first publication on measurement theory Stevens resorted to a tabular presentation of his definitions of scale types. There are essentially two versions of the table insofar as the mathematical properties of the scale types are concerned, and I have combined them in Table 4-1. Stevens himself described the 1975 verson as "adapted from" the 1946 version, which he had repeated with minor variations in his articles of 1951, 1959, and 1968a,b. Stevens (1946) was taking as his point of departure the statement "that measurement, in the broadest sense is defined as the assignment of numerals to objects or events according to rules" and asking for recognition "that measurement exists in a variety of forms and that scales of measurement fall into definite classes." The names of the classes are

TABLE 4-1.

The Stevens Classification of Scales of Measurement

Scale	Basic Empirical Operations (1946)	Operations We Perform (1975)	Mathematical Group Structure (1946)	Permissible Transformations (1975)
N	Determination of equality	Identify and classify	Permutation group $x' = f(x)$ $f(x)$ means any one-to-one substitution	Substitution of any number for any other number
O	Determination of greater or less	Rank order	Isotonic group $x' = f(x)$ $f(x)$ means any monotonic increasing function	Any change that preserves order
I	Determination of equality of intervals or differences	Find distances or differences	General linear group $x' = ax + b$	Multiplication by a constant Addition of a constant
R	Determination of equality of ratios	Find ratios, fractions, or multiples	*Similarity group* $x' = ax$	Multiplication by a constant only

learned by every graduate student in a course on statistics or "methods": the nominal scale (N), the ordinal scale (O), the interval scale (I), and the ratio scale (R).

The 1946 paper did not provide a systematic compilation of examples of these scale types, but the later papers did so; I have assembled these compilations in Table 4-2 for ease of reference. In this aspect of Stevens's discussion there were some modifications from one article to another that may have been significant to the author, although it is difficult to be sure of this, since most of the examples are not discussed. For the same reason, one cannot always be sure what specific measurement technique is meant. For example, I do not know what a "preference list" might be or how it might differ from a "rank list." Stevens does not explain what "position" (on a line) is supposed to refer to.

To my knowledge no commentator has denied Stevens's claim that the distinctions conveyed and illustrated in Tables 4-1 and 4-2 demonstrate that "measurement exists in a variety of forms." That claim, after

TABLE 4-2.

Examples of Scales of Measurement Given by Stevens

		Year Listed			
Scale	Example	1951	1959	1968b	1975
N	"Numbering" of football players	x	x	x	x
	Assignment of type or model numbers to classes	x	x	x	. . .
	Model numbers	. . .	. . .	. . .	x
O	Hardness of minerals	x	x	x	x
	Quality of leather, lumber, wool, etc.	x	. . .	. . .	. . .
	Grades of leather, lumber, wool, etc.	. . .	x	x	. . .
	Pleasantness of odors	x	. . .	. . .	. . .
	Street numbers	. . .	x	. . .	. . .
	Intelligence test raw scores	. . .	x	x	. . .
	Preference lists	. . .	. . .	. . .	x
	Rank lists	. . .	. . .	. . .	x
I	Temperature (Fahrenheit and centigrade)	x	. . .	. . .	. . .
	Temperature (Fahrenheit or Celsius)	. . .	x	x	x
	Energy	x	. . .	. . .	. . .
	Energy (potential)	. . .	x	x	. . .
	Calendar dates	x	. . .	. . .	. . .
	Time (calendar)	. . .	x	x	x
	"Standard scores" on achievement tests (?)	x	. . .	. . .	. . .
	Intelligence-test "standard-scores" (?)	. . .	x	x	. . .
	Standard scores	. . .	. . .	. . .	x
	Position	. . .	x	. . .	. . .
	Position on a line	. . .	. . .	x	. . .
R	Length, weight, density, resistance, etc.	x	. . .	. . .	. . .
	Length, density, work, time intervals, etc.	. . .	x	x	. . .
	Length, weight, numerosity, duration, and most physical scales	. . .	. . .	. . .	x
	Pitch scale (mels)	x	. . .	. . .	. . .
	Loudness scale (sones)	x	. . .	. . .	. . .
	Loudness (sones)	. . .	x	x	x
	Brightness (brils)	. . .	x	x	. . .
	Numerosity	. . .	x	x	. . .
	Temperature (Rankine or Kelvin)	. . .	x	x	x

all, was somewhat redundant when he first put it forward. In a college textbook on logic (Cohen and Nagel 1934) that Stevens could have known, we are told that

numbers may have at least three distinct uses: (1) as tags, or identification marks; (2) as signs to indicate the *position* of the degree of a quality in a *series* of degrees; and (3) as signs indicating the *quantitative* relations between qualities. On some occasions numbers may fulfill all three functions at once (p. 294).

This classification is equivalent to Stevens's classes N, O, and I and R taken together. The distinction between I and R is not entirely explicit in Cohen and Nagel, but they did warn against the error of supposing "that because we can assign numbers to different degrees of a quality, the different degrees always bear to each other the same ratio as do the numbers we have assigned to them" (p. 294). Stevens's explicit distinction between I and R scales and his demonstration that it turns on the difference in their invariance properties under transformations is, therefore, an advance beyond Cohen and Nagel and other earlier literature, although the same distinction, expounded in terms of transformations, was made by von Neumann and Morgenstern (1947, pp. 20–24; first edition 1944).

It seems to be true that making the distinction among scale types in terms of "mathematical group structure" was original with Stevens, and the importance he attributed to this contribution in the earlier articles may be suggested by the fact that he devoted two pages of the 1951 article to the concept of mathematical group. Yet the only use made of that idea was to stipulate the "permissible transformations" of scale values for each of the four types; Stevens was content to let it go at that in the 1975 presentation, where he omitted reference to "group structure."

The burden of my further discussion will be that Stevens's theory of scale types, in the form in which he left it, is flawed and requires emendation. I shall offer five major criticisms of the theory and Stevens's exposition of it. None of these criticisms will pertain to his claims for psychophysical scaling or his injunctions concerning statistics. The former are discussed elsewhere, and Stevens's attempt to legislate acceptable uses of statistical methods is better forgotten. The criticisms I offer do not gainsay the positive contributions that I have already mentioned. Nor would it be necessary to set forth any criticisms at all, in view of those contributions, but for the fact that Stevens's views continue to be influential in expositions of sociological method, wherein their deficiencies do strongly counterbalance their positive features. After all, most of what most of us know about measurement theory we learned from Stevens, if not directly then via some textbook author's secondary presentation. To improve our understanding of measurement, therefore, it may be more efficient to correct or improve upon Stevens than to discard his substantial contribution and start over. Stevens once wrote a paper, "To honor Fechner and repeal his law." My proposal is to honor Stevens and repeal, or modify, his theory of scale types.

In summary, I hold that (1) Stevens's definition of measurement is incomplete, and the deficiency is not innocuous; (2) the presentation of examples is careless and at least potentially misleading; (3) the list of scale types is seriously incomplete, although we can draw on Stevens's own text, in part, to enlarge it; (4) the discussion of nominal scales is uninformed and in some respects borders on being frivolous—in any case its defects are mischievous, not potentially but actually; and (5) criteria for recognizing or establishing the scale type of a given procedure or measuring instrument are lacking or too sketchy to be reliably applied. These themes are woven into the following discussion, but it is impractical to try to isolate the discussion of each of them.

Stevens's definition of measurement, which he referred to as a "paraphrase" of a statement by N. R. Campbell, has already been quoted. I contend that "measurement . . . is . . . the assignment of numerals to objects or events according to rules" is an incomplete statement. It is incomplete in the same way that "playing the piano is striking the keys of the instrument according to some pattern" is incomplete. Measurement is not only the assignment of numerals, etc. It is also the assignment of numerals in such a way as to correspond to *different degrees of a quality* (Cohen and Nagel, p. 294) or property of some object or event. Ordinarily one does not argue too heatedly about definitions. But in this case Stevens is attempting to make contact with a large body and long history of scientific understanding and practice. His failure to stipulate what measurement is *for* risks a dangerous alienation from that which he would join. Just to illustrate the understanding I contend exists—that the purpose of measurement is to quantify—I cite the title and subtitle of a well-known work mentioned often in these pages: *Quantification: A History of the Meaning of Measurement in the Natural and Social Sciences* (Woolf 1961). Indeed Bunge (1973) goes so far as to insist that "quantification," not measurement, is the key concept in the "adult sciences" (Bunge is the author of works on foundations and philosophy of physics): "To quantitate . . . is to introduce a functional correspondence between the degrees of a property and numbers" (p. 108). Whereas Cohen and Nagel introduced the idea that numbers can be used "as tags, or identification marks" in order to distinguish that use as something different from measurement, thereby clarifying the meaning of measurement and its utility for science, Stevens regards such a use as one "type" of measurement. A careful weighing of this issue is given by Torgerson (1958, p. 17), who otherwise finds himself in substantial agreement with Stevens: "In measurement . . . the number assigned refers to the relative amount or degree of a property possessed by the object, and not to the object itself, whereas in the different nominal scales, the numbers refer to the objects or classes of objects."

Stevens can hardly have realized how frivolous it would seem to a reader already acquainted with scientific measurement for "numbering of football players" to be his very first example of "measurement." But, of course, it is just the kind of distraction that would draw the equally frivolous (to all appearances) commentary of a contentious critic (Lord 1953). The critic could no more adduce a good scientific reason for studying such numbers than Stevens did. Actually, it was Stevens himself who administered the *coup de grace* to the example, although this can hardly have been his intention. In the 1975 text (pp. 46–47) he wrote:

Measurement is the assignment of numbers to objects or events according to rule (Stevens 1946). The rule of assignment can be any consistent rule. The only rule not allowed would be random assignment, for randomness amounts in effect to a nonrule.

But the usual method of assigning code numbers to entities or unordered classes is, in effect, to select integers randomly (without replacement) from the sequence 1, 2, . . . , k. It is because numbers so selected bear no relationship to the "relative amount or degree of a property possessed by the object" or class that the construction of such "nominal scales" is not measurement.

One can only speculate about what Stevens thought was the gain from broadening measurement to include the use of numerals as tags. It did, of course, allow him to display the whole range of the "group structures" that were so fascinating to him. It seems to me that Stevens was not actually interested in the scientific uses of numerical tags. Had he been, he could have noted the following: In the case in which each object is to have a unique tag, the obvious reason for using a numeral (rather than an arbitrary sign, such as a cattle brand or the unique shape of the punch carried by each train conductor) is to provide for a convenient catalog of the objects. Astronomers use alphanumeric (rather than strictly numeric) tags in catalogs of stellar objects. In a sample survey each respondent has an identification number. In statistical notation when we want to associate the particular observation on variable X with the object on which it was made, we write X_i for the value of X for the i-th "individual," and specify the range of i. But none of this is measurement.

A quite distinct case is the one where the N "scale" consists of a set of classes and at least some classes may have more than one member. An important example for social research is found in the conventional codebook. In a sample survey respondents may be given the codes 1 for male, 2 for female; and 1 for Protestant, 2 for Catholic, 3 for Jewish, 4 for No religious preference, and 5 for Other. The numerals are usually consecutive integers even if there is no obvious principle by which the categories are ordered. This practice is intimately related to the use of punched cards as the basic statistical record of the survey interview (in the days before the computer). Ordinarily, each item or question has codes beginning with the numeral 1 and ending with the numeral corresponding to the number of categories defined for the item being coded. An ingenious alternative, proposed by Toops (1948), is the "addend" system, designed so that different items have different sets of code "numbers which when added yield a code number uniquely identifying the ultimate breakdown society to which a given person belongs." (For example, use code 0 for male, 1 for female, and, respectively, 0, 2, 4, 6, 8 for the five religious categories; then the sum 3 uniquely represents a female Catholic.) No doubt this idea occurred independently to many people working with card-counting machines. Ford (1954) attributes to W. Parker Mauldin a version of the "trick" especially well suited to the manipulations of response codes involved in constructing a Guttman scale. Of course, the addend system is only an apparent exception to Stevens's rules concerning "legitimate manipulations" of numerals, which prohibit adding the numbers corresponding to numerals assigned to classes of a nominal scale. In the addend system, although the numerals are assigned in a systematic ("tricky") way, it is still an arbitrary decision which numeral is assigned to Protestant and which one to Catholic respondents.

I belabor Stevens's failure to discuss coding and the properties of codes only to support my conjecture that he was not very interested, after all, in the so-called nominal scale, emphatic though he was in insisting that it "is an example of the 'assignment of numerals according to rule.' " He did indicate that in working with a nominal scale we may be interested in "hypotheses regarding the distribution of cases among the classes." But his curiosity about ways of attacking those hypotheses was decidedly limited.

My experience suggests that some social scientists have become all too comfortable in the Procrustean bed of the N-O-I-R typology, so that my only hope of engendering the needed discomfort is to be downright obnoxious. This is the motivation for what some readers will feel is an unnecessarily protracted set of comments on the idea of a nominal scale. The dictionary definition of "nominal" is something like "of, pertaining to, or consisting of names." A nominal scale, therefore, is a scale consisting of names or name surrogates, such as social security numbers or the figures used to designate signs of the zodiac.

We might first take note of two commonplace scales of names: the ones we use for days and months. The names, of course, are ordered, albeit on the circle rather than the line. But the names themselves give little hint of the correct ordering, and even that hint may be misleading—December once meant the tenth (Latin *decem*, ten) month. One must consult a mental dictionary to assign to the days or months their correct ordinal numbers. We are accustomed to using these nominal scales to keep track of time as it passes. But the Balinese have a much more complicated set of nominal scales, the function of which, on the analysis of Geertz (Ch. 14), is to achieve what seems to a Westerner like the very "detemporalization" or "immobilization" of time. There are actually ten different cycles of day-names. The three main ones consist of five, six, and seven names, so that a particular trinomially designated day occurs every 210 days. The name serves to specify the quality of the day as, for some of us, Friday the thirteenth is an unlucky day. The periodicities themselves are not of interest to the Balinese: "the nature of time-reckoning this sort of calendar facilitates is clearly not durational but punctual. . . . The cycles . . . do not accumulate, they do not build, and they are not consumed. They don't tell you what time it is; they tell you what kind of time it is" (p. 393).

Less convenient nominal scales than our days and months are the various systems of eponymous years which account for most of the datings available in documentary sources from Greece and Rome as well as the ancient Near East. Some of the known eponyms are all but useless, inasmuch as we have no list that puts them in chronological order and no synchronism to other dated events. In that case, "the names float in time" (Bickerman, p. 67). Thucydides, sometimes honored as the first "scientific" historian, expressed dissatisfaction with this method of dating, which he was led to discuss upon quoting the treaty that led to a pause in the Peloponnesian war. The treaty was to come into effect "from the 27th day of the month of Artemisium at Sparta, Pleistolas holding the office of ephor; and at Athens from the 25th day of the month of Elaphebolium, in the archonship of Alcaeus." Thucydides (5:20) took the opportunity to advocate his own method of "reckoning in summers and winters" from the beginning of the war, which he took to be the occasion of the first invasion of Attica. He argued that there was "no accuracy" in calculations based on names, inasmuch as the event of interest could have taken place at any time during the year in which the named magistrate held office, and he made much of the fact that he could compute the timing of the treaty as "just ten years, with the difference of a few days, after . . . the beginning of this war." His discussion may be the first explicit argument for the advantage of an interval scale over the nominal/ordinal scale. Finley, in his introduction to the Penguin edition of Thucydides (p. 22), notes that every one of the numerous Greek cities involved in the war had its own list of magistrates and its own names for months (more than 300 of which are known to modern scholars). Thus Thucydides's chronography, which established at least roughly the timing of the main events, was no mean achievement. It should be observed that the widespread adoption of a standard calendar has not led to the abandonment of nominal scales of historical time. We still use the names of rulers to identify—indeed, to typify—periods and eras.

Let us consider some other possible scientific uses of names, commenting in each case on the issue of whether a set of names is usefully regarded as a "scale."

a. Names of individuals, or proper names. In the United States census and many household sample surveys the individuals interviewed or enumerated are named on the basic record. A common practice is to assign a unique numeral to each respondent, which then serves as an identifier on a computer tape. I contend that neither a list of names of persons interviewed nor a set of numerals matched to such names is a *scale* in any useful scientific sense of the term, nor is the assignment of the numerals to the names *measurement* on the usual understanding of measurement. Recording names and assigning interview numbers may be a preliminary or aid to measurement. But measurement proper consists in making quantitative observations. This could involve counting the number of respondents with various defined characteristics, ascertaining (that is, measuring) the income of each of them, and so on.

The individuals need not be persons. Perhaps the names are Arcturus, Betelgeuse, Polaris, Sirius, and the like. One may find such names in a catalog of stellar objects, with a unique alphanumeric designation for each. But naming stars or cataloguing them is not measurement. It is only incidental to the making of such measurements as the classification of stars by brightness or "magnitude," their distances from the earth, or their temperatures.

The individuals could be Alabama, Alaska, Arizona, and so forth. For some purposes it could be convenient to number them from 1 to 51 (including Washington, D.C.) in alphabetical, or some other, order. But the set of 51 names is not a scale, nor are the numbers so assigned a scale. Stevens might well have considered the procedure of assigning numbers to the states on some arbitrary basis as an illustration of a procedure that is *not* measurement. Instead, to the enduring confusion of discussions of measurement, he chose to regard such a procedure as a "type" of measurement. Whereas the numbering of the states in alphabetical order is not measurement, there are many things about states that can be measured: their population size, crime rates, per capita incomes, and so on. But none of these is a "nominal scale." In short, identifying by means of names, numerals, letters, or other signs the entities on which measurements are to be made may be a step in the measurement process. It is not, itself, measurement, and we do not need the idea of "nominal scale" to describe or analyze the procedure of identification.

b. Names of kinds or classes. I turn to the back of my physics text and find a table of boiling points: water 100° C, mercury 357° C, alcohol 78.3° C, helium −268.6° C, and so on. The *measurement* here has to do with assigning a number to the physical property of the substance, whereas the names water, mercury, and so forth refer to *kinds* of substance. The names are not a "scale" in any useful sense of that term, nor does naming a substance or identifying an unlabeled specimen as, say, alcohol constitute measurement. (Measurements of various properties including, say, boiling point may be needed to make such an identification, of course.) There are many thousands of different substances that have been described by chemical formulas, and a great deal of careful and precise measurement is required to arrive at these descriptions. Nevertheless, the set of formulas like CO_2 or names like carbon dioxide is regarded by scientists as a classification of substances, not as a "scale." Chemists have learned that all known substances result from combinations of the 100-odd elementary substances, and that these elements can be assigned atomic numbers—successive integers beginning with 1 for hydrogen—that correspond to theoretically important properties. But it doesn't help the chemist to tell him that the set of names of the elements constitutes a "nominal scale." And the atomic number itself is a quantification of a structural property of the element that goes beyond naming and beyond "numbering" of the kind seen on the sweaters of football players.

c. Names of qualities. If I look up a discussion on the sensing of taste in a standard text of a few years ago, I am likely to find that sapid substances can be sweet, sour, salty, or bitter. Indeed, my favorite dictionary, published in 1969, *defines* taste as the sense that distinguishes between these four qualities. Are these names, then, a "nominal scale"? I suspect that Stevens would have demurred, inasmuch as a single substance in solution may simultaneously produce more than one of these sensations. The classical view—somewhat called into question by recent work (Schiffman, Reynolds, and Young 1981) on the multidimensional scaling of judgments of similarity of the tastes of experimentally administered substances—was that sweet, sour, salty, and bitter are an exhaustive list of qualities that may be sensed as taste. But even if that were so, not all substances could be unequivocally assigned to one and only one of them. Here, again, we have a scientific classification found useful for many decades, the understanding of which is impeded rather than facilitated by referring to it as a "nominal scale."

An alternative is to suppose that what we have here are four nominal scales: sweet versus not sweet, sour versus not sour, and so on. I am going to argue that in this example we have, at last, encountered a legitimate use of the term "nominal scale." Salty and not salty are indeed names, and they do indeed distinguish (if crudely and in a somewhat artificially absolute fashion) between "degrees of a quality," inasmuch as that quality is regarded as either present or absent. It is instructive that one of Stevens's students (Marks, pp. 230–231) points out the possibility of simultaneous evaluation of all four qualities by Stevens's method of magnitude estimation. In that event, a numerical estimate replaces the dichotomous classification, or nominal scale, for each of them. That sometimes happens when a science makes progress in measurement—nominal scales, properly so called, are replaced by more precise quantifications. But we note that atomic numbers do not *replace* the names of the elements, they serve to *characterize* the elements in an elegant manner.

Names of qualities pertaining to human behavior were studied in an interesting way by Allport and Odbert half a century ago. Their method was to read through the dictionary and to record words that seemed to refer to what they called "real" traits of personality. There were some 4,500 ordinary English words on the resulting list, including assertive, introverted, sociable, honest, gay, demure, pugnacious, sulky, and truthful. An interesting feature of this list is that in many instances both a word and its antonym occur. Unassertive, extroverted, unsociable, dishonest, solemn, immodest, pacific, good-humored, and mendacious, which I take to be the respective antonyms of the names first cited, also are included. In some cases, for example, intelligent versus unintelligent, the ostensible antonym seems to refer to the mere absence of a quality. The so-called bipolar traits like introversion-extroversion are somewhat awkward in terms of the notion of scales of measurement, because one often can argue that there really are two logically separable dimensions rather than just one. In that event, a more or less balanced mixture of the two qualities would constitute ambivalence rather than neutrality. Whether bipolarity or simple presence versus absence is the relevant formulation, I would want to insist that a pair of trait names is not yet a "nominal scale" (Allport and Odbert did not propose any such thing either). Measurement even of the crudest sort is not achieved *merely* by naming. I accept salty versus not salty as a nominal scale because subjects can reliably and reproducibly distinguish between samples in these terms. For many "traits" or other qualities such experimental demonstration that measurement has been achieved is lacking.

d. Names of degrees, amounts, or magnitudes. In buying short-sleeved shirts I have learned to choose the one marked M when the alternatives are S, M, L, and XL. The letters stand for names of the "sizes," small, medium, large, and extra large. I suppose the names work well enough for their purpose; I am usually satisfied with the fit of my shirts. This is literally a "nominal" scale—a scale of names. But I suspect that Stevens would have called it an O scale, on the grounds that the categories are ordered. Names can be ordered sometimes, but they do not thereby cease to be names. Hence a scale might be both nominal and ordinal. That is true, for example, of the 63 British "titles of honour" (in order of precedence) that I mentioned in Chapter 3. But in that case, the names themselves do not denote rank or degree; one has to learn in some other way that "treasurer of the household" precedes "gentlemen." Similarly, the ten minerals named in the original Mohs hardness scale are merely ten kinds of substance until you learn that experiments have established their ordering with respect to the ability of one to scratch another. Notice that the scale defines "degrees" of hardness by naming the substances and not the degrees, but we cannot dispense with the names by replacing them with a set of ten numbers. For the only way to find out the hardness of a new specimen is to see which of the particular substances designated by Mohs will scratch it and which ones it will scratch. The Mohs scale, therefore, is like the orders-of-precedence scale, rather than the scale of shirt sizes, in this respect.

A little later, we will encounter a historically interesting example of "strictly qualitative categories" that were supposed to represent "degrees" of hot and cold. It would appear that Galen's proposal for such a scale anticipated the idea (often attributed to Galton) of the rating scale. In modern psychology there are many variants of this notion and I don't want to review them here. The adjectives large, medium, and small could, I suppose, be used to rate sizes of almost anything conceived as varying extensively—in size or amount of some property—thus large, medium, and small cars; apartments, men, countries, or whatever. In survey research, such "scales" of adjectives or adverbs are popular. A widely used question reads, "Would you say that you are very happy, pretty happy, or not too happy?" To reiterate, these terms "very happy" and so on are purportedly names of degrees or intensities of the property happiness. The question, therefore, is intended to serve as a nominal scale for "measuring" happiness. We also understand as part of our comprehension of vulgar English semantics that "very" is more than "pretty" which, in turn, is more than "not too." Is it then to be taken for granted that Smith, who says she is "very happy," is actually happier than Jones, who says she is "not too happy"? Does the "scale" actually order *respondents* as well as adverbs? Try to design an experiment that would demonstrate that it does so. I am not saying it cannot be done, but I am conceding I do not know how to do it. More important, I am contending that social and behavioral scientists in-fluenced by Stevens in their thinking about measurement have been all too willing to claim success in achieving O scales that purportedly measure (admittedly very crudely) properties or qualities of subjects, respondents, clients, or patients, when all they in fact have are seman-tically ordered names of degrees or intensities. Surely this observation helps to explain why "measurement" is so easy for us and why our "measures" have proliferated into the thousands. We are to blame, of course, not Stevens. He was explicit enough about the limitations, as he saw them, of "category scales" (see that entry in the index of his 1975 text).

To recapitulate, I have observed that a "scale of names" might comprise (a) the names of individual *entities* which are to be counted or otherwise measured; (b) the names of *kinds* or *classes* of objects, events, or phenomena; (c) the names of *qualities* construed as defining a scale through the contrast with their opposites or with their simple absence; or (d) the names of the magnitudes, amounts, or *degrees* of a property that are to be recognized. I do not think that (a) and (b) can be regarded as scales of *measurement* in any proper scientific sense. In particular, the implication that all classifications are tantamount to a crude form of measurement is obfuscatory. One charitably presumes that it originates in simple ignorance or misunderstanding of the func-tion of classification in science. I hold that nominal scales of kind (c) do sometimes arise in a natural way in scientific inquiry and that the attempt to replace them with more precise forms of measurement is correctly regarded as a desirable development. In regard to (d), al-though I have made no systematic survey of their use, I have suggested that the practice of turning nominal scales of adjectives or adverbs into ordinal scales by merely appealing to ordinary linguistic usage is extremely hazardous. The implication is that we may have far fewer actual O scales than we now claim.

Inasmuch as both Hempel (p. 54) and Carnap (p. 51) enjoin us to replace "classificatory concepts" with "characteristics capable of gradations" (Hempel) or "quantitative concepts" (Carnap), it behooves us to consider that advice seriously. At the same time, we can take note of the extreme mischief caused by Stevens's conflation of crude nominal scales (such as salty versus not salty, or Aristotle's "primary contrarieties," hot versus cold and dry versus moist), which it makes sense to regard as a primitive effort at measurement—with genuine scientific classifications—which are in no useful sense to be regarded as failed attempts at measurement or mere prolegomena to measurement. The main actual example of "replacement" Hempel offers is the use of wind speeds in miles per hour instead of the Beaufort scale of wind strengths, which comprises a graded set of twelve strengths (calm, light air, and so on) together with signs such as vertically rising smoke or white caps on waves used to recognize them. The advice is well taken, I suppose, if there happens to be an anemometer right where you want to estimate wind speed. Carnap gives a good deal of attention to temperature, an example I take up presently. Both of these philosophers ignore the classification of substances in chemistry and give the most meager and uninformative explication of what is at stake in biological taxonomy. But surely we have learned from Thomas Kuhn not to take the word of philosophers for what is or is not done, or what is or is not useful in actual science. I have found that sociologists are handicapped in understanding the function of classification not only by their acceptance of the Stevens classification of scale types and their reliance on the hearsay evidence of philosophers of science, but also by their own addiction to typology. My best recommendation, to anyone who can open his mind on this matter, is to read a scientist like George Gaylord Simpson on "The Diversity of Life" (Ch. 7 in his 1953 book).

When organisms are stated (for example, by Simpson and co-authors, pp. 477–484) to belong to one of the three "kingdoms," protists, plants, and animals (protists are one-celled or noncellular organisms that may resemble both plants and animals in various ways, although some of them are not much like either plants or animals), we are confronted with (part of) a classification, not a "nominal scale." Protists, plants, and animals are different *kinds* of "objects" (or, for that matter, "events"). They are not categories that speak to differences between objects or events in regard to degrees of some quality. If I am not misreading him, Stevens (1975, Table 9, p. 169) offered just such a classification, prothetic versus metathetic sensory continua, for his own field.

Stevens misled us in implying that all classifications are attempts at "measurement," inferior attempts at that. On the contrary, classification is a basic procedure of science that may be related to or may intersect with measurement in a bewildering variety of both obvious and subtle ways. Cohen and Nagel wrote (p. 223), "the process of classifying things really involves, or is a part of, the formation of hypotheses as to the nature of things." In biological taxonomy, as Simpson and co-authors point out, the "nature of things" that is scientifically relevant is the phylogenetic relationship of species, and species are defined as populations. Taxonomic categories are not "types"; they are groupings of lower-order taxonomic categories, ultimately of species:

typological systematics maintained that organisms belong to the same systematic unit because they have the same anatomical pattern. Modern systematics has learned that they have the same anatomical pattern (to the extent that they really do) because they belong to the same biological, evolutionary population or groups of populations. The systematist is not engaged in classifying anatomy or any other sort of evidence. He is engaged in using the evidence to classify populations of organisms (p. 465).

The "evidence" used may, of course, be quantitative; it may derive from measurements, though it need not do so. Similarly, the chemist uses quantitative evidence to classify (*not* typify) substances. The atomic theory developed from and was substantiated by some simple proportionalities discovered when complex substances were compared as to proportions by weight (Guerlac 1961). But the classification of elements is not a "nominal scale." Elements are *kinds* of substance, not a categorization of substances according to "degrees" of some quality. It turns out, remarkably, that these kinds can indeed be placed in a serial order, the atomic number, which has profound theoretical implications. But that number, again, is not a "measure" of the degree of some quality like acidity or combustibility. Elements differ in regard to many qualities, some of them measurable. Indeed, measurement of a very sophisticated kind is involved here. But the classification of the elements is a classification, not an N scale.

In sociology Protestant (P), Catholic (C), Jewish (J), "Other," and "None" is *not* a "nominal scale" of religiosity or any other quality of persons or groups. It is a crude, very crude, classification of *kinds* of religious denominations that are prevalent in North America. It may be that these categories can be ordered in regard to one or another quantitative criterion. *For some rough purposes only*, that might entitle us to use religious preference, so classified, as an indicator of such a quantitative variable. But too much sociology is already built on such rough and ready (or unready) procedures, and proliferating them, even with refinements, is not the way to go, the formidable wisdom of some eminent quantitative methodologists to the contrary notwithstanding. (Stevens, of course, is not responsible, directly, for their views.) If P, C, and J are anything, they are categories in a taxonomy of religions. They are real, not merely nominal, although they do have names. If sociology were to get serious about the "religion variable" (a revealing locution from the professional argot), the way to go is to make careful and detailed taxonomic categories and to study the religious "species" (the most elementary category in the taxonomy such as, perhaps, the American Lutheran Church, Free Will Baptist, Jehovah's Witnesses, Greek Orthodox Archdiocese of North and South America, Plymouth Brethren, Roman Catholic Church, United Methodist Church, Apostolic Overcoming Holy Church of God) in their natural habitat. There are many things about such species to be measured, but the species classification itself is not measurement and it may not, in any significant way, be the outcome of measurement. To argue that such "nominal scales" as a taxonomy of religions should be discarded as too "imprecise" or "inaccurate" for scientific purposes and be replaced by some number is to argue that one should not study the actual, historical facts of social process and social structure but some Platonic geometry of strictly imagined quantities. Stevens is not (directly) to blame for the mess we have worked ourselves into in this regard. But his pronouncements have often been taken as the text for some counterproductive exhortations that are put forward in tracts on "methodology" in the social sciences.

Nominal scales (of the hot versus cold variety) are a crude form of measurement, and science does indeed try to replace them with some more precise or powerful form of measurement. Classifications are something quite different. Yet they play a role in measurement. It is indeed measurement to *count* the units belonging to each category of our classification in the ecosystem we are studying. Counts of organizations, members, and memberships turn up in a literature on the dynamics of affiliation that is demonstrating the productivity of ecological and structural models, elaborated mathematically, which apparently can explain well-known differentials in social participation among social strata (McPherson 1981 and literature cited). Thus, sociologists willing to take classification seriously may find something they need to learn in quantitative ecology, where the study of relative prevalence of different species is a central problem. We also have as tools for analyzing counts the apparatus of formal demography, survey analysis, log-linear statistical models, and so on. I do not go into that here, but only emphasize that we sold ourselves very short when we conceded that in working with N scales we are just barely measuring at all. On the contrary, in working with counts we take advantage of the most powerful scale of all, as I shall mention again.

With actual nominal scales—crude attempts to distinguish degrees of some quality or property—the assignment of numerals is premature and invites the very abuses of statistics and quantitative methods that Stevens was concerned about. With true classifications, by contrast, the assignment of numerals is a mere convenience and not an invitation to illicit arithmetic. When I worked with occupational data I had to learn to use both an "alphabetical index" of occupations, in which occupation titles were entered in alphabetical order, and a "classified index," in which one could find an ordering by their code numbers. It is true that the code numbers correspond, very roughly, to what someone long ago had supposed was a socioeconomic ranking of major groups of occupations, although within groups the codes were assigned to occupation titles alphabetically. But one was unwise to use the code numbers for anything but mere tags. The occupation classification is a taxonomy—though hardly a perfect one—and not a "nominal scale."

There is, however, one special case that is tricky, the binary classification. I am not thinking of N scales like hard vs. soft or hot vs. cold, where there is a tacit agreement that greater refinement of discrimination can be had if desired or if an appropriate measuring instrument can be designed. I have in mind genuine binary classifications such as present vs. absent; switched on vs. switched off (as applied to nerve impulses, "all-or-none events"—Stevens 1975, p. 203); plant or animal (for multicellular organisms); male or female (for sexual organisms); voted for proposition 101 vs. voted against proposition 101 (for voters); dead or alive; pregnant or not. Sometimes, of course, there is difficulty in applying the classification, as in determining for legal purposes whether death has occurred or whether a woman is pregnant. Difficulties and ambiguities notwithstanding, the rationale of the binary classification is straightforward—for all cases to which it applies we classify them into the one or the other category. Now, it is well known that there are various ways to "score" a binary classification so that appropriate arithmetic applied to the numerals yields legitimate and useful results. Thus, if I define the scores, voted for $= 1$ and voted against $= 0$, the mean score for a sample of voters is just the sample proportion voting for. That proportion estimates a probability, and estimation of probabilities is one of the fundamental inventions in social measurement. All this, though commonplace, is not in Stevens. Moreover, it directly contravenes his injunctions concerning permissible arithmetical operations on N scales. Stevens's measurement theory requires revision in regard to this matter.

The O scale "arises from the operation of rank-ordering," according to Stevens. Again we see the merit of Bunge's contention that it is dangerous to try to understand measurement apart from the context in which it occurs. Stevens has grouped under one "operation" procedures that may have quite distinct rationales. For one thing, he fails to distinguish the strict case of ranking, in which each object gets a unique rank (recall the Borda-Condorcet-Laplace proposal for preferential voting), from the case in which objects are classified and the classes are ordered or graded. Within both of these cases there might be reason to distinguish between the case in which the differences among objects or classes are held to be, in principle, of the kind produced by a quantity that varies continuously, and the case in which such variation is clearly discrete. A teacher might be asked to rank her 30 students in order of ability to write English, understanding that such an ability could reasonably be assumed to have many more than 30 grades—to be, in effect, continuous. But in the preferential ballot there are just as many slots (and no more) to be filled with ranks as there are candidates, notwithstanding the possibility that a voter could imagine a candidate intermediate in attractiveness between two to whom he has assigned adjacent ranks. In the case of ordered classes, the usual idea of grades (for example, course grades in college) is that they represent a more or less arbitrary partitioning of what one might otherwise want to conceive as a continuous scale of accomplishment. But when I was in the army there were exactly seven grades of enlisted men, four grades of sergeant, followed by corporal, private first class, and private (other titles being equated with these as far as grade was concerned).

Inasmuch as a modern school of mathematicians has gone to a great deal of trouble to create a subject of finite mathematics, supposedly because of its special applicability in social science (for example, Kemeny, Snell, and Thompson 1956; Kemeny and Snell 1962), we might do well to take cognizance of finite or discrete aspects of our measurement operations where they turn up. Stevens, of course, was not in the business of forecasting what kind of mathematical structures would be useful in all the sciences that try to measure. But his classification of scale types becomes an impediment to productive thinking if it smears over distinctions in kinds of measurement that are fundamental to the uses that will be made of the measurements. We might even entertain the possibility that it was a strategic error for him (or anyone) to try to develop measurement theory that would be applicable in some way "apart from both substantive theories and the praxis of measuring" (Bunge, p. 121).

A more serious failure is the casual fashion in which Stevens gives intelligence test raw scores as a "typical example" of the O scale. Like many of his critics, he clearly thought that the important issue in regard to such scores is whether we are justified in treating them as I, and not merely O scales. He evidently did not see any difficulty in regarding test scores, along with hardness of minerals or grades of leather, as providing at least ordinal measurement. But there are difficulties. To illustrate the difficulties in principle it suffices to consider a test with just three questions—A, B, C—each marked right or wrong. There are $2^3 = 8$ possible patterns of right and wrong answers for examinees who complete the test. To be quite general, we suppose that each item contributes to the raw score the value zero if it is

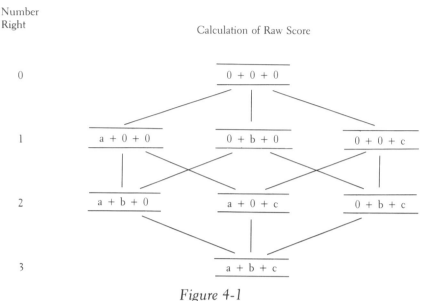

Figure 4-1

Response Patterns and Raw Scores on a 3-Item Test

answered incorrectly and a positive value if the answer is correct. These values are a, b, and c for items A, B, and C, respectively. Figure 4-1 shows how the aggregate test score ("raw score") is obtained for each response pattern. If no restrictions are put upon the item values, and in the absence of any other specification of a model that might underlie the observed responses, all we can get from the test is a *partial order* (Coombs 1953, pp. 474–475) of patterns (and, thereby, of the examinees who produce them). We have no basis for saying that examinees getting exactly one item right are equal in achievement, or that they are not equal, inasmuch as a, b, and c are unspecified. Similarly, examinees passing just two items may neither be compared with nor tied with other such respondents passing a different pattern of two items. Within the partial ordering of the eight response patterns there are, however, $3 \times 2 = 6$ sets of four patterns each that are strictly ordered. To construct such a set, trace from the top down along connecting line segments in Figure 4-1. If it should happen that only the four patterns in one of these sets ever occur, then the test would be a Guttman scale (just such a three-item test was mentioned as a hypothetical example in Guttman's original presentation of his idea, in

1944). In that case, Stevens would be correct: it is an O scale, not an I scale. But this never happens with achievement tests of the usual variety. (It can be made to happen by constructing items such that getting a correct answer to C presupposes a correct answer to B which, in turn, presupposes a correct answer to A. But ordinarily it is thought undesirable to build in such dependencies among items in a test.)

Where Stevens went wrong is in assuming that the operation of "scoring" is admissible in constructing an ordinal scale. We see that it involves addition of item values. But each item, by itself, is an O scale, and Stevens's own rules prohibit adding the numbers (numerals) pertaining to the categories of an O scale. Once scoring is admitted it is a contradiction to deny that the resulting score is an I scale. That is, once item values are specified, the raw score is uniquely determined. (It is an I scale, not an R scale, however, since our formula assigning zero to any wrong answer is arbitrary.) The foregoing remark holds *a fortiori* if we adopt the usual scoring rule—surely the one most likely to have been followed in the achievement tests known to Stevens— that item values are uniform: $a = b = c = \ldots = 1$.

More than one writer has suggested that equality of intervals is sometimes obtained by fiat or convention. Torgerson (1958, p. 24) observes:

For example, a major share of the results of the field of mental testing and of the quantitative assessment of personality traits has depended upon measurement by fiat. Measurement of morale, efficiency, drives, and emotion, as well as most sociological and economic indices, is largely measurement of this type.

Coombs somewhat earlier (1953, p. 487) put this matter into a sociological context in noting "a curious but valid, reason for the social scientist to choose a stronger level of measurement than is satisfied by the data," to wit, "common social necessity." And he remarked as well that such "enforced mapping of a partial order into a stronger system may be one of the sources of social conflict." The "grade-point average," which we academicians have become accustomed to use with little question, surely has its main justification in purported "social necessity" rather than in logic. And the possibility of "social conflict" is always open—despite the acknowledged "social need to have an accepted yardstick" of prices—when "Abrupt events give abrupt characteristics to inflation which destroy the possibility of an effective summary by any single number" (Afriat, pp. 4–5).

Later chapters include further remarks on popular procedures for constructing social "measures" that take psychometric methods and economic index numbers as paradigms. If, as we shall see, the results of these endeavors cannot be conceded to provide I measurement, it appears that sociology is virtually bereft of examples bona fide of this level of the mensurative art. Wolins (p. 1) puts the matter succinctly:

The meaning of interval measurement in physics stems from well supported theory which specifies the procedures for making measurements and provides the explicit functional relationship between variables derived from different measurement procedures. The concept of interval measurement may be heuristic but in applied fields of psychology and education it is not scientifically relevant because theory is inadequate to either specify how to obtain measurements or to specify the function which relates different measures.

I would hope that an honest confrontation with this state of affairs might occasion a reappraisal of our present conventions of data analysis, hypothesis testing, and theory verification.

Of the examples of supposed I scales given by Stevens, the strategic one is *standard* scores on achievement tests or intelligence tests (any purported distinction between the two being irrelevant for the present discussion and, so far as I can see, for Stevens, since he nowhere alludes to the notion of "mental age"). It is strategic because most of the social scientists who have taken issue with Stevens have been investigators interested in, if not committed to, the use of test scores as I scales or, perhaps we should say, quasi-I scales. Unfortunately Stevens does not really tell us what, in general (ignoring social necessity), justifies the assumption of equal intervals. His remarks amount to a restatement of the problem. "Most psychological measurement aspires to create interval scales, and it sometimes succeeds. The problem usually is to devise operations for equalizing the units of the scales—a problem not always easy of solution but one for which there are several possible modes of attack" (1946). If you ask, "What modes?" the only answer (1968b, p. 174) leads back around the circle: "The admissible transformations by which a scale type is defined are those that accord with or at least do not offend the scientist's judgment about a matter that is thoroughly empirical. . . . The size of the departure from equal intervals that can be tolerated in a given circumstance will depend . . . on . . . the purpose to which the answer is put." But how is one to know anything about the "size of the departure" if one does not already know something about the "size" of the intervals?

What, then, are we to make of the citation of "Intelligence test raw scores" as a "typical example" of an *O* scale and "Intelligence test 'standard scores' (?)" as a "typical example" of an *I* scale? Stevens does not explain the interrogation point following "standard scores," which is missing from the 1975 version, where Stevens no longer puts quotation marks around standard scores. One is not sure what Stevens understood by standard score. An authoritative work on *Educational Measurement* (Lindquist 1951) defined a whole cafeteria of "units, scores, and norms," but "standard scores" are said to "be obtained by adding or subtracting a constant value to or from all raw scores and multiplying the results by another constant" (p. 722)—in other words, by a linear transformation. If the first constant is the mean and the second the reciprocal of the standard deviation, the result is the "z-score" or "standard measure." Surely Stevens did not intend to imply that a linear transformation of an *O* scale results in an *I* scale. Perhaps he was thinking of one of the recipes found in the mental testing cookbooks for producing scores approximately normally distributed in a population of interest. So it can be inferred from the wording in the 1951 article (pp. 27–28), where this is called "a kind of magic—a rope trick for climbing the hierarchy of scales." Elsewhere he described as an "infraction" the "assertion that a variable is normally distributed when the variable is amenable only to ordinal measurement" (1968a, p. 853). The assumption of a normal distribution is not part of the usual definition of standard score.

I imagine the reason for the ambiguity about the intervalness of *I* scales was that Stevens was interested in *R* scales, not *I* scales. But the result of his casual exposition is a substantial "methodological" literature that, at least in sociology, has produced absurd claims and counterclaims about the appropriateness or inappropriateness of the assumption of *I* scaling for test scores and other such composite indexes. There is no way out of this morass short of the uncompromising position taken by Adams, Fagot, and Robinson (1965, pp. 122–123):

. . . the theory of appropriate statistics . . . would not appear to be applicable to systems of measurement for which there are not clearly defined sets of permissible transformations. For example, this would appear to rule out test scores and other measurements of this kind. It might be argued that in the case of such measurements as test scores, we should allow as permissible transformations any which do not alter the measurements in any obviously nonarbitrary feature, but unfortunately it is not at all clear what is and what is not arbitrary about test scores.

The importance of this limitation cannot be over-stressed. Test scores are the sorts of measurements over which disagreement most often arises concerning questions of appropriateness. We believe that the failure to provide a precise definition of permissible transformations for such scales is not just a defect in our formulation—the imprecision of the concept in these applications is inherent, and no deeper analysis can discover what the permissible transformations "really are" in these cases. This has an important bearing on the controversy over the validity of Stevens' theory of appropriate statistics, since much of this has centered around measurements whose classes of permissible transformations are undefined.

. . . Critics of Stevens, in arguing that the type of scale should have no effect on the choice of statistical technique, do not distinguish between measurements such as [test scores] and fundamental measurement systems for which there are clearly defined sets of permissible transformations. In any event, as stated in the preceding section, neither Stevens' theory nor our formalization of the theory of appropriate statistics is applicable to such scales (i.e., these theories do not offer any relevant normative strictures). However, this is not to say that questions of appropriateness and significance cannot legitimately be raised about uses of statistics in connection with these scales, only that our theory (and, we believe, any theory based on the idea of a permissible transformation) will not help much to resolve them.

Although the foregoing quotation is in a paper discussing Stevens's ideas about "permissible statistics," the basic issue is not one of choosing the appropriate method of data reduction, but of justifying a claim that one is working with *units* of measurement. That some real social mischief is done when such a claim is put forward or accepted without adequate justification has been argued in strong language by Wolins, but here it may suffice to note that test scores generally are conceded to be intractable from the "foundations" point of view, unless much stronger models for test theory are entertained than were widely known in Stevens's time. Without blaming Stevens for failing to anticipate the possibility of an item response theory which can conceivably define a coherent logic of measurement for mental tests, we can again take note of the futility of trying to reach conclusions about measurement in a theoretical void (again, see Bunge).

The bulk of Stevens's discussion of R scales has to do with claims made on behalf of his own methods for ratio scaling of sensations. Here, in contrast to his treatment of N, O, and I scales, we can appreciate how the author's engagement with the substantive theory fortifies the approach taken to measurement and vice versa. It would be quite wrong to suppose that his psychophysical scaling experiments were undertaken merely to illustrate an a priori specification of a measurement technique. In this essay we are not interested in psychophysics as such but in what its methods may have to offer the enterprise of social measurement. This topic has seemed important enough to require separate treatment, so I make no further comment on it here.

That restriction might seem to leave little to say about Stevens's presentation of R scales. He notes correctly that ratio scales ("the type of scale most useful to science," 1975, p. 50) occur commonly in physics and we will review the benign consequences of its measurement system for physical science in the following chapter, which will allude to some matters Stevens did not go into. As I have already stated, one of Stevens's contributions was to clarify the distinction between I and R scales, although he (1951, p. 23, fn.) conceded that von Neumann and Morgenstern independently presented the "gist" of his notion. It was implicit but not carefully expounded in Cohen and Nagel and, of course, physical scientists had in effect recognized the distinction in their search for an "absolute" temperature scale, a search which, by Middleton's account, lasted for a century and a half, during which time there was much experimentation with alternative units. That experience does bear on the question of how to recognize that a proposed R scale is actually a mere I scale. But the more difficult question is how to know if one has an I scale when it is certain that there is not (yet) a corresponding R scale. On this, Stevens is not as helpful as one might wish. We can only regret that he did not elect to consider the temperature example more fully. Just as test scores turned up in both the O and I types, so temperature appears in both I and R. What Stevens says about this is the textbook information that, whereas the Kelvin scale has an absolute zero (at approximately $-273°$ C), the Fahrenheit and Celsius scales have zero points arbitrarily defined by convention or convenience, although the numerical value of temperature on one of these can be obtained from the other by a linear transformation, $°F = 32 + 1.8 °C$. This is indeed how things are said to stand today. But for disciplines trying to learn how to measure, it might be ever so much more instructive to appreciate, if only vaguely, how this equation was established and what the situation was before that came about.

Actually, Stevens could have listed temperature under all four scale types. For Aristotle, "hot" and "cold" were primary qualities, and he "opposed on principle the notion that these qualities, which we would consider secondary or derived, might be reduced to more fundamental primary ones, that is, to properties denotable by quantitative symbols" (Barnett, p. 270). It would appear from this account that Aristotle really believed in an N scale. The great physician Galen (died A.D. 200), influenced by Aristotle,

introduced the conception of "degrees" of hot and cold, to indicate the extent to which these qualities were present in a body. Cold bodies . . . were assigned to the 1st, 2nd, 3rd, or 4th degrees of cold. Similarly, hot bodies were relegated to four classes, according as they were hot in the 1st, 2nd, 3rd, or 4th degree. These degrees of hot and cold were strictly qualitative categories associated with the physician's perception (Barnett, p. 272).

Thus Galen seems to have provided the first O scale of temperature. Even in antiquity, however, it was understood that substances expand upon heating, and the ancient literature describes devices not unlike Galileo's air thermometer. As Barnett points out, the invention of such an instrument amounts to the substitution of an objective procedure for reliance on sensation. Hence, the import of the invention is not merely that measurement becomes more precise or reliable as we move to a new type of scale, but that its theoretical basis has shifted. From Galileo to Fahrenheit, Celsius, and other creators of modern thermometry is a long and tortuous tale. Shortening and straightening it, I observe only that it required much experimentation to determine the properties of air, mercury, alcohol, and other thermometric substances, as well as methods for constructing and calibrating instruments. In this work the investigators learned the hard way that not all fluids have the same laws of expansion, so that a number of inconsistent "interval" scales were being advocated at one time or another and it was *not* in general possible to convert readings on one to readings on another by a linear transformation. Middleton (Table 5.1, p. 118) presents a table by Deluc showing discrepancies up to 5° between two instruments, his own mercury thermometer, and a thermometer using Réaumur's liquid, when the two were calibrated to agree at 0° (melting ice) and 80° (boiling point of water). Incidentally, the modern so-called Réaumur scale with these two fixed points does not agree closely with the scale he devised for his own very different instruments. So our Réaumur, Celsius, and Fahrenheit scales are actually misnomers from the historical point of view. During this period attempts to get an "absolute" scale by extrapolation from experiments with mercury and alcohol thermometers gave wildly discrepant results.

The solution to the discrepancies among alternative scales came with still another shift in the theoretical basis of measurement, when Kelvin showed that Carnot's theory of the heat engine implied the possibility of defining a scale that is independent of the physical properties of any substance. The Kelvin scale, therefore, is not merely a centigrade scale with its origin shifted to absolute zero, although it does define such a zero. Subsequently it was shown that a constant-volume hydrogen thermometer agrees very closely with the absolute scale at all temperatures ordinarily observed, although it was ultimately replaced as a standard by the platinum resistance thermometer (Middleton, pp. 114, 180). This standard defines not only the K but also the F and C scales, although in applications the older mercury and alcohol thermometers continue to be used with their own calibration.

I hope it is clear that most of the story of temperature measurement has to do with experimental determination of the quantitative laws of expansion of substances and with the deepening of the theoretical understanding of heat and thermodynamics, as well as learning how to construct reliable and sturdy instruments. There is not really much to be learned from the concomitant contentions about how to assign numbers to objects (Celsius actually ran his scale backwards relative to our convention), except that the strictly numerical part is quite secondary. The Kelvin scale is a scientific achievement of the first order, not merely because it provides a scale with mathematically powerful properties, but because it incorporates a profound understanding of how a certain class of phenomena works.

Actually, in some branches of science or applied science it is not clear that having a ratio scale of temperature helps a great deal. Medicine seems to get by with the older I scales. In meteorology, improving instruments for use under field conditions and standardizing methods of exposing them seem to be of greater concern than the exploitation of the R properties of the Kelvin scale.

Perhaps there is a lesson here for social measurement: after you get a ratio scale, then what? I have seen a textbook on statistical methods for sociologists that cited age as an example of an R scale. I have not seen any mathematical models or quantitative data analysis using age as a variable that exploits this fact. Indeed, I am waiting for an example showing why it is useful to be able to assert that age ten is twice as old as age five. If ratios are taken seriously, what follows from that statement should also follow from the statement that age 60 is twice age 30. Absent the theory that provides meaning for such comparisons, perhaps it is merely pretentious to claim R measurement.

To continue the discussion of Stevens's measurement theory I call attention to the serious imcompleteness of the list of four scale types, N, O, I, and R. We note that "numerosity" was included as a typical example of the R scale in 1959, 1968, and 1975. Its omission in 1951 may only mean that it was not an especially salient example for Stevens, inasmuch as he had written in 1946:

Foremost among the ratio scales is the scale of number itself—cardinal number—the scale we use when we count such things as eggs, pennies, and apples. This scale of the numerosity of aggregates is so basic and so common that it is ordinarily not even mentioned in discussions of measurement.

In a fugitive note of 1969 (which came to my attention after the remainder of this discussion was written) Stevens took note of the view I am urging: "Much activity in the social sciences involves two processes, categorizing and counting . . . . Important knowledge is produced thereby, not the least of which is the census." Again in 1975 Stevens wrote both emphatically and insightfully on the "measurement of numerosity." In at least two places (1951, p. 23, fn.; 1959, p. 34) he mentioned (without explicit reference to "numerosity") a scale where the constant of the similarity group is $a = 1$. That is, the scale has a "natural unit" which cannot be altered without changing its meaning. But "numerosity" is an example of precisely this kind of scale and it was potentially misleading not to make the absolute (A) scale explicit. This was done however by others (Marks 1974, Table 7.1, p. 246; Roberts 1979, Table 2.1, p. 64) who provided modified versions of the Stevens classification.

Whatever Stevens's intentions may have been, I suspect that his usual compliance with the norm according to which counting "is ordinarily not even mentioned" has been stultifying for social science. Another sociologist who thought so is James Coleman, who issued (1964, Ch. 2) a sharp challenge to the programmatic priorities implicit in Stevens's presentation, a challenge unfortunately not noted by the latter. In sociology, Coleman suggested (p. 73), "it seems most reasonable to use counting, together with theory-validation, rather than to use measurement validation" in the style of Stevens, whose work Coleman pointedly criticized (p. 63), albeit possibly on the basis of superficial study of Stevens's experimental and theoretical papers. But sociologists too have largely ignored Coleman on this issue, and there's not much mention of A scales in our methodology literature.

Stevens himself called attention to other omissions from his list of scale types, observing that N, O, I, and R are the types most commonly used (forgetting counting!). The 1959 article gives an instructive account of the logarithmic interval scale along with references to discussions of still other types of scales. More recent references would include Marks (1974, pp. 247–249) and Roberts (1979, section 2.3). We might glance at Marks's ingenious proposal for defining scale types. He suggests the following formula for a transformation:

$$x' = (a + 1)x^{(b + 1)} + c$$

and considers possibilities defined by the alternatives that each of the constants is positive (+) or zero (0). We obtain 8 scale types in this fashion. (See listing in Table 4-3 and note the formal resemblance to Figure 4-1.) In the light of earlier discussion, one is pleased to find that the so-called nominal scale has disappeared. A peculiarity of this proposal not mentioned by Marks is that the foregoing 3-parameter transformation, when all parameters have arbitrary positive values, is not as general as the Stevens definition of the transformation permitted for the O scale, $x' = f(x)$, where f is any monotone function. But the scheme is attractive in providing "a measure of the power of a scale,"

TABLE 4-3.

Scale Types Proposed by Marks

Scale	Value of Constant			Power
	a	*b*	*c*	
Ordinal	+	+	+	0
Hyperordinal	0	+	+	1
Interval	+	0	+	1
Log interval	+	+	0	1
Difference	0	0	+	2
Power	0	+	0	2
Ratio	+	0	0	2
Absolute	0	0	0	3

to wit, "the number of unspecified parameters" in the transformation. If it is not too great a digression, one might ask, what is the scale type of this "measure"? Offhand, it would appear to be an A scale, since what is involved is a counting of parameters. I wonder, though, if we shouldn't consider that we have here another kind of measurement altogether, one based on geometric properties of a formal structure and not on degrees of a quality or property. I ran across such a thing in a work on geochemistry (Ahrens 1965) in which the author gives a table of "coordination numbers of cations" in ionic structures: "The coordination number is the number of ions or atoms which lie closest to the central ion (or atom). In other words . . . the number of 'nearest neighbors' " (p. 43). For geometric reasons, there are just five possible coordination numbers, 3, 4, 6, 8, and 12. If sociology gains proficiency in measuring complex social structures, we may end up using quantifications resembling coordination numbers more than they do scales derived from mental tests or psychophysical experiments.

Returning to our task of emending Stevens, I call attention to his failure to consider as an example, typical or otherwise, the probability scale. His 1951 essay actually does devote three pages (44–47) to the concept of probability and the discussion indeed suggests that the probability calculus is of use in predicting "the behavior of molecules and death rates and election votes." This discussion, however, is quite separate from that of scales of measurement.

It is uncertain whether Stevens recognized that estimating the probability of death, say, conditional on age, sex, color, and socioeconomic level, is a kind of measurement with its own kind of scale. In a letter of 17 October 1957 of an eminent statistician, Leonard J. Savage, to S. S. Stevens, a separately numbered paragraph calls attention to the usual probability measure as a ratio scale with a natural unit, and also to the percentage scale used to describe mixtures. (The letter is in the collection of Savage's papers in Manuscripts and Archives, Yale University Library.) In the 1959 volume to which Stevens contributed, another author, Suppes (p. 131), was quite clear on this: "Other formally different kinds of measurement" (different, that is, from R and I scales) "are exemplified by . . . the measurement of probability, which is absolutely unique (unique up to the identity transformation)," and so forth. Inasmuch as Stevens (1968a) cited Ellis (1966), he may have known of the latter's (p. 177) purported demonstration "that a normal probability scale is a ratio scale" although it "is not subject to scale-transformation." The statements of Suppes and Ellis as to the uniqueness of the probability scale are potentially misleading (like other statements, taken out of context, that one encounters in the discussion of scale types). It is true that the addition and multiplication theorems of the probability calculus do not hold under transformations of the probability scale. On the other hand, in estimating probabilities with the aid of a model or in testing hypotheses about probabilities, there may be very good reasons to make use of transformations, nonlinear transformations, moreover. For example, a widely used and wonderfully useful transformation of the probability p of an event is the logit, or (natural) log $[p/(1 - p)]$. Logits turn up in bioassay, models of the diffusion of culture traits, and log-linear models for dichotomous response variables in surveys; they might well be used in a formal model for Stevens's own "poikilitic function for absolute threshold" (1975, p. 174), which he later suggested might be extended to problems in social measurement.

If the questions about what kind of scale the probability scale is can be answered, we could entertain other such questions. What about the variant of the O scale in which categories (for example, seasons of the year) are ordered on the circle rather than on the line? (This example was mentioned in a letter of W. H. Kruskal to S. S. Stevens, 15 January 1958, which is filed with the Savage papers at Yale.) To take another example, does the correlation parameter ρ of a bivariate normal population or the correlation statistic r used to measure assortativeness of marriage have an "absolute" scale of its own? It is, of course, a dimensionless number, in the sense that will be explained in the next chapter. But what I want to note is that with the algebraic limits, -1.0 and 1.0, where zero represents complete absence of (linear) association of two variables, the correlation scale is bipolar and in that respect different from any scale considered by Stevens. In some contexts it is advisable not to evaluate an association with the correlation coefficient r but to use its transform r^2. Again, we see that there may be good reason to violate the property that an absolute scale is absolutely invariant. I am not sure whether it is wise to extend the theory of scale types, as such, to include scales like those for the coordination number or the correlation coefficient, or, perhaps, the scales used to measure similarity and agreement. But if the theory cannot comfortably handle the probability scale and its transformations, something is seriously wrong with it. And if theory of measurement, more broadly conceived than the theory of scale types, stops short of accounting for these measures which are among our main working tools, we must create a more comprehensive theory of social quantification. A beginning would be to redefine measurement as the assignment of numbers, according to rules, to objects or events to represent degrees of a quality or property, or the assignment of numbers to represent degrees of relationship between variables, objects, or events. That would widen the domain of "measurement" in a way that Stevens, for consistency with his own attitude, should have approved. (Another proposal, to broaden "measurement" to include nonnumerical structures, is beyond the scope of this essay.)

I conclude that the Stevens theory of scale types, pruned of its terribly misleading confusion of classifications and binary variables with N scales, augmented to take more explicit account of the scales used in measuring numerousness and probability, and specified more clearly so that the examples could be properly understood and assessed, has utility in suggesting the appropriate mathematical and numerical treatment of the numbers arising from different kinds of measurement. Still, a theory of scale types is not a theory of measurement. And I, for one, am doubtful that any amount of study devoted to either of those topics can teach you how to measure social phenomena, though it can conceivably be helpful in understanding exactly what is achieved by a proposed method of measurement or measuring instrument. Thus, it is more instructive to watch Stevens in his own laboratory carrying out the kinds of measurement he invented than it is to read his obiter dicta about other scientific approaches he did not choose to study closely. It is another of the ironies of historical metrology that Stevens is in danger of being remembered mainly for the less robust part of his contribution to measurement.

REFERENCES

Adams, Ernest W. "Elements of a Theory of Inexact Measurement." *Philosophy of Science* 32 (July 1965): 205–228.

Adams, E. W., R. F. Fagot, and R. E. Robinson. "A Theory of Appropriate Statistics." *Psychometrika* 30 (June 1965): 99–127.

Afriat, S. N. *The Price Index.* Cambridge: Cambridge University Press, 1977.

Ahrens, L. H. *Distribution of the Elements in Our Planet.* New York: McGraw-Hill, 1965.

Allport, Gordon W., and Henry S. Odbert. *Trait Names: A Psycho-lexical Study. Psychological Monographs* 211, Vol. 48 (1936).

Barnett, M. K. "The Development of Thermometry and the Temperature Concept." *Osiris* 12 (1956): 269–341.

Bickerman, E. J. *Chronology of the Ancient World.* London: Thames and Hudson, 1968.

Bunge, Mario. "On Confusing 'Measure' with 'Measurement' in the Methodology of Behavioral Science." In *The Methodological Unity of Science,* edited by M. Bunge, Dordrecht-Holland: D. Reidel, 1973.

Campbell, N. R. *Physics: The Elements.* Cambridge: Cambridge University Press, 1920. Reprint as *Foundations of Science.* New York: Dover, 1957.

Carnap, Rudolf. *An Introduction to the Philosophy of Science.* New York: Basic Books, 1966.

Cohen, Morris R., and Ernest Nagel. *An Introduction to Logic and Scientific Method.* New York: Harcourt, Brace, 1934.

Coleman, James S. *Introduction to Mathematical Sociology.* New York: Free Press, 1964.

Coombs, Clyde H. "Theory and Methods of Social Measurement." In *Research Methods in the Behavioral Sciences,* edited by Leon Festinger and Daniel Katz, Ch. 11. New York: Dryden Press, 1953.

Ellis, Brian. *Basic Concepts of Measurement.* Cambridge: University Press, 1966.

Ford, R. N. "A Rapid Scoring Procedure for Scaling Attitude Questions." In *Sociological Studies in Scale Analysis,* edited by M. W. Riley, J. W. Riley, and J. Toby. New Brunswick, N.J.: Rutgers University Press, 1954.

Geertz, Clifford. *The Interpretation of Cultures.* London: Hutchinson, 1975.

Guerlac, Henry. "Quantification in Chemistry." *See* Woolf (1961).

Guttman, Louis. "A Basis for Scaling Qualitative Data." *American Sociological Review* 9 (April 1944): 139–150.

Hempel, Carl G. *Fundamentals of Concept Formation in Empirical Science.* Chicago: University of Chicago Press, 1952.

Kemeny, John G. and J. Laurie Snell. *Mathematical Models in the Social Sciences.* New York: Blaisdell, 1962.

Kemeny, John G., J. Laurie Snell, and Gerald L. Thompson. *Introduction to Finite Mathematics.* Englewood Cliffs, N. J.: Prentice-Hall, 1956.

Krantz, D. H., R. D. Luce, P. Suppes, and A. Tversky. *Foundations of Measurement,* Vol. 1. New York: Academic Press, 1971.

Leaning, M. S., and L. Finkelstein, "A Probabilistic Treatment of Measurement Uncertainty in the Formal Theory of Measurement." In *Measurement for Progress in Science and Technology*, Acta IMEKO 1979, Vol. 1. Amsterdam: North-Holland Pub. Co., 1980.

Lindquist, E. F., ed. *Educational Measurement*. Washington, D.C.: American Council on Education, 1951.

Lord, Frederic M. "On the Statistical Treatment of Football Numbers." 1953. Reprint, in *Readings in Statistics*, Ch. 3, edited by A. Haber, R. P. Runyon, and P. Badia. Reading, Mass.: Addison-Wesley, 1970.

Marks, Lawrence E. *Sensory Processes: The New Psychophysics*. New York: Academic Press, 1974.

McPherson, J. Miller. "A Dynamic Model of Voluntary Affiliation." *Social Forces* 59 (March 1981): 705–728.

Middleton, W. E. Knowles. A *History of the Thermometer and Its Use in Meteorology*. Baltimore: John Hopkins Press, 1966.

Nagel, Ernest, and James R. Newman. *Gödel's Proof*. New York: New York University Press, 1958.

Pfanzagl, Johann. *Theory of Measurement*. 2d rev. ed. Würzburg: Physica-Verlag, 1971.

Roberts, F. S. *Measurement Theory*. Reading, Mass.: Addison-Wesley, 1979.

Schiffman, Susan S., M. Lane Reynolds, and Forrest W. Young. *Introduction to Multi-dimensional Scaling*. New York: Academic, 1981.

Simpson, George Gaylord. *Life of the Past*. New Haven: Yale University Press, 1953.

Simpson, George Gaylord, Colin S. Pittendrigh, and Lewis H. Tiffany. *Life: An Introduction to Biology*. New York: Harcourt, Brace, 1957.

Stevens, S. S. "On the Theory of Scales of Measurement." *Science* 103 (June 1946): 677–680. Reprint, in *Philosophy of Science*, edited by Arthur Danto and Sidney Morgenbesser. New York: Meridian Books, 1960. Reprint, in *Readings in Statistics*, edited by A. Haber, R. P. Runyon, and P. Badia. Reading, Mass.: Addison-Wesley, 1970.

Stevens, S. S. "Mathematics, Measurement, and Psychophysics." In *Handbook of Experimental Psychology*, edited by S. S. Stevens. New York: Wiley, 1951.

Stevens, S. S. "Measurement, Psychophysics and Utility." In *Measurement: Definitions and Theories*, edited by C. W. Churchman and P. Ratoosh. New York: Wiley, 1959.

Stevens, S. S. "Measurement, Statistics, and the Schemapiric View." *Science* 161 (30 August 1968): 849–856. [a]

Stevens, S. S. "Ratio Scales of Opinion." In *Handbook of Measurement and Assessment in Behavioral Sciences*, edited by D. K. Whitla. Reading, Mass.: Addison-Wesley, 1968. [b]

Stevens, S. S. "Measurement and Social Science." *et al*. 2 (Summer 1969): 5–6.

Stevens, S. S. *Psychophysics*. New York: Wiley, 1975.

Suppes, Patrick. "Measurement, Empirical Meaningfulness, and Three-Valued Logic." In *Measurement: Definitions and Theories*, edited by C. West Churchman and Philburn Ratoosh. New York: Wiley, 1959.

Sydenham, P. H. *Measuring Instruments: Tools of Knowledge and Control*. Stevenage, U.K.: Peter Peregrinus, 1979.

Thucydides. *History of the Peloponnesian War*. Trans. by Rex Warner, with introduction by M. I. Finley. Harmondsworth: Penguin Books, 1972.

Toops, H. A. "The Use of Addends in Experimental Control, Social Census, and Managerial Research." *Psychological Bulletin* 45 (January 1948): 41–74.

Torgerson, Warren S. *Theory and Methods of Scaling*. New York: Wiley, 1958.

von Neumann, John, and Oskar Morgenstern. *Theory of Games and Economic Behavior*. 2d ed. Princeton: Princeton University Press, 1947.

Wolins, Leroy. "Interval Measurement: Physics, Psychophysics, and Metaphysics." *Educational and Psychological Measurement* 38 (Spring 1978): 1–9.

Woolf, Harry, ed. *Quantification*. Indianapolis: Bobbs-Merrill, 1961.

5

MEASUREMENT: THE REAL THING

$\mathbf{I}$F ONE WERE TO WRITE an essay on measurement of social phenomena—even if "measurement" were to have only a metaphorical significance in such a phrase—it would seem prudent to become informed about what "measurement" means in the domain that is sometimes called the science of measurement, that is, physical science and its applications. Although I am not well informed about physics, it seemed important to consider how and why social measurement resembles and, especially, differs from physical measurement. There are two terms to the comparison, and I am as well qualified as your average physicist to discourse on one of them. Among the other things I was pleased to learn about the other is that even at the community-college level there are courses in fundamentals of physical measurement. I recommend the text for that course by Zebrowski (1979). I wish we had a similar text for social measurement.

Measurement to a physical scientist (I am vague about the extension of that category, but I mean to include engineers and applied scientists of whatever denomination who work primarily with physical variables and systems) usually means comparing a physical quantity with a standard. This is accomplished, ordinarily, with a specialized instrument which comprises a sensor and a display unit. The sensor detects change in the particular quantity and transmits that information to the display unit, which might be a digital readout, a micrometer scale, a dial with pointer, a cathode ray tube, or any of various other devices. The display yields a numerical value which is a fraction or multiple of a permanent or readily reproducible standard unit. Every measuring instrument is calibrated, indirectly if not directly, against that primary standard.

The same physical variable may be measured under a wide variety of conditions, to which the instrument—in particular, its sensor—must be suitably adapted. Thus, while it is estimated that there are on the order of a hundred physical variables that are commonly measured, there are thousands of different instruments for measuring them. Maintenance of the standards to which these instruments are calibrated is the responsibility of the National Bureau of Standards (NBS), which works through a

hierarchy of federal, state, and private laboratories employing working and field standards. The NBS provides state, county, and local officials with technical and operational guides that contain measurement specifications, standard tolerances, and model laws designed to support the measurement system. In many cases this is done in close collaboration with the National Conference on Weights and Measures, a forum for the exchange of measurement information staffed by the Office of Weights and Measures of the NBS (Hunter 1980, p. 869).

(I know of no sociological study of this complex organization.) The primary standards today are those of the International System of Units (SI units) and are seven in number. I list the fundamental physical quantities, with their SI units and the symbols for them in parentheses: length (metre, m); mass (kilogram, kg); time (second, s); electric current (ampere, A); temperature (kelvin, K); luminous intensity (candela, cd); amount of substance (mole, mol). In addition, the plane angle (radian) and solid angle (steradian) are recognized as SI supplementary units.

Although it is easy to turn up persuasive presentations of the International System of Units, you should be aware not only of lingering resistance to the metric system (which SI presumes to incorporate) but also of the view that SI "is even opposed to the Metric System which was concerned with a view to its use in commerce." Danloux-Dumesnils continues (p. 137):

With the *candela* the SI leaves the field of physics and enters that of calibration. By putting this unit on the same footing as the other five basic units, the General Conference is mixing sand with the salt. Its presence paves the way for other even less well-defined units such as the acoustical units and the unit of penicillin. The Twelfth General Conference has had to take steps already to repel such an invasion by declaring that the *curie* is not part of the SI but can be accepted only as a unit "outside the system," a step which is an admission of the inadequacy of the "system."

I do not presume to evaluate the issues raised by this paragraph or to estimate how much support this critic's opinion may have.

According to exponents of SI, all of the hundred or so physical variables mentioned previously can be defined as combinations of these fundamental quantities. Indeed:

Most equations encountered in the [physical] sciences are definitions of quantities, or equations derived mathematically from such equations. Occasionally, however, we use equations derived directly from a set of measurements. Such relationships are called *empirical equations* (Zebrowski, p. 148).

It turns out that some "empirical equations" are much like the regression equations one encounters in an elementary textbook of social statistics or econometrics.

The definitional and mathematically derived equations, however, are something quite different. A remarkable characteristic of the definitions is that they generally have the rather simple mathematical form of a product of quantities each raised to a small integral power (positive, zero, or negative). Thus, Table 16 in Dresner (1971, p. 212) defines 20 common mechanical quantities in terms of the three dimensions, $[M]$, $[L]$, $[T]$ (mass, length, and time). For example, $P = E/t$ defines power (in watts) in terms of energy (in joules) and time (in seconds). The dimensional formula, written with brackets $[\ ]$, which considers only the pattern of exponents of the fundamental quantities, is $[P] = [M\,L^2\,T^{-3}]$, inasmuch as energy is defined as $E = Fs$, where F is force (in newtons), with the dimensional formula $[E] = [M\,L^2\,T^{-2}]$, and force, in turn, is defined as $F = ma$, where m is mass (in kilograms) and a is acceleration, with dimensional formula

$[F] = [M \; L \; T^{-2}]$; and so on. Although my example pertains to mechanical quantities, the principle extends to thermal, photometric, electrical, and magnetic quantities (Dresner, Tables 21-25). There are also dimensionless variables which combine quantities in such a way that the dimensions cancel—for example, the Mach number, a ratio of two velocities.

The fact that physical variables can be expressed in terms of equations with simple dimensional formulas is the basis for a technique called dimensional analysis. Its first principle is that all the terms in an equation must be dimensionally identical. This enables equations to be checked for consistency; it gives guidance as to the form of functions to be expected in complex problems; and it may be of aid in making scale models for experiments in wind tunnels and the like (Dresner, pp. 218–224). There are a number of textbooks on the subject, including one (Schepartz) that explores biological applications of dimensional analysis (see also Stahl). (I doubt that this terse statement will convey much to social scientists whose experience with dimensional analysis is as limited as mine. I can only recommend recourse to the cited publications.)

The idea of dimensional analysis has also been considered in economics. Boulding (1955, pp. 241–242) used it, in particular, to emphasize the distinction between capital stock or fund and income or flow concepts, which he contends are often confused in economic arguments. Indeed they are. A far-reaching consequence of such confusion is the delusion that GNP, a flow concept, measures welfare—as though how well off you are depends on how fast you have been spending in the last year and not on your present state or what you now have. (We might add that stock-flow accounting is basic to all demographic models, including their applications in studies of such specific populations as college and university students, prisoners, hospital patients, and economically active persons.)

According to Christ (pp. 52–53):

The two major types of dimensions used in economics are *physical* dimensions and *money* dimensions. Physical dimensions include time, distance, weight, volume (which itself has distance cubed as its dimensions), and horsepower, and also ones or pairs or dozens, that is, the simple counted total of objects. . . . For some purposes it is convenient to use another dimension—utility.

His table 1.1 lists 23 "common economic magnitudes" and their dimensional formulas; for example, price of a single good has the dimensions Money/Quantity. The accompanying discussion presents the rules that must be observed to maintain dimensional consistency, but there is no attempt to illustrate how dimensional analysis aids in making theoretical derivations. There is at least one work that does this, however. De Jong (1967) makes a careful distinction between "theoretical equations or economic equations" which "are mathematical formulations of laws . . . to be explained by economic science (economic laws)" and "empirical equations" or "mathematical formulations of functional relationships which are detected by mere experiment, that is, regression analysis, making only a very global use of theoretical knowledge" (p. 50). The author presents a number of examples from economic theory (the evaluation of which is best left to economists) to illustrate his contention (p. 51) that "dimensional analysis presents a method of defining, at least partially, the form of the functional relationship between a number of variables, if and when we know that just one relationship must necessarily connect these variables." An important remark (pp. 76–77) calls attention to the distinction between dimension as a concept of measurement (as it occurs in the present discussion) and dimension as a geometrical property (as it occurs, for example, in the notion of degrees of freedom in statistics). Since there is a large amount of social science—and even popular literature—with titles like "dimensions of X" (particularly research using factor analysis, cluster analysis, and related multivariate models), we should note that the geometrical meaning is much the more prevalent one (leaving aside purely metaphorical usages) but is not the one considered here.

For sociologists I might also point out that Dodd's *Dimensions of Society* (1942) was not an exercise in dimensional analysis, as the author made clear in a brief remark (p. 918). But it must have been written with some vague analogy to that subject in mind. It considered the four "sectors" (not dimensions), space, time, population, and "indicators" or "characteristics" and proposed a notation (including exponents) which when applied to them could supposedly be used to describe any social phenomenon capable of quantitative expression. The system of "indices" in the so-called general formula of Dodd's S-theory was quasi-mathematical, but in fact the "theory" produced no mathematically derived equations, only an elaborate coding scheme. Although the formalization attempted in this work was misguided and/or premature, it presented an astonishing collection of examples of quantitative description and analysis. Its virtually complete neglect, therefore, was not wholly justified.

With the possible and, in any event, limited exception of economics, we have in social science no system of measurements that can be coherently described in terms of a small number of dimensions. Like physical scientists, we have thousands of "instruments," but these instruments purport to yield measurements of thousands (not a mere hundred or so) variables. That is, we have no system of units (much less standards for them) that, at least in principle, relates all (or almost all) of the variables to a common set of logically primitive quantities. There are no counterparts of mass, length, and time in social science—except, of course, that mass, length, and time and perhaps other physical variables are used in social science. This is most obviously so in economics, where "quantity" means literally physical quantity—weight of product, distance transported, hours of work, and so on. To the physical dimensions economics adds money, so that dimension too becomes available to the other social sciences and to operations research, whose "basic classes of dimensions" are "time, quantity, and money" (Naddor, p. 508).

The fact that social science (beyond economics, if that exception is valid) does not have such a system of measurements is, perhaps, another way of saying that theory in our field is fragmentary and undeveloped, or that our knowledge is largely correlational rather than theoretical (cf. Torgerson, Ch. 1). One could agree with such a characterization without necessarily agreeing that the social sciences should put high priority on attempts to improve their measurements. For example, at least in his youth, Talcott Parsons, who understood that "mathematics in its application to physics *is* theory" (1938, p. 18), also believed that "measurement as such" (or, I suppose, mathematics) "is not logically essential to science" (p. 19). And he stated that "numerical data" are not of great scientific importance "until they can be fitted into analytical categories" (p. 19), a remark that could be read as deploring attempts at measurement where the theoretical role of the concept measured is indeterminate.

I shall return to the issue broached here. In the meantime there is another way to look at physical measurement. How dependable is it, after all? Different cases must be considered: the problem alluded to thus far has to do with the fundamental units of physical measurement. It is here that the performance is impressive indeed. Consider the official SI definition of the metre: "the length equal to 1 650 763.73 wave lengths in vacuo of the radiation corresponding to the transition between the energy levels $2p_{10}$ and $5d_5$ of the krypton–86 atom," as given by Dresner (p. 68), who states that this length is reproducible to 1 part in 10^8 and that "standardization with a laser beam will probably increase the accuracy to 1 part in 10^{10}." Klein (p. 188) notes that the metre as defined in the eighteenth century (one ten-millionth of the quadrant from the pole to the equator) was accurate to about 1 part in 10^4. There seems to be general agreement that the U.S. system of scientific measurement works well at the level of standards for SI units and measures closely related thereto (Hunter 1980). For recent and impending changes in standards for fundamental physical measurements and an account of the impact of increased precision of measurement on estimates of the fundamental constants and tests of physical theory, see Pipkin and Ritter (1983).

When we turn to the data generated by physical measurements in the applied sciences—that is, to the actual measurement process in everyday scientific work—the multiplicity of kinds of instruments mentioned earlier becomes relevant, and even more so the fact that many different instruments (of the same or different kinds) are used by different laboratories at different times. One broad class of problems has to do with determining the physical properties of substances:

Density, viscosity, boiling points, conductivity; the list of properties is very long. A great amount of effort goes into the revision of old values and into the determination of properties for the unending production of new substances (Youden 1961/1969, p. 119).

Here, a disconcerting variability of numerical results is often encountered. In the mid-1960s the National Standard Reference Data System (NSRDS) was created to undertake continuing compilation and evaluation of numerical values for "well defined physical and chemical properties of well characterized materials or systems," properties that presumably do not vary with place or time. Both Hunter (1977) and Lide (1981) have pointed to the "remarkable variability" or "scatter" of

alternative determinations of the thermal conductivity of copper as a
function of temperature, and both indicate that there are many other
such examples of widely discrepant readings from different laboratories
on supposedly invariant physical qualities.

The difficulties are only aggravated when a different measurement
problem is considered, the one referred to by Lide (p. 1345) as

. . . observational data. Here we include the results of measurements that are
dependent on time or space and cannot, in general, be checked by remeasure-
ment. This category includes much of the data from the geosciences and
environmental monitoring data.

Here the danger is that the between-method or between-laboratory
variation already mentioned will be confounded with true variation
between locations and time periods. (Do the difficulties here begin to
sound like those encountered by medical and social scientists?) Lide
suggests that the "most effective way to maintain the quality" of observational "data may be by careful control of the measuring instruments
prior to acquisition of data" (p. 1346). Hunter (1980) goes into greater
detail on the requirements of a measurement *system* and notes a basic
problem: many measurement methods, as described in documents
specifying standards, do not include adequate provision for estimates of
precision:

The record indicates that, for most measurement methods, repeatability is
poorly estimated, reproducibility is not estimated, and no continuing effort is
made to stabilize or control the associated measurement system across the
nation's laboratories. This statement . . . is true for almost all measures
exclusive of the SI units (Hunter 1980, p. 873).

The problem is exacerbated by the fact that

. . . the quantity of the scientific measurements now required by our measure-
ment-intensive laws and regulations are piling up, while many of the desirable physical and statistical characteristics of good measurement systems are
being given short shrift. The result is that the quality of many scientific
measurements is suspect (p. 874).

An astonishing statistic, attributed to the NBS, indicates (if not measures) the need for concern: it is estimated that the cost of taking

measurements of all kinds amounts to 6 percent of the gross national product.

In Chapter 2, I noted Bridgman's warning that astronomical distances are measured with "restricted accuracy." William Kruskal has pointed out to me in informal communications that discrepancies in regard to some theoretically crucial astronomical measurements are much greater than we would tolerate for some of the more politically sensitive kinds of social measurement. The 1981–1982 report of the president of the Carnegie Institution documents an illustration.

Scientists yet do not agree on such basic questions as the age and size of the universe, the rate of deceleration of its expansion, and whether . . . the expansion will continue forever. It has been known . . . from the work of . . . Hubble and . . . Humason . . . in the 1920's, that distances to nearby galaxies are in near-linear proportion to their velocities from us . . . . But the calibration of this relation— . . . the so-called Hubble Constant—remains highly controversial. . . . The reciprocal of the Constant represents approximately the age of the universe (p. 15).

Work beginning in 1963 yielded a value implying 19 billion years as the age of the universe, a much higher estimate than Hubble's own earlier determination. But subsequent work, using a different method, lowered this estimate to 10 billion years. Now, we are told, the most recent results tend to confirm the figure of 19 billion.

We turn to a different kind of skeleton in the closet of physical measurement—the lingering presence of apparently primitive scales of measurement. The favorite example in discussion of measurement theory is the Mohs (German mineralogist 1773–1839) hardness scale, which is stated to provide only ordinal measurement. A century ago Sir William Thomson (Lord Kelvin) described the

. . . "scale of hardness" for stones and metals used by mineralogists and engineers . . . as a mere test in order of merit in respect to a little understood quality, regarding which no scientific principle constituting a foundation for definite measurement had been discovered. Indeed it must be confessed, that the science of strength of materials, so all important in engineering, is but little advanced, and the part of it relating to the quality known as hardness least of all (p. 242).

The present situation appears to be much as Kelvin described it:

> The general concept of hardness as a quality of matter having to do with
> solidity and firmness of outline is easily comprehended, but no single mea-
> sure of hardness, universally applicable to all materials, has yet been devised.
> The fundamental "physics" of hardness is not yet clearly understood (Davis
> and others 1964, p. 184).

Among the concepts of hardness for which tests or measurements have
been developed are indentation hardness, rebound hardness, scratch
hardness, wear hardness, and machinability. The Mohs scale employs
a scratch test. In its original form it is based on a series of ten substances ordered by the ability of each to scratch those lower in the
series, from the hardest, diamond (10), to the least hard, talc (1). (A
revision of the scale makes use of 15 substances.) According to Adams
(who seems to be the only writer on measurement theory to have
looked carefully at the Mohs scale), its major use is as an aid in
mineral identification under field conditions where, in the absence of
laboratory facilities, a tentative identification is useful as a screening
device. We note that the scale does not purport to provide quantification of a theoretical concept of hardness and its shortcomings
from that point of view (such as they may be) are not really relevant to
its purpose.

A different concept of hardness and a different use of a test procedure are illustrated by an example in the classic work on statistical
quality control (Shewhart 1931, pp. 33–34, 41–42, 112–115, 394–
400). The problem considered is that of "measuring some physical
quality such as tensile strength which cannot be measured except
through the use of some statistical relationship unless we resort to a
destructive test" (p. 394). The solution is to find, for a sample of
specimens of a given kind of metal piece, the multiple regression of
tensile strength (measured in a breakage test) on Rockwell E hardness
and density. This is, of course, an "empirical equation."

Rockwell hardness is one of several tests described by Davis and
others for use in different situations. A special machine puts a known
load on a steel ball indenter and the depth of indentation is sensed and
converted into an arbitrary number. Different indenters and loads are
used for different kinds of materials, so that there is no direct comparison between them, but only between specimens of a given kind of

material. The somewhat similar Brinell hardness test yields numbers that actually have the nominal physical dimensions of pressure per unit area, so that if there were any reason to do so, one could treat the data as if they arose from measurement on a ratio scale. But the Brinell numbers are not derived from a general physical law and the uses to which they are put by engineers do not depend on knowledge of such a law or, really, on the ratio-scale property:

> Although all the hardness measures are, no doubt, functions of inter-atomic forces, the various hardness tests do not bring these fundamental forces into play in the same way or to the same extent; thus no method of measuring hardness uniquely indicates any other single mechanical property. Although some hardness tests seem to be more closely associated than others with tensile strength, some appear to be more closely related to resilience, or to ductility, etc. In view of this situation, it is obvious that a given type of test is of practical use only for comparing the relative hardness of similar materials on a stated basis (Davis and others, p. 185).

Such limitations notwithstanding, the various tests and the measurements resulting from them are widely used for grading products, determining their suitability for various uses, controlling quality, and inferring other properties of materials (as was illustrated in the preceding paragraph).

Another ostensibly primitive scale well known to engineers is the binary "go" versus "no go" gage used to determine whether a particular component is within permissible limits. Although interchangeable parts were introduced around 1790, the ideas of the "go" and the "no go" tolerance limits did not come into use until about 1840 and 1870 respectively. This is a case where the speed and reliability of the binary measurement more than compensate for the greater precision obtainable with a micrometer. The gages themselves are, of course, precision calibrated. (By this example I do not intend to convey approval for the lazy habits of sociological survey analysts of "dichotomizing" polytomous or quantitative variables. In survey research we seldom have any clear idea of the relevant tolerances.)

I was interested to learn of the existence of works on a subject called "engineering metrology," which deals (among other things) with measurement of qualities like straightness, flatness, roundness, and surface finish. The actual physical quantities sensed are often lengths, areas, and angles. But the measure generated from them may be something like a least-squares center and radius computed from systematically chosen points of the polar diagram produced by a roundness-measuring machine (Scarr, pp. 117–129). One is impressed by the ingenuity of such work but also by its "empirical" and statistical rationale; the final result is interpreted in relation to a standard developed from experience in use, not in absolute terms on the basis of derivation from theory. Yet the possibility of achieving high precision in specifying the shape of components derives from the establishment of an internationally accepted standard for the dimension of length which is extremely accurate. Hence, the distinctive kind and precision of measurement achieved in physics is always in the background in a way that would not be true for the "empirical sciences."

In the foregoing discussion, problems in applied science and technology comprise much of the agenda. But in concluding I want to mention the issue of how measurement relates to basic physical science. The only historically informed and philosophically sophisticated discussion of this issue known to me is an essay by Kuhn, which begins by giving reasons for distrusting most of what is said about it in science textbooks and philosophies of science. The essay is specifically not concerned with "measurement done simply to gather factual information . . . such . . . as specific gravities, wave lengths," and other parameters to be inserted into theories, which do not, however, predict their values. I cannot hope to abstract Kuhn's line of argument but will only try to summarize his main contentions in the hope that they will challenge the interested reader.

The measurements shown in physics textbooks always show "reasonable agreement" with theory, since textbooks select for presentation those experiments that are successful by comparison with theoretical expectations. Most quantitative experiments represent efforts to design apparatus and procedures that will be successful in this sense. Often the data obtained do not agree with theory, but this is usually regarded as a stimulus to new or better designed experiments.

Because most scientific laws have so few quantitative points of contact with nature, because investigations of those contact points usually demand such laborious instrumentation and approximation, and because nature itself needs to be forced to yield the appropriate results, the route from theory or law to measurement can almost never be travelled backwards. Numbers gathered without some knowledge of the regularity to be expected almost never speak for themselves. Almost certainly they remain just numbers (Kuhn 1961, pp. 44–45).

Apparent exceptions to this generalization usually pertain to the case in which qualitative understanding of a phenomenon is well developed but measurements are needed to disclose the mathematical form of the regularity being studied.

Nevertheless, there are abnormal situations in which disagreements between measurement and theory do produce revisions of theory, and quantitative anomalies are more productive than qualitative ones in this regard when "relevant measurements have been stabilized" (Kuhn, p. 52). But this function of measurement depends on the availability of an alternative theory. "In scientific practice the real confirmation questions always involve the comparison of two theories with each other and with the world, not the comparison of a single theory with the world" (p. 54). It is only in this sense that Kuhn permits use of the term "confirmation" to describe the role of measurement in physical science. The effectiveness of quantitative experiment seems to be greatest in the "context of a fully mathematized theory." Hence, while "full and intimate quantification of any science" is a desideratum, it cannot "effectively be sought by measuring." In his Appendix, Kuhn wonders whether "the social sciences are really sciences at all" (p. 61).

I share his uncertainty and perhaps feel some greater sense of urgency about the question. I do not think the relationship between theory and measurement in the social sciences is much like what Kuhn describes for physics. Talcott Parsons was right about the lack of interaction between the two in sociology. If Kuhn is right about the preconditions for such interaction in physics, and if physics is the model for sociology, then it will be a long time before measurement makes an important contribution to sociology as a basic science.

But sociology is not like physics. Nothing but physics is like physics, because any understanding of the world that is like the physicist's understanding becomes part of physics, as Sommerhoff (p. 33) has argued persuasively. Other sciences investigate kinds of phenomena that, although they are subject to physical laws, are governed by other laws as well (Simpson, p. 107). Here is not the place to go over the argument for that claim. (It is well known to social scientists, but for that very reason I prefer to have a biological scientist make my point for me.) Anyone who thinks there will be a positive payoff to the strategy of imitating physics in respect to either its pattern of theorizing or its methods of measuring is free to choose and defend that strategy. I shall be interested in seeing the results but will only insist that a program not be mistaken for the accomplishment.

REFERENCES

Adams, Ernest W. "On the Nature and Purpose of Measurement." *Synthese* 16 (1966): 125–169.

Boulding, Kenneth E. *Economic Analysis.* 3d ed. New York: Harper, 1955.

Christ, Carl F. *Econometric Models and Methods.* New York: Wiley, 1966.

Danloux-Dumesnils, Maurice. *The Metric System.* Trans. by Anne Garrett and J. S. Rowlinson. London: Athlone Press, 1969.

Davis, Harmer E., George Earl Troxell, and Clement T. Wiskocil. *The Testing and Inspection of Engineering Materials.* 3d ed. New York: McGraw-Hill, 1964.

De Jong, Frits J. *Dimensional Analysis for Economists.* Amsterdam: North-Holland Pub. Co., 1967.

Dodd, Stuart Carter. *Dimensions of Society.* New York: Macmillan, 1942.

Dresner, Stephen. *Units of Measurement.* Aylesbury, England: Harvey Miller & Medcalf, 1971.

Ebert, James D. *Report of the President 1981–1982.* Washington, D.C.: Carnegie Institution of Washington, 1982.

Hunter, J. S. "The National System of Scientific Measurement." *Science* 210 (21 November 1980): 869–874.

Hunter, J. Stuart. "Quality Assessment of Measurement Methods." In Study Group on Environmental Monitoring (National Research Council). *Environmental Monitoring*, Volume 4a, Supplement, Ch. 1. Washington, D.C.: National Academy of Sciences, 1977.

Klein, H. Arthur. *The World of Measurements.* New York: Simon and Schuster, 1974.

Kuhn, Thomas S. "The Function of Measurement in Modern Physical Science." In *Quantification*, edited by Harry Woolf. Indianapolis: Bobbs-Merrill, 1961.

Lide, David R., Jr. "Critical Data for Critical Needs." *Science* 212 (19 June 1981): 1343–1349.

Naddor, Eliezer. "Dimensions in Operations Research." *Operations Research* 14 (1966): 508–514.

Parsons, Talcott. "The Role of Theory in Social Research." *American Sociological Review* 3 (February 1938): 13–20.

Pipkin, Frances M., and Rogers C. Ritter. "Precision Measurements and Fundamental Constants." *Science* 219 (25 February 1983): 913–921.

Scarr, A.J.T. *Metrology and Precision Engineering.* London: McGraw-Hill, 1967.

Schepartz, Bernard. *Dimensional Analysis in the Biological Sciences.* Springfield, Il.: Charles C. Thomas, 1980.

Shewhart, W. A. *Economic Control of Quality of Manufactured Product*. New York: D. Van Nostrand, 1931.

Simpson, George Gaylord. *This View of Life*. New York: Harcourt, Brace & World, 1964.

Sommerhoff, G. *Analytical Biology*. London: Oxford University Press, 1950.

Stahl, W. R. "Similarity and Dimensional Methods in Biology." *Science* 137 (20 July 1962): 205–212.

Thomson, William. "Electrical Units of Measurement" [Abstract]. *Chemical News* 47 (May 25, 1883): 242–243.

Torgerson, Warren S. *Theory and Methods of Scaling*. New York: Wiley, 1958.

Youden, W. J. "Physical Measurements and Experiment Design," 1961. Reprint, in *Precision Measurement and Calibration*, edited by Harry H. Ku. NBS Special Publication 300, Vol. 1, Ch. 2.6. Washington, D.C.: GPO, 1969.

Zebrowski, Ernest, Jr. *Fundamentals of Physical Measurement*. North Scituate, Mass.: Duxbury Press, 1979.

PSYCHOPHYSICS

W ITH THE PUBLICATION of G. T. Fechner's *Elements of Psychophysics* in 1860 (English translation 1966), the first of the four main histories of measurement in psychology identified by Boring was formally inaugurated, although experimental work on sensation and perception antedates Fechner by a century or so. Kelley quotes O. Klemm, *A History of Psychology* (1914, p. 218): "It is certain that there is not one of the methods of psychical measurement that did not exist in its broad outlines before the time of Fechner." During the first several decades after Fechner's epoch-making contribution, psychophysics took rather little note of matters relating to social measurement, although Fechner himself published some papers on esthetic judgments. Nor is there much evidence of interest in sensory psychology on the part of sociologists. True, the great German sociological theorist and pioneer of quantitative empirical social research, Max Weber, carried out in 1908 a detailed study of "Psychophysics of Industrial Work," which is summarized by Oberschall (1965, pp. 115–125), but this had to do with task performance and worker productivity in relation to personal characteristics and factors in the occupational environment rather than the psychology of sensory processes.

By some accounts (e.g., Ekman and Sjöberg 1965) the two main lines of development in psychophysics in the last half century or so are those stemming from the contributions of L. L. Thurstone (see his collection of articles, 1959) and S. S. Stevens (see his text, 1975). Both of them took more than a passing interest in problems of scaling social as well as physical stimuli. Indeed, Thurstone gave relatively little attention to classical psychophysics because "Instead of asking students to decide which of two weights seemed to be the heavier, it was more interesting to ask, for example, which of two nationalities they would generally prefer to associate with, or which they would prefer to have their sister marry, or which of two offenses seemed to them to be the more serious" (1959, p. 16). Incidentally, Thurstone made a sharp distinction (p. 15) between "subjective measurement" of this kind and the other topic for which he is famous, "test theory." Inasmuch as his work in the latter field relied heavily on correlation statistics, it is interesting to read, in the discussion of attitude measurement (p. 267):

When a problem is so involved that no rational formulation is available, then some quantification is still possible by the calculation of coefficients of correlation or contingency and the like. But such statistical procedures constitute an acknowledgment of failure to rationalize the problem and to establish the functions that underlie the data.

Thurstone's early studies included investigations of opinions on prohibition, seriousness of criminal offenses, preferences for different nationalities, attitude toward the church, and attitude toward the movies. In connection with these and other inquiries, he developed a variety of scaling models, including those adapted to data collected by means of pair comparisons, categorical ratings, ranking, and opinion questionnaires calling for acceptance or rejection of a number of statements on a social issue.

I suspect that the particular procedure of Thurstone best known to sociologists is the one he used to assign scale values to statements of opinion. A large number of statements on a social object (such as the church) or issue (such as the desirability of prohibiting the manufacture and sale of alcoholic beverages) are sorted into eleven categories, numbered consecutively 1, 2, . . . , 11, by each of a few hundred "readers" or judges, so that the statements "*seem* to be fairly evenly spaced or graded" from "opinions most strongly affirmative to those most strongly negative," where the middle category is for "neutral opinions" (1928; 1959 reprint, p. 226; italics in original). For each statement on which there is a sufficiently close approximation to agreement on the part of the judges, the scale value is estimated by the median value of the category numbers assigned to it by the several judges. From among the scaled statements the investigator selects a small number (say, 25) spread fairly evenly over the range of opinion to comprise the final instrument for use in investigating the distribution of attitudes in populations. To measure a respondent's attitude, one has only to ask him to signify which of the statements he agrees with and to compute the average of the scale values of the statements he endorses.

Actually, the method just described is not very representative of Thurstone's general approach to psychophysical scaling. He explicitly notes that "the direct application of the law of comparative judgment . . . is considerably more laborious than the method here described" (1928/1959, p. 232). I don't want to try to exposit the "law of comparative judgment" or the model(s) to which it gives rise in the present context. Anyone interested in using it for this kind of scaling problem would refer to the treatment in terms of modern statistical methods given by Bock and Jones (1968, Ch. 8) rather than Thurstone's own presentations. But I do want to look carefully at the rationale of Thurstone's approach, which is of more general interest.

Let us note the clear separation between two tasks: first, to scale the statements, or to infer their locations on a linear attitude continuum defined in terms of the polar contrast of "strongly affirmative" with "strongly negative"; and, second, to place respondents on that *same* attitude continuum insofar as their locations on it can be inferred from the selection of items they choose to endorse. Not only are the two problems logically distinct and operationally separated, but also the former—the scaling of statements—precedes and is presupposed by the latter. (By contrast, psychometric or "test theory" methods of attitude measurement either attempt to accomplish the two tasks simultaneously and jointly or even to bypass the scaling of items altogether.) In both problems, the attitude continuum is not directly observed, being, in our contemporary jargon, a "latent trait." Thurstone was quite explicit about this. The statements themselves he referred to as "opinions," so that opinions are verbal expressions of attitudes while overt actions are also expressions of attitudes. Either opinions or actions may, in particular circumstances, be distorted expressions of attitude. "Therefore we must remain content to use opinions, or other forms of action, merely as indexes of attitude" (1929/1959, p. 217) and "truth" must be sought in the relative consistency of these fallible indexes.

A different issue arises when we focus on the first problem of scaling items and note that different judges put the same statement in different categories; their judgments are variable, scattered, or dispersed. In Thurstone's view, this manifest dispersion between judges is only an aspect of the more fundamental postulate that each individual's judgments are variable. That is, in hypothetically independent repeated presentations of the same stimulus (statement) to one judge, we would observe fluctuations in the category assigned, or "discriminal dispersion." It is as though his judgments are produced by sampling from a probability distribution. Various assumptions are made about the form and parameters of that distribution in the several Thurstone models derived from the law of comparative judgment, notably that it is a normal distribution (although that assumption is not actually used in the simplified scaling procedure described above). Note that this variability is intrinsic to the judgment process. It has nothing to do with either the differences among the several stimuli (statements) in regard to their scale values or the distribution on the attitude continuum of a sample or population of respondents whose attitudes are measured. With respect to the latter, Thurstone remarked, "It goes without saying that the frequent assumption of a normal distribution in educational scale construction has absolutely no application here, because there is no reason whatever to assume that any group of people will be normally distributed in their opinions about anything" (1928/1959, p. 222).

I shall mention here three issues with respect to Thurstone's technique that will bear upon later discussions. First, the procedure of category scaling of statements is challenged by Stevens as inferior to his own magnitude estimation procedure, as we shall note presently. Second, there is the issue raised by Thurstone himself in a discussion that begins with these memorable words (1928/1959, p. 228):

A measuring instrument must not be seriously affected in its measuring function by the object of measurement. To the extent that its measuring function is so affected, the validity of the instrument is impaired or limited. If a yardstick measured differently because of the fact that it was a rug, a picture, or a piece of paper that was being measured, then to that extent the trustworthiness of that yardstick as a measuring device would be impaired. Within the range of objects for which the measuring instrument is intended, its function must be independent of the object of measurement.

Thurstone proposed to establish the requisite invariance by showing, experimentally, that "the scale values of the statements [are] not affected by the opinions [attitudes?] of the people [i.e., the judges] who help to construct it" (p. 228). I am not sure whether Thurstone thought that this issue could be settled in general terms by a comprehensive experiment, but subsequent investigators have sometimes written as though this would be possible. On the contrary, I contend that it must be addressed over again for each proposed new scale. A failure could be due to the particular statements under study, or in some sense it could be a consequence of the particular attitude issue being investigated, and not a fault of the scaling technique as such. (Of course, if the technique never worked, it would be discarded.) In any event, invariance (within limits of random experimental and sampling errors) of statement scale values with respect to the attitudes of those whose judgments are used to estimate scale values is a sine qua non of a valid instrument. Similarly, the scale values must be the same for all respondents, whatever their positions on the attitude continuum.

Third, as Thurstone observed, the fact that statements can be scaled with respect to the particular property of their location on the attitude continuum does not guarantee that respondents will be influenced in their endorsement or rejection of statements, only by their own attitudes and the scale values of the statements. Thurstone suggested a kind of item analysis (as his maneuver later came to be called) to detect and eliminate items responses to which are apparently affected markedly by irrelevant factors. There is no need to summarize the obsolete technique of item analysis Thurstone suggested, but I want to underscore the importance of the criterion of "relevance" for the validity of an instrument that purports to measure a single variable.

Stevens's research, in contrast to Thurstone's, emphasized the classic problem of psychophysics, the scaling of sensation as inferred from responses to physically measured stimuli, such as tones varying in sound pressure, which are perceived as varying in loudness. His main innovations included the invention of new methods of eliciting responses to physical stimuli (including the cross-modality matching experiment comparing two or more ways to elicit response) and a proposed revision of the "psychophysical law." In his earlier work Stevens required his subject (or "observer") to make judgments concerning the ratios of sensations, but beginning in 1953 he relied most heavily on their judgments of magnitudes as such, although the instructions suggested that attention be given to the ratios of the magnitudes. For example (Stevens 1975, p. 57):

> I am going to present a series of noises. Your task is to judge the loudness of each noise. The loudness of the first noise will be called 10. Assign to each of the succeeding noises a number proportional to its apparent loudness; remember that the loudness of the first noise was called 10. For example, if the second noise sounds four times as loud, call it 40; if half as loud call it 5, and so forth.

From data provided by several subjects Stevens computed the median or the geometric mean of the subjective magnitudes and plotted its logarithm against the stimulus values in decibels (a logarithmic scale of sound intensity) and found a close fit to a straight line with slope approximately $\frac{1}{3}$. This led to the formulation of the psychophysical law as:

$$\psi = \alpha\phi^{\beta}$$

where ψ is the sensation magnitude pertaining to a particular value of the stimulus (as realized in the average of the magnitudes estimated by the subjects), ϕ is the stimulus magnitude in physical units, α is a constant that depends on the units of measurement, and β is a parameter of the sensory continuum under investigation. In logarithmic form the law is linear:

$$\log \psi = \log \alpha + \beta \log \phi$$

with $\log \alpha$ the intercept and β the slope. Stevens, his associates, and his followers have found a large number of sensory continua for which the power function appears to be at least approximately valid. Exponents have been found to vary across sensory continua from as low as .33 for brightness (of a 5° target in dark) to 3.5 for electric shock.

With respect to the discussion in the preceding chapter, we may note that this psychophysical law is of the kind there characterized as "empirical," and it does not share the dimensional properties of physical laws. That, of course, is not to deny its utility. Indeed, the power function featured in Stevens's research has also been used to describe such diverse phenomena as allometric growth in biology and, in chemistry, the dependence of the size of a polymer chain on the number of monomer units in the chain.

Stevens himself did little work on the scaling of social stimuli, and he credited Thurstone with bringing psychophysical methods to bear upon this problem. A few years after the method of magnitude estimation was proposed, however, various investigators began to apply it to such problems as the scaling of opinion statements (a reconsideration of the scaling problem treated by Thurstone, which was reviewed above), seriousness of criminal offenses, preferences for wrist watches, esthetic judgments, occupational preferences, aggressiveness of acts, and so on. Reviewing this research, Stevens (1966) provided the attractive slogan, "A Metric for the Social Consensus," and the topic was re-emphasized in his posthumous 1975 text. (I have been told that late in his career he came to feel that this would be the most important area for applications of his methods in the future.) The 1975 presentation enlarged the range of examples with the inclusion of studies on judgments of the social status conferred by income and education, occupational prestige, perceptions of national power, and scaling of acts of conflict and cooperation by nations.

Stevens's claim for his methods in this context is bold: "The direct measures of subjective magnitude . . . lead to ratio scales," and "The fallout from the development of the direct methods . . . has introduced ratio-scale quantification into sociology, criminology, and political science" (1975, pp. 229, 227). And, as we have seen, Stevens held that "the ratio scale . . . is the type of scale most useful to science" (1975, p. 50). By contrast, the category scaling procedure of Thurstone (which we reviewed earlier) at best results in an interval scale, while the Thurstone scaling models strictly derived from the law of comparative judgment—even when improved by the incorporation of Stevens's own assumption of a lognormal form for the "discriminal dispersion"—at best can produce a "logarithmic interval scale— . . . a type of scale with few practical uses" (1975, p. 232). How startling it is, therefore, to read in the text of a prominent student of Stevens (Marks 1974, p. 249):

The so-called ratio procedures, like magnitude estimation, yield, under given conditions, psychophysical power functions whose exponents often vary from one experiment to another. To the extent that the exponents do vary . . . the sensory scales may be considered to be invariant up to exponentiation as well as multiplication: that is, they may be considered more properly logarithmic interval, rather than ratio scales.

This ostensible difference of opinion within the fraternity of magnitude-estimation experimenters has complex sources. Resolving the issue as it applies to psychophysics—if that were possible—does not interest me as much as considering how it manifests itself in applications of magnitude estimation to social measurement. I hope also to indicate the wide scope of potential applications of the technique in our field. I will refer mostly to work that has proposed such applications, with only occasional reference to Stevens's own writing.

A significant part of the literature I am concerned with is addressed to the comparison of scales obtained by magnitude estimation and those obtained from comparative or categorical judgments. Lodge and Tursky (1979) refer to this kind of investigation as a "scale confrontation study." Such a comparison was included in the first study cited by Stevens as an example of a metric for the social consensus, an unpublished memorandum by Finnie and Luce on scales of attitude items (1960). Since I have not seen the report, I rely on Stevens's (1966, 1975) account of it. These investigators looked again at some of the statements about the church that had been scaled by Thurstone and Chave in 1929. Stevens reports that they were able to replicate Thurstone's scale values when using his method, despite the lapse of three decades. They also estimated values for what Stevens calls a poikilitic scale (from Greek *poikilos*, which refers to variability, as in poikilothermal, a zoological term for animals whose body temperature fluctuates with the temperature of the environment). Presumably they used one of the Thurstone models derived from the law of comparative judgment. And they also had their subjects give magnitude estimates of the strength of attitude expressed by each statement. Stevens shows a graph in which poikilitic scale values are curvilinearly related to magnitude estimation values; he comments that "the relation . . . is approximately logarithmic." I take this to mean a function of the form:

$$poi = constant + slope \times \log (mag),$$

so that the poikilitic scale is (approximately) a linear transformation of the logarithm of the magnitude estimation scale. That could explain why Stevens asserted that Thurstone's methods provide only a logarithmic interval scale.

Another study (Lodge and others 1975) yielding a similar result involved the scaling of adjectives that might be used to express political support, as in the statements, "The U.S. Senate is so-so, . . . very good, . . . inadequate," and so on. In that study magnitude estimation of the "strength of support" implied by each statement was actually accomplished in three modes: the verbal designation of a number, the force exerted by the subject in squeezing a hand dynamometer, or the sound pressure of noise made by a generator which the subject adjusts to the desired loudness. The final magnitude estimate was derived from an average of the three responses (together with an adjustment for "regression bias" that I shall not describe here). The category scale, separately reported by Lodge (1981, p. 39), involved nine categories numbered with the integers 1, . . . 9, with the end categories labeled "strong approval" and "strong disapproval." Lodge's plot of mean category number against magnitude scale value for 13 adjectives is curvilinear, and he shows a fitted line that I read as having the equation, approximately:

$$\text{cat} = -2.25 + 4.5 \log_{10} (\text{mag}).$$

Similar results are obtained with three more different (but overlapping) lists of adjectives inserted into statements concerning support for the local Suffolk County police, the Supreme Court's decision on abortion, and President Nixon's handling of domestic affairs. In view of the similarity of ratings for each adjective occurring in two or more of these replications, the four sets of scale values were merged by taking geometric means over replications. The result is a scaling of 30 adjectives or phrases, ranging from 3 for "disgusting" through 29 for "inadequate" to 332 for "absolutely perfect." The adjective "so-so" receives a score of 50 because the instructions for the verbal mode provided this value to the subject as a "modulus." (In the handgrip and sound pressure modes, the same adjective was to be set at a "comfortable" level by the subject.)

We note that the recommended use of the adjective scale for measuring respondent's inclination to support the political entity or act in question is somewhat parallel to Thurstone's use of scaled opinion statements. However, Lodge and co-authors recommend that the respondent be asked to choose a statement from a shorter list developed from the whole set of 30 as the one that "best expresses" his own opinion, as well as second and last choices. No attention is given to the psychometric properties of this choice task, and the researchers report no findings or analysis making use of it. My hunch is that a rigorous analysis of data collected in this fashion will encounter obstacles not anticipated by the authors.

The use of three modes of responding—verbal statement of numerical estimates, handgrip, and loudness adjustment—was calculated to take advantage of Stevens's work on the cross-modality matching procedure. I describe one of his experiments as briefly as possible (Stevens 1975, pp. 111–115). Consider three tasks you, as a subject, might be asked to perform in separate experiments: (1) match the subjective or apparent force (H) you exert on a precision hand dynamometer to the perceived intensity of a criterion stimulus S_j (for example, j = sound pressure, perceived as loudness); (2) provide your numerical (N) magnitude estimate of that intensity; (3) match your handgrip (H) to a numerical value N provided by the experimenter. With respect to the first experiment, Stevens reports that the power function

$$H_j = \alpha_j \, S_j^{\beta_j} \qquad (1)$$

holds for each of nine continua: j = electric shock, warmth, lifted weight, pressure, cold, vibration, loudness of white noise, loudness of 1000-hertz tone, or brightness of white light. Each continuum has its own exponent, ranging from 2.13 for the first named down to 0.21 for the last. In the second experiment, power functions are obtained of the form,

$$N_j = \gamma_j \, S_j^{\delta_j} \qquad (2)$$

with exponents varying from 3.5 for j = electric shock down to 0.33 for j = brightness of white light. In the third experiment, with handgrip matched to number, a power function is observed once more:

$$N = \lambda \, H^{1.7} \qquad (3)$$

Substituting (3) into (2) we obtain

$$\lambda \, H_j^{1.7} = \gamma_j \, S_j^{\delta_j} \text{ or } H_j = [(\gamma_j/\lambda) \, S_j]^{\delta_j/1.7}$$

This is of the same form as (1) and, therefore, implies that

$$\beta_i = \delta_i/1.7$$

Comparing the nine exponents β_i with the nine predictions of them, $\delta_i/1.7$, Stevens finds an average error (calculated without regard to direction) of 4.4 percent, which he takes to be small enough to permit the inference of a "transitive relation among the power function exponents" (Stevens 1975, p. 106).

Now, consider the adjective scaling experiment of Lodge and co-workers. We have a set of statements, say $\{A_i\}$, $1 \le i \le 13$, where i identifies the statement (or adjective included in it). For each statement we obtain a magnitude estimate in numeric form:

$$N_i = f_N (A_i), \tag{4}$$

another in the form of a handgrip adjustment

$$H_i = f_H (A_i), \tag{5}$$

and a third as an adjustment of sound pressure

$$P_i = f_P (A_i). \tag{6}$$

(In these expressions A_i is non-numeric, so the functions only mean that a magnitude estimate is made for each statement; the functional form is wholly arbitrary.) We know from Stevens's work that power functions obtain for

$$N = \lambda H^{1.7} \tag{7}$$

and

$$N = \mu P^{.67} \tag{8}$$

Hence we expect (7) to describe the relationship of N_i to H_i when N_i from (4) is paired with H_i from (5), and we expect (8) to describe the relationship of N_i to P_i when N_i from (4) is paired with P_i from (6). Moreover, the relationship of H_i to P_i should be described by a power function with exponent $.67/1.7 = .39$. Lodge and co-investigators (1975, p. 628) find that the indirectly established relationship of N to H (using N_i and H_i from the adjective scaling) and the indirectly established relationship of N to P (using N_i and P_i) are well described by power functions (linear regressions after log transformation). The

comparison of exponents in the indirect relationships with their pre-
dicted values is as follows: 2.14 vs. 1.7 for N and H, .77 vs. .67 for N
and P, and .36 vs. .39 for H and P. The authors attribute the discrepancies partly to random error (only 16 subjects participated) and
partly to what they call regression bias. I am unable to follow their
argument and adjustments concerning the latter effect, and some aspects of the statistical methods are described in insufficient detail for
the reader to learn exactly how the estimates were computed. Moreover, I am unable to reconcile the figures just quoted with those given
by Lodge in his 1981 monograph, p. 36. My concern here, however,
is not with these details but with the general idea of cross-modality
matching as a means of validating scales of the kind described and of
establishing "the claim that the numeric estimation procedure produces ratio scales" (Lodge 1981, p. 23).

As we have noted, in scaling attitude statements, the stimulus is
non-numeric, but the response, a magnitude estimate, is numeric. If
the psychophysical experiment with a physical quantity as stimulus is
our paradigm, it appears that we must postulate a social quantity
which, though not observed or directly measurable, serves as the *quantitative* stimulus. Let us call it S_A^*, the subscript A for attitude and the
asterisk to emphasize the hypothetical character of the variable. We
suppose, following the paradigm, that (4), (5), and (6) are the observable counterparts to the actual psychosocial laws,

$$N = f_N (S_A^*) \tag{4'}$$

$$H = f_H (S_A^*) \tag{5'}$$

and

$$P = f_P (S_A^*) \tag{6'}$$

Now, it may seem reasonable to assume that f_N, f_H, and f_P are power
functions (with unknown parameters), since the power function is
encountered so often in psychophysics. But a power function is not
universal in psychophysics. It does not hold for metathetic continua,
such as pitch (Stevens 1975, pp. 13, 169), and for all we know attitude
may be a "metathetic" continuum. It does not always hold even for the
"prothetic" continua, although it is typical there. In Stevens's first
cross-modality matching study he found curvilinear relationships be-

tween electric shock and noise and between shock and vibration (1975, pp. 104–106), even though the usual linear relationship (on logarithmic coordinates) held for noise and vibration. Suppose we had an instrument by which we could vary the shock current, but we had no means of knowing the amount of current administered as a stimulus. This would be analogous to the scaling of $\{A_i\}$ where S_A^* is unknown. And the linear relationship between the two responses (loudness and subjective vibration) to measured stimuli (sound pressure and amplitude of vibration) would tell us nothing about how responses in either of those modes relate to electric current. Ergo, cross-modality "validation" does not establish a power function for (4′), (5′), or (6′).

Let us suppose (nevertheless) that these are in fact power functions; that is,

$$N = \alpha_N \, S_A^{*\,\beta_N} \tag{4″}$$

$$H = \alpha_H \, S_A^{*\,\beta_H} \tag{5″}$$

and

$$P = \alpha_P \, S_A^{*\,\beta_P} \tag{6″}$$

Unless β in such a function is exactly unity, the equation does not establish a ratio scaling of S_A^*. And even if $\beta = 1$ in one of these equations, we would not know which one. Each of them is a power transformation of S_A^*, and the scale for which a power transformation is admissible is the log interval scale. The *best* we can do in regard to a metric for the S_A^* variable, therefore, is the log interval metric, already achieved by Thurstone, as Stevens observed. At worst—that is, if (4′), (5′), and (6′) are not power functions—it appears that we obtain only an ordinal scaling of S_A^*, that is, a scaling that subjects the unknown metric of that quantity to an arbitrary monotonic transformation.

A possible rejoinder is that we are not really interested in scaling the stimuli—notwithstanding Stevens's claim (1975, p. 279; cf. p. 228), "The outcome of a scaling by magnitude estimation places each nonmetric stimulus on a ratio scale"—but only their "affective values," to use Thurstone's terminology. *Not good enough!* Before I elaborate, let me quote an honest statement on "A Limit on the Method" by an advocate of magnitude estimation who thinks it is, or may be, good enough (Shinn 1969, p. 140):

. . . these methods . . . can only be used to study an individual's *perceptions* of the real world, they can never be used to study, or to measure variables in, the real world itself. County election returns, levels of the gross national product, the sources of a politician's support, and the weather are all real world variables, and data concerning these could be analyzed to determine patterns of relationship, but the analysis must proceed without any help from psychophysics. It is only when one is willing to assume that it is the perception of these real world variables in the minds of political decision makers which should be studied that these techniques may become useful.

Indeed, "decision makers" (that's all of us) proceed on the basis of their perceptions. But the perception process is situation-specific. I shall demonstrate this by referring to research on psychosocial measurement where the social stimulus is actually known to be measured on a ratio scale—to wit, money. As we shall note subsequently, Sellin and Wolfgang (1964) found that the magnitude estimate of the "seriousness" of a theft is a power function of the dollar value of the property taken, with exponent 0.17, and Figlio (1978) in a somewhat comparable study estimated the exponent at 0.24. The exponent was more than twice as large when Hamblin ascertained the subjective "status" (Y) attributed to "a man who makes \$X per year." He obtained the functions $Y = c(X - 1000)^{.54}$ from the estimates of 22 college students and $Y = d(X - 1000)^{.51}$ from the responses of 30 U.S. Navy seamen. This may be regarded as a power function with a threshold correction; without the correction, the exponent would have to be a bit larger to give the best linear fit. Data collected by Coleman and Rainwater on the status value of income are shown by Stevens (1975, p. 245) with a fitted power function having an exponent of 0.73, although he notes some departure from linearity. Hamblin (1974) reports additional status-income functions, with stress on their departure from the strict form of the power function.

    There may be difficulty in determining empirically which of these transformations of the income scale—supposing all of them to be power functions—is the sociologically relevant one as far as the perceptions of "decision makers" are concerned. It is interesting that Sellin and Wolfgang (pp. 327–328) find their seriousness scores to be related to the maximum legal penalties for the several crimes by a power function, approximately. That is, when log seriousness score is regressed on log penalty, the regression is seemingly linear. But this result does not depend on the assumption of a ratio scale for seriousness. Any power transformation $(y' = ay^b)$ of y (seriousness score) will likewise be related by a power function to legal penalty. I do not question the sociological relevance of the Sellin-Wolfgang finding—although it is contrary to the result obtained by Rose and Prell (1955), which they do not cite. I only want to show that the finding is not uniquely dependent on the exponent in their scaling of offenses, different as it is from the exponents in other scalings of stimuli with monetary values. On the other hand, we know that for some transactions, like buying groceries or paying the rent, the relevant metric is the money value itself (whether the unit be the dollar or the cent) and not some subjective counterpart to it. If the relevant metric for money depends on whether we are making purchases, conferring status, or punishing thieves, might not the same be true of attitude? I am echoing, in the context of different subject matter, an argument of N. H. Anderson, paraphrased thus by Marks (1974, pp. 276–277):

. . . scaling and the determination of substantive relations among variables go hand in hand, particularly with regard to the validation of scales. Rescaling of response values may, for example, be necessary in order to correlate the scales with behavioral laws.

We come back to Coleman's (p. 73) warning against seeking "measurement validity" separately from "theory-validation."

Behind this discussion lurks a broader issue: whether the "ratio-scale" property of magnitude estimation holds by virtue of the instructions to the subject and the way in which the subject naturally makes judgments of magnitude, or whether it holds by virtue of the functional form of Stevens's psychophysical law, $\psi = \alpha\phi^\beta$, where ϕ is known to be measured on a ratio scale. It seems to me that Stevens is himself quite inconsistent on this matter. In some passages he alludes to the demonstrated ability of subjects to make ratio judgments—contrary to the preconceptions of some scientists prominent in the history of psychophysics (for example, 1975, p. 111). On the other hand, he often appeals to the psychophysical law and in particular to the cross-modality matching experiment as though it validated the claim that subjects actually are judging ratios of sensation (for example, 1975, p. 230). I am not the first to find Stevens's position somewhat obscure. Measurement theorists routinely complain that the term "ratio scaling" is ambiguous (Luce and Galanter 1963, p. 280). Does it refer simply to the magnitude estimation procedure, or is it implicitly a claim to the scale type produced by that procedure? Roberts (1979, p. 69) characterizes as "vague" Stevens's proposal to define "admissible transformations" of scale values as those that keep "intact the empirical information depicted by the scale." He goes on (pp. 186ff.) to propose a "measurement axiomatization for magnitude estimation and cross-modality matching" which does implicate the power function in the measurement theory, following Krantz (1972). But Luce (1972, p. 99) notes that for Krantz's axiomatization to be applicable, "it will be necessary for the exponents . . . to be independent of the subject" and expresses pessimism as to the possibility of establishing such invariance. And Cross, who has made important contributions to the methodology of magnitude estimation, finds (1979 preprint, p. 14) that Krantz's theory fails because the required invariance does not obtain.

I suspect Stevens's response to all this—in conformity with his "schemapiric" (1968) position—would be that invariance is where you find it or, rather, where you can design and execute the experiment capable of revealing it. Hence, he could appeal to the considerable body of evidence supporting his formulation of the psychophysical law and verifying the predictions implicit in the cross-modality experiment as support, not for a strictly axiomatic demonstration that ratio-scale measurement has been achieved, but for the ability of that assumption to order the experimental data.

Still, the bulk of this evidence is indeed psychophysical, not psychosocial. I ask the reader, with Stevens (1975, p. 93), to note "the long-standing misconception that each perceptual attribute reflects a physical dimension of the stimulus" and to consider whether the statement would make good sense with "social dimension" replacing "physical dimension." And, lest we conclude too quickly that psychophysical methods will solve problems of social measurement, let us recall a little of the history of physical measurement. As I pointed out in an earlier discussion, the measurement of temperature made real progress by abandoning the effort to scale sensation and adopting an entirely different approach, based on observations concerning the physical expansion of materials when they are heated. Can we take for granted that the best way to measure "social temperature"—or whatever social magnitude(s) might be its counterpart—is to quantify the sensations it produces? Stevens was fond of noting that the first category scale of sensation was invented by the Greek astronomer Hipparchus about 150 B.C. to estimate brightness, or stellar magnitude, visually and was used by astronomers until it was replaced in recent times by objective photometry, even though the results of the measurement continue to be stated in (modified) magnitudes. Thus, astronomy found its own scale of measurement at last, rather than taking advantage of advances in psychophysics to improve the scaling of perception.

I continue my discussion of issues arising in the use of psychophysical methods by describing summarily and commenting on three main lines of work: the scaling of seriousness of criminal offenses, the scaling of social status, and the use of "direct" magnitude scaling of "strength of opinion."

The work on seriousness of offenses has already been mentioned. The earlier study (Sellin and Wolfgang 1964) provides rough estimates of seriousness for some 120 offenses and more careful estimates for a selection of 21 offenses that were used to construct an index of delinquency. That index is not discussed here, and I really want to make only a few comments on the scaling exercise itself. One of the interesting features of the research was the use of several groups of subjects, including university students, police officers, and juvenile court judges. This makes possible various comparisons, most of which the authors interpret (p. 268) as supporting the conclusion that there is a "pervasive social agreement" as to the "estimated numerical degree of seriousness of these [21] offenses." They caution that "Because of the inherent ratio quality of the magnitude judgments, the particular numbers used by the raters are not especially relevant; rather, it is the ratios of offense seriousness that are preserved intact"—that is, the seriousness of one offense as compared with another. The implication of this qualification can be brought out by looking at the regression of seriousness score (Y) on maximum legal penalty (X), already mentioned. Over 18 of the offenses (excluding those carrying the death penalty) with penalties ranging from one to 276 months, this regression is estimated as $Y = 1.665 \, X^{.6568}$ for a group of student subjects and $Y = 2.146 \, X^{.7419}$ for a group of police officers. Because no standard errors are provided, we cannot tell whether the difference in exponents is significant. However, for each of the offenses, the police gave the higher seriousness score. From the foregoing regressions we find that the police score was (on average) 1.3 times as high at $X = 1$ and 2.1 times as high as the student score at $X = 276$. On the face of the matter police take crime more seriously than students, regardless of the gravity of the offense. That seems like a reasonable finding, possibly a banal but not a sociologically meaningless one. We are told, however, that because of their "inherent ratio quality," such a comparison is not "relevant." I note that in his graphic presentation of this regression Stevens (1966, p. 539) stated, without elaboration, "For plotting purposes the police ratings were multiplied by 0.5." Perhaps he, too, considered the comparison of levels not "relevant." Indeed, I know of no work in the entire literature on magnitude estimation where such a comparison is attempted. If comparisons like this cannot be made because of the "inherent ratio quality" of the judgments, the results of magnitude estimation will have but modest utility for studies in social psychology and cultural values, the focus of which is on comparisons between groups.

Presumably the need for caution arises—here one must conjecture, in view of the silence of the literature—because the difference in level could merely reflect a different choice of units, as though police measured seriousness in centimeters and students measured it in inches. But that, of course, is the difficulty: *There are no units of sensation* within the usual meaning of the term "unit" in the practice of measurement.

Something akin to the specification of a unit is sometimes attempted in the instruction concerning the "modulus," or experimenter-defined magnitude estimate for a standard stimulus. Apparently this was done in the Sellin-Wolfgang study; the printed instructions to the subjects state (pp. 254–255):

The first violation has been done as an example. It shows a violation which is given a seriousness score of 10. Use this violation as a standard. Every other violation should be scored in relation to this standard violation. For example, if any violation seems ten times as serious as the standard violation, write in a score of 100. If a violation seems half as serious as the standard, write in a score of 5. If a violation seems only a twentieth as serious as the standard, write in a score of ½ or .50. You may use *any* whole or fractional numbers that are greater than zero, no matter how small or large they are just so long as they represent how serious the violation is compared to the standard violation.

But we are not told what the "standard violation" was or whether it was the same violation for all subjects. And none of the analysis sheds light on whether the instructions as to modulus were effective.

In the later study (Figlio 1978), there is additional information. (Only a progress report on the study was available to me, so that the results quoted are subject to correction.) I have mentioned that the 1978 study produced estimates of the seriousness of thefts involving various dollar amounts. For five offenses, with the value of the property taken ranging from $10 to $10,000, the regression of seriousness on dollar value was estimated as $Y = 21.88 X^{.27}$. In this study, the data for which were collected by the U.S. Bureau of the Census, considerable attention was given to the standard stimulus and the modulus. The instructions to the respondent began:

The first situation is, "A person steals a bicycle parked on the street." This has been given a score of 10 to show its seriousness. (PAUSE) Use this first situation to judge all the others.

Then three additional "situations" were described—a robbery resulting in the victim's hospitalization, a 16-year-old person playing hooky from school, and a victim stabbed to death. For each of these, the interviewer was to say, "Compared to the bicycle theft with a score of 10, how serious do YOU think this is?" The three responses were then reviewed and for each the respondent was asked whether he or she understood that the number given meant that the "situation" was (more/less/as) serious (than/as) the bicycle theft. All of this was done by way of training. Each respondent then scored 21 additional "situations," one at a time, for a total of 25, counting the four used in training. Before situations 5, 6, 11, 16, and 21 were described, the instruction was repeated: "Compared to the bicycle theft scored at 10, how serious is . . . ?" Using 12 different versions of the interview schedule with different (but overlapping) lists of "situations," the survey produced seriousness scores for 204 offenses. Only two offenses, playing hooky (scored 5.4) and being a vagrant (6.7) received scores (geometric means) below 10. "A person steals property worth $10 from outside a building" was scored 37.8. The regression for the five thefts mentioned earlier implies a seriousness score of 10 when X = .055; that is, a bicycle is implicitly valued at 5½¢ by this equation. Clearly the American people do not regard a "bicycle parked on the street" as "property," do not have any conception of the value of a bicycle, or cannot be trained to use a modulus that approximates the smallest degree of seriousness they can perceive. Perhaps the effort to standardize the subjective scale would be more successful if respondents were instructed to measure seriousness in feet rather than millimeters.

The investigator concedes: "Our experiments with college students indicated that the assignment of a value to the modulus compared to self-assignment by the respondent had little effect on the scale values produced" (Figlio 1978). Indeed, my impression is that recently the opinion of specialists has shifted to the view that no modulus should be specified. Stevens (1975, p. 252) remarks: "The form of the function determined by the geometric means is not altered when each subject's judgments are based on a different unit." Exactly! And if there can be no standard unit, measurement is not on a ratio scale; it is on a log interval scale. Or perhaps we should say that each subject uses his personal "absolute" scale so that no calibration between persons beyond the log-interval level is possible.

Economists would not be surprised. The weight of opinion in economics has long been that interpersonal comparisons of utility are impossible or meaningless. Von Neumann and Morgenstern in their axiomatic theory, which aimed at treating utility as "a number up to a linear transformation," emphasized (p. 29) that they were "considering only utilities experienced by one person. These considerations do not imply anything concerning the comparisons of the utilities belonging to different individuals." (I was a little uncomfortable with letting this unembroidered remark stand as a summary of a very complicated issue in economic thought, until I reread Meeks's recent review paper. She does, however, point to a diversity of professional opinion on some aspects of the issue and leaves open some hypothetical possibilities for "meaningful" utility comparisons. Georgescu-Roegen, to whom I owe my earlier observation on the nonexistence of the hedonimeter, is similarly guarded on the issue of interpersonal comparisons.)

To be fair, it should be stated that no proponent of magnitude estimation, to my knowledge, has defended inter-individual or inter-group comparisons on the subjective scale in the absence of a physically measured stimulus (or, for that matter, in psychophysics proper). Stevens was careful to limit his advocacy of scaling social stimuli to the case of the "social consensus"—that is, the case in which individual and group differences are of no interest. This case is a very important one—sociologists influenced by Emile Durkheim's concept of *représentations collectives* should be ready to insist on that—but it does not account for all the problems on which the quantitative sociologist might have hoped to get help from psychophysics.

Let us turn the matter around. Suppose we *could* devise an experimental procedure which, with a reasonable choice of modulus, insured that respondents would use it correctly. (I dodge the difficult question of what experimental design would be appropriate for showing this.) What would our predicament then be? A ratio scale, of course, has a "natural" zero. In the Census Bureau interview respondents were told, "If YOU think something should not be a crime, give it a zero." If the standard stimulus is assigned a constant prespecified value (which is respected by respondents), and if the psychosocial law relating perceived seriousness (what YOU think) to society's definition of seriousness is

$$N = \mu S_C^{*\,\nu},$$

then we have but one degree of freedom. Everything is determined but the respondent's personal value of ν, since the curve of this function must pass through the origin and the point describing the standard stimulus and its modulus. It would appear that we might then compare respondents with respect to the parameter ν, assuming that variation in the estimates of it for individuals reflects something more than intraperson response variability. Dawson (p. 53) reports that "most studies have found that individual exponents vary widely across subjects." I note that ν is rather like what the economist calls an "elasticity" and that econometric literature (for example, Leser 1966) might be suggestive in this connection. Of course, since S_C^* is not observed, we can only estimate ratios such as ν_p/ν_0 from the plot of one person's seriousness estimates against another's. Here ν_0 is the exponent for one individual arbitrarily chosen as a standard and ν_p is the exponent for the p-th respondent, or (say) ν_p is the mean of exponents for the police and ν_0 the mean exponent for students. (The statistical problem of estimating such ratios is an interesting one, since both N_p and N_0 are doubtless subject to random error.)

Perhaps some sociological use can be found for the "elasticities" of the psychosocial law (if the power function can be assumed to hold). But it is disconcerting to realize that the argument has painted us into a corner where we cannot make statements like "Police take all crimes more seriously than students," but only statements like "Crime K is twice as serious as the standard crime for students, but it is three times as serious as the standard crime for the police." Yet that is the kind of limitation to relativistic statements we must accept if we must rely on subjective scaling of variables like "seriousness," for which (on our present understanding of the problem) no unit can be defined.

By contrast, if we asked police and students to specify appropriate monetary fines for a range of offenses, we might observe that police suggest a stiffer penalty for every offense (my guess is that this is what would happen, but I have no evidence). In that event, there would be no hesitation in stating that police are, let us say, in favor of penalties twice as severe as those endorsed by students, inasmuch as their fines on average are twice as large. Thus, with a true ratio scale, money— one that actually has a unit—our conclusion is more robust than it can be with the log interval scale (with no real unit), subjective seriousness. N. R. Campbell (1920/1957, pp. 359–360) was not mistaken when he wrote:

It must be admitted then that an arbitrary system of measurement may lead to a numerical law. And this law will involve constants. Are these constants derived magnitudes? Actually they are not; the law based on an arbitrary system of measurement is always empirical. Here is the great and fundamental difference between true and arbitrary systems of measurement: the former do and the latter do not define true derived magnitudes. The recognition of derived magnitudes is one of the most fruitful sources of scientific progress and the search for them one of the most powerful instruments in the hands of an investigator. But that weapon cannot be used until true and not arbitrary systems of measurement are established. That is why the development of a science may be fitly estimated by the part that measurement plays in it, and why all other sciences rely ultimately on physics which provides them with their systems of measurement.

Redefining "true measurement" (as Stevens did), while it opens up the possibility for a lot of beautiful experiments and mathematical models, does not really change the nature of the profound contrast between physical and psychophysical measurement. It just enables us to rediscover it from a different point of view.

My remarks on scaling of social status will be brief. I have already mentioned some interesting results of experiments on scaling the (perceived) social status of income levels. Similar work has been done on levels of educational attainment (Hamblin; Shinn; Coleman and Rainwater). If the stimulus is years of schooling—regarding each year as the same on the social scale regardless of whether it is a year of elementary school, of high school, of college, or of postgraduate study—then the psychosocial law is evidently not in the form of the power function. Instead, the status accorded to a year of schooling increases at an accelerating rate as the level of schooling rises (Coleman and Rainwater, pp. 68ff.). The curve could perhaps be described by an exponential function. Or, as Hamblin suggests, if we add a constant, 4 or 6, to the number of years of schooling (to shift the origin), the fit of the power function is greatly improved, as though an individual is "credited" with a certain number of years of culturally prescribed pre-school acculturation as well as the number of years spent in the school system. Coleman and Rainwater explored some relationships among schooling, its status value, the public's perception of the monetary rate of return to education, and the actual relationship of income to educational status. Results were presented only in verbal form, so I surmise they were regarded as tentative. The work is valuable, nonetheless, in showing that an exercise in scaling social status needs to be embedded in a system of relationships for its substantive implications to be developed.

In scaling occupational status or prestige we come back to the situation where the stimuli are nominal rather than numerical. Unfortunately, none of the more substantial pieces of research on this problem (Reiss with others 1961; Siegel 1971; Goldthorpe and Hope 1974; Treiman 1977) includes experiments with magnitude estimation, whereas studies using that technique have been of very modest dimensions in regard to number of occupations rated and number of respondents participating (Shinn 1969; Cross 1981) or have provided only a cursory analysis (Coleman and Rainwater 1978). My distinct impression is that category scaling will, if properly carried out, yield a set of occupational prestige scores linearly related to the logarithm of scores produced by magnitude estimation. I have already given reasons why I think it best to regard the latter as limited to the log interval rather than ratio scale, so that it is far from obvious that magnitude estimation makes a decisive contribution here. Nevertheless, the crucial experiment has yet to be done. I have a notion that it might be done as a problem in calibration (Ku 1969), carrying out magnitude estimation on a small scale with intensively trained interviewers and respondents, and category scaling (or more sophisticated extensions thereof) on a large scale to produce scores for a large number of occupations. The scores resulting from the category scaling could then be calibrated to the magnitude estimation scores.

But the most problematic aspect of this work is not the method of eliciting responses or the formula used to calculate scores from the responses. It is the occupation classification itself. Coleman and Rainwater indicate that their real interest is in jobs, not occupations in the traditional meaning of the term. They are quite right, of course, that its occupational classification is only one—perhaps not the most important—of the aspects of a job that may affect the jobholder's social standing. Thus "Senior partner of a Wall Street law firm" (to mention one of their "occupation" titles) surely has higher status than "Lawyer" (the title ordinarily used). But one should, for comparability, specify "Distinguished professor at Harvard University" rather than "College professor," which is the title they give for the academic job. Or, rather, the attempt should be made to separate the status value of the occupation as such from the status that derives from success or seniority in the occupation, the status of the employer, the size or dominance of the employing organization, and other job characteristics. Here and elsewhere a multivariate approach to the determinants of status is called for. Prototypical research designs are available in studies using either magnitude estimation (Hamblin 1971) or category scaling (Rossi 1979). Again one would like to see a careful but extensive study optimally combining complementary strengths of the two methods. The time for "scale confrontation studies" for their own sake is past.

In his most recent work, Lodge (1981) reports experiments on what he calls "direct" scaling of opinion. The preliminary scaling of stimuli, such as adjectives or opinion statements in the fashion of Thurstone and Lodge's earlier research, is bypassed. Instead, the respondent is asked to make a magnitude estimate of his own strength of opinion on an issue, such as whether the government should increase or decrease defense spending. The procedure begins, however, with a categorical response, exactly as in the conventional survey: the respondent chooses between "Increase defense spending"; "Same as now"; and "Decrease defense spending." Next he is asked to draw a reference line representing an arbitrary magnitude that will correspond to the present level of defense spending. Finally, he draws a response line to "say how much you favor an increase (decrease) in defense spending" (p. 64). The procedure is repeated with the stating of a number replacing the line-drawing task. This gives two measures that may be averaged to reduce random response error and to provide cross-modality validation (concerning which I have already stated reservations). The ratio of the length of the response line to that of the reference line (or the response number to the reference number) is calculated, and the reciprocal of this ratio is taken for respondents who favor "Decrease." Apparently, respondents who say "Same as now" are assigned a response ratio of unity. Upon transformation to logarithms their strength of opinion will become zero. Persons favoring decreased spending will have various negative values, and those favoring increased spending will have positive values. *There is no zero on the original magnitude estimate scale* which, therefore, cannot be a ratio scale (Stevens 1946). At its present stage of development, Lodge's "direct" technique appears not to recognize that the initial categorical response may be unreliable. The technique, therefore, is subject to the same reservations that apply to conventional survey data when categorical response data are treated as though error-free. Another limitation of the conventional technique also applies here: the implicit equating of complete indifference between alternatives (arising from lack of interest in either or ignorance about both) to ambivalence (the respondent is unable to choose between two alternatives found equally attractive or unattractive). With bipolar issues, such as the government spending item, it should be possible to adapt Hamblin's (1974, p. 80) device of securing both "like" and "dislike" magnitudes for the two main alternatives. Hamblin allowed respondents to indicate a magnitude of zero on either the "like" or the "dislike" scale (or both) and observed that with a numerical stimulus (wage rate for a job) the curve describing median level of "liking" as a function of the stimulus value crosses the curve for median "disliking" at a point well above the zero on either response scale. Also suggestive are the psychophysical experiments in which respondents judge both a quality (for example, roughness of a surface) and its inverse (smoothness) varying over a set of specimens (Stevens 1975, p.

124). In the attitude case, the respondent could judge both the degree to which he favors increased spending and the degree to which he opposes it and likewise his feelings of both kinds concerning decreased spending.

The salient feature of the attitude problem, as distinct from measures of the "social consensus," is that each respondent may have a unique location on the unobservable pro-con continuum and only he or she can estimate that location, whether indirectly by making choices or directly by emitting magnitudes. A great deal of experimentation will be needed to understand what is at stake in such a statement of the alternatives. Lodge begs the issue by grafting magnitude estimation onto a category-choice procedure. Since he collects the conventional data and something more, he can hardly do worse than the conventional one-question approach, cost considerations neglected. Another approach, however, is to augment the one-question procedure with additional questions on the same issue. I shall have something to say about this in my discussion of psychometrics.

REFERENCES

Bock, R. Darrell, and Lyle V. Jones. *The Measurement and Prediction of Judgment and Choice*. San Francisco: Holden-Day, 1968.

Campbell, N. R. *Physics: The Elements*. Cambridge: Cambridge University Press, 1920. Reprint, *Foundations of Science: The Philosophy of Theory and Experiment*. New York: Dover, 1957.

Coleman, James S. *Introduction to Mathematical Sociology*. New York: Free Press of Glencoe, 1964.

Coleman, Richard P., and Lee Rainwater. *Social Standing in America*. New York: Basic Books, 1978.

Cross, David V. "On Judgments of Magnitude." *Harvard-Yale Preprints in Mathematical Sociology* 13 (August 1979); Reprint, in *Social Attitudes and Psychophysical Measurement*, edited by B. Wegener. Hillsdale, N.J.: Erlbaum, 1981.

Dawson, William E. "An Assessment of Ratio Scales of Opinion Produced by Sensory-Modality Matching." In *Sensation and Measurement: Papers in Honor of S. S. Stevens*, edited by H. R. Moskowitz, B. Scharf, and J. C. Stevens, 49–59. Dordrecht-Holland: D. Reidel, 1974.

Ekman, Gösta, and Lennart Sjöberg. "Scaling." *Annual Review of Psychology* 16 (1965): 451–474.

Fechner, G. T. *Elemente der Psychophysik*, 1860; trans. by H. E. Adler as *Elements of Psychophysics*. New York: Holt, Rinehart & Winston, 1966.

Figlio, Robert M. *National Survey of Crime Severity: Progress Report, 1978*. Marvin E. Wolfgang, Project Director. Philadelphia: Center for Studies in Criminology and Criminal Law.

Finnie, B., and R. D. Luce. "Magnitude-Estimation, Pair-Comparison and Successive-Interval Scales of Attitude Items." Memorandum MP-9. Philadelphia: Department of Psychology, University of Pennsylvania, 1960.

Georgescu-Roegen, Nicholas. "Utility." *International Encyclopedia of the Social Sciences* 16: 236–267. New York: Macmillan, 1968.

Goldthorpe, J. H., and K. Hope. *The Social Grading of Occupations.* Oxford: Clarendon Press, 1974.

Hamblin, Robert L. "Mathematical Experimentation and Sociological Theory: A Critical Analysis." *Sociometry* 34 (1971): 423–452.

Hamblin, Robert L. "Social Attitudes: Magnitude Measurement and Theory." In *Measurement in the Social Sciences*, edited by H. M. Blalock, Jr., Ch. 3. Chicago: Aldine, 1974.

Kelley, Truman Lee. *Interpretation of Educational Measurements.* Yonkers-on-Hudson, N.Y.: World, 1927.

Krantz, D. H. "A Theory of Magnitude Estimation and Cross-Modality Matching." *Journal of Mathematical Psychology* 9 (1972): 168–199.

Ku, Harry H., ed. *Precision Measurement and Calibration.* Washington, D.C.: GPO, 1969.

Leser, C.E.V. *Econometric Techniques and Problems.* New York: Hafner, 1966.

Lodge, Milton. *Magnitude Scaling: Quantitative Measurement of Opinions.* Beverly Hills, Calif.: Sage, 1981.

Lodge, Milton, and Bernard Tursky. "Comparisons between Category and Magnitude Scaling of Political Opinion Employing SRC/CPS Items." *American Political Science Review* 73 (March 1979): 50–66.

Lodge, Milton, David V. Cross, Bernard Tursky, and Joseph Tanenhaus. "The Psychophysical Scaling and Validation of a Political Support Scale." *American Journal of Political Science* 19 (November 1975): 611–649.

Luce, R. Duncan. "What Sort of Measurement is Psychophysical Measurement?" *American Psychologist* 27 (February 1972): 96–106.

Luce, R. Duncan, and Eugene Galanter. "Psychophysical Scaling." In *Handbook of Mathematical Psychology*, Vol. I, Ch. 5, edited by R. Duncan Luce, Robert R. Bush, and Eugene Galanter. New York: Wiley, 1963.

Marks, Lawrence E. *Sensory Processes: The New Psychophysics.* New York: Academic, 1974.

Meeks, J. G. Tulip. "Utility in Economics: A Survey of the Literature." In *Surveying Subjective Phenomena*, Vol. 2, edited by Charles F. Turner and Elizabeth Martin. New York: Russell Sage Foundation, 1984.

Oberschall, Anthony. *Empirical Social Research in Germany 1848–1914.* Paris: Mouton, 1965.

Reiss, Albert J., Jr., with Otis Dudley Duncan, Paul K. Hatt, and Cecil C. North. *Occupations and Social Status.* New York: Free Press of Glencoe, 1961.

Roberts, Fred S. *Measurement Theory.* Reading, Mass.: Addison-Wesley, 1979.

Rose, Arnold M. and Arthur E. Prell. "Does the Punishment Fit the Crime?" *American Journal of Sociology* 61 (November 1955): 247–259.

Rossi, Peter H. "Vignette Analysis: Uncovering the Normative Structure of Complex Judgments." In *Qualitative and Quantitative Social Research: Papers in Honor of Paul F. Lazarsfeld*, edited by Robert K. Merton, James S. Coleman, and Peter H. Rossi, Ch. 14. New York: Free Press, 1979.

Sellin, Thorsten, and Marvin E. Wolfgang. *The Measurement of Delinquency.* New York: Wiley, 1964.

Shinn, Allen Mayhew, Jr. "The Application of Psychophysical Scaling Techniques to Measurement of Political Variables." Working Papers in Methodology, No. 3. Chapel Hill: Institute for Research in Social Science, University of North Carolina, 1969.

Siegel, Paul M. "Prestige in the American Occupational Structure." Ph.D. diss., University of Chicago, 1971.

Stevens, S. S. "On the Theory of Scales of Measurement." *Science* 103 (1946): 677–680.

Stevens, S. S. "A Metric for the Social Consensus." *Science* 151 (1966): 530–541.

Stevens, S. S. "Measurement, Statistics, and the Schemapiric View." *Science* 161 (1968): 849–856.

Stevens, S. S. *Psychophysics*. New York: Wiley, 1975.

Thurstone, L. L. "Attitudes Can Be Measured." *American Journal of Sociology* 33 (1928): 529–554. Reprint, in Thurstone (1959, Ch. 19).

Thurstone, L. L. *The Measurement of Values*. Chicago: University of Chicago Press, 1959.

Treiman, Donald J. *Occupational Prestige in Comparative Perspective*. New York: Academic, 1977.

von Neumann, John, and Oskar Morgenstern. *Theory of Games and Economic Behavior*. 2d ed. Princeton: Princeton University Press, 1947.

7

PSYCHOMETRICS

THE QUANTITATIVE STUDY of individual differences in ability and mental processes is often considered to have begun with Francis Galton about a century ago, although as I mentioned earlier some nineteenth-century experiments in educational measurement preceded his inquiries into human faculties and their inheritance. E. G. Boring credits Galton with being the inventor of the mental test (the term itself, however, was coined by J. McK. Cattell in 1890), but Galton's tests of sensory discrimination and reaction time were not much like the individual and group tests of intellect that were developed shortly after the turn of the century by Alfred Binet in France and his followers in America and England. Galton is, nevertheless, an appropriate symbolic father of psychometrics and no less so because he happened to be a cousin of Charles Darwin. Darwin's emphasis on the variation among individuals in any natural population and the heritability of such variation actually provides the general conceptual framework for psychometrics and makes clear its affiliation with the population sciences. (Psychophysics, by contrast, has usually taken a typologically oriented interest in the species norm, as represented by "the" observer, and has only grudgingly conceded the existence of interindividual variation, regarding it as a nuisance rather than a primary object of inquiry.)

The decisive developments in psychometrics occurred within a few years after 1900. They included Binet's invention of the individual test, comprising a variety of tasks arranged in order of difficulty and interpreted by reference to age norms of mental development; Charles Spearman's proposal for a "correlational psychology" deriving from his correction of correlation coefficients for "attenuation" (unreliability of test scores) and leading to a theory of hierarchy in intellectual functions (later formulated in terms of a single "general factor" and various "specific factors"); the widespread adoption of Stern's concept of IQ (intelligence quotient), originally defined as the ratio of "mental age" to chronological age but later defined in terms of standard scores for age levels; and the development of the group test for military application in World War I, with items devised for ease of administration and scoring. All this history is succinctly recounted by Anastasi (1965). The extension of mental testing methods to the measurement of personality traits, interests, values, and attitudes got under way a bit later.

Beginning at least as early as C. H. Cooley's criticism (1897) of Galton's studies on inheritance of genius, sociologists have generally taken a skeptical view of the proposition that intellectual achievement is determined largely by genetic factors, a claim defended by many, though not all, exponents of testing. But in other respects the sociological fraternity has enthusiastically supported the mental testing movement. From the 1920s on, social scientists took cognizance of the differences by nationality, "race," sex, social class, and rural-urban residence in test performance turned up in psychologists' studies of military and school populations, although some of the inferences drawn from these data were criticized. There was also considerable interest—or "intense controversy and speculation," as Thomas (1938) described it—in the problem of selectivity of migration according to "intelligence."

After World War II the attention of social researchers was directed to the use of test scores in investigations of educational opportunity, social mobility, and achievement of occupational and economic status. It is curious that a measurement technology developed with a view toward immediate application should be so turned to the account of basic research in another discipline, although I suppose precedent for this could be found in the history of the natural sciences. In any event, it is in such investigations as Sewell's longitudinal study of a Wisconsin cohort of high school seniors that we begin to get a quantitative sense of how individual differences in measured ability interact with social factors to produce variation in life chances. It is found, for example, that social status of the family of origin does not affect academic performance in high school independent of ability, yet it has a strong bearing upon continuation to college, with ability scores and high school grades held constant. On the other hand, while it is true that ability, as measured, reflects the advantages or disadvantages of favorable or unfavorable home backgrounds, its bearing upon success or failure in the socioeconomic career is by no means limited to the intergenerational transmission of status. On the contrary, the meritocratic principle is continuously balanced in the social process against the class principle in regard to educational attainment beyond high school, vocational aspirations, occupational achievement, and earnings from employment (Sewell and Hauser 1980). The rigorous demonstration of these counterpoised effects of social origins and individual ability is one of the major achievements of contemporary social science, even though the evidence, based on conventional mental tests, is vulnerable in ways that I shall mention later.

Policy implications of the social distribution of intellectual ability and achievement were explored in a congressionally mandated large-scale application of testing technology, the 1965 Educational Opportunities Survey (Coleman and others 1966) in which sociologists played a leading role. By the time of this vast enterprise, the testing industry had grown to a large scale and had itself become an object of sociological study—the report by Goslin (1963) initiated a series of important studies on "Social Consequences of Testing" by the Russell Sage Foundation—as well as public controversy continuing to the present time (see Committee on Ability Testing 1982). And the annual changes in average scores on college-entrance examinations have received increasing attention as a de facto social indicator (Advisory Panel on the Scholastic Aptitude Test Score Decline 1977). It could happen that work of this kind, including analyses of the continuing "IQ controversy" (Berger 1978), will provide the raw materials for an important chapter in the sociology of social measurement one would like to see develop in the next couple of decades.

In all these and various other ways, social science has involved itself in psychometrics, largely in the role of consumer of the statistical results of mental testing. Its role as producer of cognitive tests has been slight. Early criticisms of purported biases in these tests were followed by a short-lived effort, instigated by social scientists, to develop "culture-fair" measures of ability. But for the most part, social scientists have been content to use and to criticize tests of intellectual aptitude and achievement rather than to involve themselves in the technical procedures of test development. But the use of mental test scores in social research, extensive as it is (more so than my cursory summary may suggest), probably represents the lesser part of the impact of psychometrics on social measurement. It is as a methodological paradigm and source of specific measurement techniques that I want to look at psychological "tests and measures" in more detail. Three markers of their pervasive influence are our dependence on the psychometric definitions of "reliability" and "validity" of measures; the popularity of factor analysis and its derivatives in the treatment of multivariate data; and the adoption of a psychometric approach to the development of "instruments" or "scales" to measure a host of variables, ranging from the economic development of nations to the relative power of spouses in a marriage, and including, in particular, a great many scales of attitudes, feelings, and the like.

All this traces back to the "correlational psychology" proposed by Spearman in 1904, the foundation of which is an argument concerning the implications of measurement error, and the apparatus of which is the statistical theory of correlation developed by Galton and Karl Pearson. Consider a test on which the i-th examinee's obtained score is x_i. We imagine that this score differs from the "true" score t_i for that examinee (on the ability measured by the test) by reason of an error of measurement e_i. Hence, the definition or identity,

$$x_i \equiv t_i + e_i \tag{1}$$

Nothing is asserted by this expression, except that an error is possible; but then, nothing follows from it either without further definitions and assumptions. The same equation appears in the theory of measurement of a single physical quantity when repeated measurements are taken to provide evaluation of precision and accuracy (Eisenhart 1963/1969). But the assumptions of the psychometric approach are radically different from those of the laboratory physical scientist, and the two versions of measurement theory are, therefore, quite different. A major concern in physical measurement is to be confident that the measurement process is in a state of so-called statistical control, so that the errors behave like a sample of values from a fixed probability distribution. In that event, considering $t_i = \tau$ to have a fixed value, the expected value of a measurement (over repetitions) is $E(x) = \tau + E(e)$, and $E(e) = E(x) - \tau$ is called the *bias* (or systematic error) of the measurement process. Inasmuch as τ is ordinarily unknown, as a practical matter it is of interest to measure bias with respect to the outcome of an "exemplar method" or "preferred procedure" adopted as a standard. In classical test theory (which is the basis for the vastly larger part of contemporary psychometrics) true score is merely defined in such a way that $E(e_i) = 0$, so that measurements x_i are by fiat unbiased.

The theory erected on such a foundation is appropriately characterized by Lord and Novick as "weak." They refer to the idea of true value suited to the physical case as a "Platonic conception" and remark (p. 28):

If conditions are precisely specified, it seems correct to speak of the true velocity of light, the true weight of a bag of potatoes, and the true distance between two points, assuming of course that a measurement procedure and hence a scale of measurement have been specified. However, this conception of true score does not provide a satisfactory axiomatic basis for psychological theories, since these theories are typically based on unexplicated, inexact constructs.

A "correlational psychology" (Spearman's term) of "inexact constructs" is what psychometrics has indeed produced. I will reproduce just a few of its equations to try to convey the flavor of psychometric models and arguments, without any attempt at rigor.

If an equation like (1) is assumed for each of several tests, linear models for their multivariate structure are developed from convenient assumptions as to the mutual independence of measurement errors across tests and their independence of all true scores. The derivations are mathematically elegant and statistically sophisticated in the treatise of Lord and Novick (1968), although many of the results are available in elementary texts on psychological measurement. The reliability of a test is defined as

$$\rho_{xt}^2 = \text{Var}\ (t)/\ \text{Var}\ (x) = 1 - \text{Var}\ (e)/\ \text{Var}\ (x) \qquad (2)$$

where ρ_{xt} is the correlation between observed and true scores in a "well-defined population" of examinees. The "validity" of a test is assessed with respect to any other test or variable that it may be related to and is defined as

$$\rho_{x_1x_2} = \text{Cov}\ (x_1x_2)\ /\ \sqrt{\text{Var}\ (x_1)\ \text{Var}\ (x_2)} \tag{3}$$

where $\rho_{x_1x_2}$ is the population correlation between x_1 and x_2, the two variables of interest. It is easy, given the assumptions mentioned before, to express the validity in terms of the corresponding correlation between true scores and the reliabilities:

$$\rho_{x_1x_2} = \rho_{x_1t_1}\rho_{x_2t_2}\rho_{t_1t_2}$$

or

$$\rho_{t_1t_2} = \rho_{x_1x_2}/\rho_{x_1t_1}\rho_{x_2t_2} \tag{4}$$

which is the theoretical form of Spearman's "correction for attenuation." Although $\rho_{x_1x_2}$ can be estimated directly from a sample of paired measurements of x_1 and x_2, special methods for estimating the reliabilities must be used. Much of the practical technique of testing has to do with obtaining these estimates.

The step to factor analysis involves a conceptualization of a test score as a linear combination of values of hypothetical variables, in the fashion of the equation:

$$x_{hi} = \Sigma_j\ a_{hj}F_{hij} + d_hu_{hi} \tag{5}$$

where x_{hi} is the score of the i-th individual on test h, F_{hij} is his score on the j-th common factor that enters into that test (a hypothetical or latent variable), a_{hj} is the weight of the factor for the particular test (the same for all examinees), u_{hi} is the contribution to the score of the i-th individual on test h made by the unique factor for that test, and d_h is its weight (the same for all individuals). If we are considering a set of p tests ($1 \leq h \leq p$), and if there are $p - 1$ factors ($1 \leq j \leq p - 1$), equation (5) is tautologically true (although the weights a_{hj} and d_h are indeterminate) and, in this respect, resembles equation (1). If there are fewer factors, say $m < p - 1$, equation (5) becomes a (possibly false) *model* describing the way in which test scores are generated in the population. In the simplest case—factors are uncorrelated among

themselves and each has unit variance—the correlation between any
two tests, say $h = 1$ and $h = 2$, is given by:

$$\rho_{12} = \Sigma_j \, a_{1j} a_{2j} \qquad (6)$$

and the weight a_{hj} is interpreted as the "factor loading" or the correlation of test h with factor j, that is, $\rho_{x_h F_j} = a_{hj}$. The technology of factor
analysis has to do with the estimation of the loadings from the observ-
able correlations and the determination of the acceptability of the
model, which is assessed by its ability to reproduce those correlations
within the limits of sampling error. If the model is accepted, there is
still an indeterminacy in the estimation of factor loadings inasmuch as
systems of factors differing from those in (6), but mathematically
equivalent to them in the sense that they produce exactly the same
correlations on the left-hand side of (6), may be chosen in an infinity
of ways. Stating criteria for the choice of a preferred way is the gist of
the so-called rotation problem. Its solution has considerable bearing
upon the substantive or conceptual interpretation of the "factors." In
so-called confirmatory factor analysis, strong assumptions—supposedly with theoretical justification—serve to remove most of the indeterminacy. Typically these assumptions specify zero values a priori
for a considerable number of the factor loadings, so that each factor is
involved in only a few of the tests (or other observed variables). In one
of the most highly developed procedures—Jöreskog's LISREL—quite
a variety of such a priori specifications can be made (Jöreskog and
Sörbom 1981), including those suggested by the kinds of linear structural equation models developed in econometrics (Aigner and Goldberger 1977).

The extension of the factor model from the Spearman case of a
single common factor to multiple common factors in the fashion of (5)
and (6) was accomplished by 1930, in large part through the work of
Thurstone. By 1948 he noted that already "several thousand papers on
multiple-factor theory and experimental results" had been published
(Anastasi, p. 58). Thurstone always insisted that factor analysis should
be regarded not as a mere statistical method for analyzing just any
correlation matrix, but as a strategy for developing a theoretical model
of psychological structure. He cherished the hope that research ultimately would isolate a modest number of "primary mental abilities"
that could be regarded as "functionally distinct," and he thereby cast

his lot, described in this way by Lumsden (1980, p. 7): "During the 1920s [in his psychophysical research] Thurstone stole fire from the gods. (As a punishment they chained him to factor analysis.)" By 1968, it was apparent to a participant observer that the "number of variables and the number of factors have grown astronomically, and the end is not yet in sight." Humphreys (p. 286), thus pessimistically assessing the quest for "psychological meaning" via factor analysis, could only offer a feeble justification of the technique: "An economical description of complex data is itself an important scientific goal."

By my own judgment, consistent with the remarks just quoted, factor analysis is a failure. I am not really concerned to defend such a conclusion in regard to strictly psychological material such as cognitive and personality tests. However specialists may assess those areas, in applications drawing upon sociological ideas we certainly see nothing more than a "correlational" science of "inexact constructs." I shall refer to what may be the strongest case to the contrary, passing over in melancholy silence a wasteland of ill-considered, mechanically executed, and carelessly interpreted factor analyses of correlations among every conceivable kind of social variables. The strong case is presented in Schuessler's recent monograph on Social Life Feeling Scales (SLFSs). The author performs a major service in demonstrating the prevailing chaos in which there is a multiplicity of "tests," "scales," or "instruments" ostensibly serving as "measures" of a collection of ambiguous and poorly discriminated concepts like morale, alienation, external-internal control, life satisfaction, cynicism, optimism-pessimism, demoralization, estrangement, anomia, anomy, normlessness, powerlessness, social isolation, affect-balance, disenchantment, confidence, psychological well-being, usefulness, faith in people, job morale, depressive affect, worry, perceived purposelessness, efficacy in public affairs, meaninglessness, personal control, anxiety, personal efficacy, and others. Schuessler found many instances of the same items (questions, or statements calling for an agree/disagree response) in tests intended to measure different constructs, different and dissimilar items in tests with the same or similar names, a widespread habit of arbitrarily modifying tests when applying them in new research (thereby precluding comparison or any benefit of standardization), and the replacement of old scales by new ones without cross-calibration between them and without demonstration of improved validity.

Ransacking the literature recording these disorderly pre-scientific practices, Schuessler turned up around 1,000 items occurring in about one-tenth that many distinct questionnaires. Eliminating duplicates and near duplicates reduced the number to 500-odd items that could be reasonably classified by topical similarity. Pilot studies led to a final questionnaire incorporating 237 life feeling items administered to a national sample of 1,522 adults living in households in 1974. Factor analysis of these items was then carried out to determine the number of common factors, estimated at 17. The attempt was made to construct a scale for each of them in such a way that each scale would have only the one factor in common and would meet other stated criteria pertaining to length, reliability, representation of the subject-matter domain, and validity (as inferred indirectly from correlations with social background variables). The result was a dozen new scales, each of which is assessed as to its statistical properties, including its score distribution in the U.S. adult population, and described in terms of plausible meanings that could be ascribed to high and low scores. It is noted that "scale interpretations came after item screening and selection," a reversal of "the usual procedure of defining a concept first, and then finding a set of items expressive of that concept" (Schuessler, Ch. 2). But this kind of bootstrap strategy has always been prominent in the applications of factor analysis to batteries of tests rather than collections of items. Moreover, the investigator took great pains to compare the new scales with the old ones from which items were taken and to make use of whatever resources the literature offered to aid in achieving and refining conceptualization. In the end, the scales are characterized in everyday language. SLFS1 is called "Doubt about Self-Determination" rather than "anomia," despite its correlation of .78 with Srole's Anomia scale, and SLFS3 is named "Feeling Down," although it is regarded as substantially equivalent (r = .84) to Bradburn's Negative Affect Scale. Some of the other scales are 4 − Job Satisfaction, 7 − People Cynicism, 9 − Future Outlook, and 12 − Career Concerns. All have to do in one way or another with a person's outlook on society (such as cynical, pessimistic, fatalistic, and so on) or the person's frame of mind as a member of society (such as demoralized, estranged, or alienated). An open-minded reader, I feel, can hardly help being impressed by the investigator's judiciousness in characterizing the meaning of his scales and his ingenuity in generating statistical evidence to control the interpretations. Nevertheless—and I can't imagine Schuessler would contest the description—what we have are "inexact constructs." The research report, moreover, is almost compulsively meticulous in pointing out repeatedly the arbitrary aspects of decision criteria and their application, and also the method-dependent character of the resulting scales. Claims for validity are muted: "some scales approximated" the criterion of "face validity in the strict sense that all . . . items referred directly to the concept" supposedly measured. None had "criterion validity in the strict sense of predicting an independent criterion of that feeling, since in no case was such a criterion available" (Ch. 7). I doubt that stronger claims could be justified for any of the earlier scales surveyed by Schuessler, although some writers have made heavy pronouncements concerning the conceptual underpinning of their instruments. The investigator warns that meanings of items are uncertain, may vary from one population to another, and may change from time to time, thereby destroying the scale pattern. But he provides no technique for recognizing or coping with such problems.

While expressing appreciation of the quality of the research that produced Schuessler's SLFSs, I have hinted at dissatisfaction with the outcome, predestined as it was to produce a "correlational" social psychology of "inexact constructs." I must be more specific about the seriousness of these limitations.

In regard to "inexact constructs," we cannot lay all the blame at the investigator's door. He is working in a notoriously "soft" area—one in which much of the research that has been done has been motivated by the perceived urgency of the social problems to which negative social life feelings are related, rather than by theoretical concerns. Indeed, one could probably show that the applied rather than the theoretical motivation has been dominant in most of psychometrics and its social science derivatives. Whatever the prospects may be for fundamental theoretical clarification of a domain like social life feelings (not to mention "intelligence" or mental ability), we can hardly expect such clarification to be achieved singlehandedly by specialists in measurement and scale construction. I take it this is what Blalock (1982, p. 263) may have had in mind in writing—at the close of a book-length examination of the interaction of conceptualization and measurement models of the kind made available by structural-equation systems of the LISREL type—"multiple measures without a theory will only lead to chaotic results." The one thing a measurement specialist might be asked to do, nevertheless, is to provide strong criteria that should be met by any scale proposing to make a hitherto "inexact" construct into one that corresponds to a unidimensional magnitude. I believe that the traditional claim of factor analysis to provide a good estimate of the "dimensionality" of a domain is not credible. (Earlier I quoted Humphreys much to this effect.) Schuessler makes a somewhat weaker claim: "We found a close correspondence between our 12 empirical scales and the more numerous [scales of previous authors]. We took this to mean that sociologists have operationally distinguished no more than 12 social life feelings, however many nominal distinctions they have drawn" (Ch. 7). This may be one of the least adequately defended conclusions of the study. It amounts to an assertion that no other "real" (that is, not merely "nominal") distinction is reflected in or registered by any of the some 400 items discarded in the process that led to the dozen scales comprising some 95 items. Or, to put it differently, the claim seems to be that each of the 400 discarded items could be shown actually to belong to one (if not more than one, since some items appear in more than one scale) of the final dozen scales. That is difficult to believe.

Admittedly I am forcing the argument a bit for the sake of my point, which is that multiple factor analysis is not really a method of measuring at all; it is a method of obtaining a minimum estimate of how many distinct hypothetical variables, operating as common causes of a set of observed variables, are required to account for the intercorrelations of the latter in some population. Whether any one of these hypothetical variables, or an estimate of scores on it derived from a selection of items, is a *measure* of any construct simply cannot be determined by the method. (The "measurement model" of LISREL or other linear equations methods may seem to finesse this difficulty by making much stronger assumptions, with whatever conceptual justification, about how a construct is reflected in or evidenced by fallible indicators. Even in LISREL, however, we have only correlational evidence to use in assessing the model specification and no rational means of turning the correlation results into an explicit measuring instrument.)

Apart from its tolerance of inexactitude in constructs, correlational

TABLE 7-1.

Score Distribution and Scale Characteristics Computed from
Correlation Analysis of Simulated Data (n = 2,500)

	Simulation						
	I	II	III	IV	V	VI	VII
Score							
4	1590	709	1272	188	829	34	4
3	589	534	182	422	333	213	65
2	252	431	114	588	201	472	252
1	65	358	387	730	329	585	589
0	4	468	545	572	808	1196	1590
Mean	3.48	2.26	2.50	1.57	2.02	0.92	0.52
Standard deviation	0.79	1.47	1.70	1.22	1.70	1.06	0.79
Item means							
A	.97	.74	.72	.64	.62	.42	.28
B	.88	.56	.61	.37	.50	.21	.11
C	.83	.50	.59	.30	.46	.16	.08
D	.80	.46	.57	.25	.44	.13	.06
Factor loadings							
A	.21	.65	.72	.48	.77	.66	.58
B	.38	.69	.87	.52	.83	.49	.41
C	.45	.67	.88	.50	.82	.42	.34
D	.47	.64	.88	.47	.81	.38	.30
Reliability	.39	.76	.91	.56	.88	.55	.43

knowledge produced by aggregation of item responses is not good enough for another reason. It confounds two entirely different things: (a) the structure of meaning-relationships among the items, and (b) the population distribution over the dimension or dimensions measured by the items. I will try to make this assertion plausible without demonstrating it as a general theorem, by means of an exercise involving simulated data.

In Table 7-1 I show calculations based on hypothetical data obtained from seven simulations. In each simulation I consider a scale constructed from four dichotomous items, A, B, C, and D, each of which may be answered in the "positive" or the "negative" direction. The item mean, or proportion, is simply the number answering it positively divided by the sample size. The respondent's score is the number of items he answers positively. Table 7-1 shows the observed score distribution under each simulation. For each simulation I calculate the factor loadings under Spearman's model, which assumes that a single common factor pertains to all four items. According to this model, the theoretical correlation between two items is the product of their respective loadings. The model fits well in all of my simulations. All but one of the theoretical correlations differ from the actual correlations by less than .01, and that one differs from the actual correlation by only .0115. Thus, I have apparently achieved in these simulations the kind of unidimensionality Schuessler was aiming for in his empirical work. Finally, following Schuessler, I estimate the so-called α–reliability as $m\bar{r}/[1 + (m - 1)\bar{r}]$, where m (here 4) is the number of items and $\bar{r}$ is the mean of the correlations (here, 6 of them) for pairs of items in the scale. It will be noted that in some of the simulations the scale performs well as judged by α–reliability, although in others it does not. (Schuessler accepts scales with reliabilities as low as .53 and .62.)

In these simulations I have used a measurement model that keeps separate, rather than confounding, the item structure and the (unknown) distribution of the population on the latent variable of which the item responses are taken to be observable indicators. Inasmuch as I am not simulating random sampling variation, the quantities shown in Table 7-1 may be regarded as population values or, in the case of the frequency distributions of scores, as expected values in a sample of 2,500 respondents, subject to the rounding errors incurred in expressing them as whole numbers.

Having provided the array of summary measures describing a scale that would be exhibited under the conventional psychometric approach, I now offer you a challenge. I have indicated that my model keeps separate the structure of item parameters and the population distribution on the latent variable. Some of these simulations have the same scale structure, as described by item parameters, and differ only in regard to the population distribution. My challenge problem is as follows: *For any two simulations, determine whether the item parameters are the same or different* (making a reasonable allowance for rounding errors, but none for sampling errors). You are to make this determination by inspection of the figures given in Table 7-1 or from other quantities that may be derived from them using conventional factor-analysis methods. For convenience, in each simulation I have listed the items in order of their means, calling the one with the highest mean A and the one with the lowest mean D. Although there are similarities for some pairs of simulations in the pattern of means, no two simulations have exactly the same item means. We also see that the simulations include a variety of observed score distributions, although some similarities in form, location, or spread of the distributions may be discerned. The several sets of factor loadings likewise are heterogeneous.

Accordingly, if you play my game honestly, I believe you will acknowledge that few pairs of simulations show close similarities in terms of the correlational statistics, and hardly any exhibit actual mathematical invariances of the kind suggested by my criterion of "the same scale structure" defined in terms of "item parameters." If the several simulations represented distinct population strata, evidence of the kind shown in Table 7-1 would mainly point to a lack of invariance across strata.

Yet, such invariance is there, for I put it there. You can find it in the following manner. Within each simulation, use the factor loadings to reconstitute (approximately) the inter-item correlations; and from these, the item means, and the sample size, derive the pairwise cross-classifications of items. For example, for items A and D in IV, we have the correlation $(.48)(.47) = .2256$ and the covariance $(.2256)$ $[(.64)(1 - .64)(.25)(1 - .25)]^{1/2} = .0468901$, whence the four frequencies in the cross-classification of A and D are $F_{11}^{AD} = n(\text{Cov AD} + p_A p_D) = 517$; $F_{12}^{AD} = p_A n - F_{11}^{AD} = 1600 - 517 = 1083$; $F_{21}^{AD} = p_D n - F_{11}^{AD} = 108$; and $F_{22}^{AD} = n - F_{11}^{AD} - F_{12}^{AD} - F_{21}^{AD} = 792$. The subscripts refer to the first and second row and the first and second column, respectively, of the A-by-D cross-classification, and p_A and p_D are the item means. Now compute $F_{12}^{AD}/F_{21}^{AD} = 1083/108 = 10.02$, which is in approximate agreement with the ratio $a/d = 9.6601$ actually used in my simulation. (The small discrepancy is due to rounding errors and to the approximation involved in using factor loadings to compute the correlation.) This same ratio (aside from the errors mentioned) applies in *all* the simulations. Moreover, similar ratios computed for all six pairs of items are invariant across *all* the simulations I through VII. The structure of item parameters is actually the same in all of them, even though that fact is not brought to light in any way that I can see by the results of the correlational analysis pertaining to the Spearman model.

Moreover, within each simulation another kind of invariance ob-

TABLE 7-2.
Item Cross-Classifications, Simulation IV (n = 2,500)

Positive response to	Negative response to				Total Positive	Item Parameter
	A	B	C	D		
A	. . .	855	992	1079	1603	9.6601
B	187	. . .	512	568	935	2.1170
C	139	327	. . .	441	750	1.3526
D	112	269	327	. . .	636	1.0
Total Negative	897	1565	1750	1864	. . .	. . .

Computed Ratios

$a/b = 4.57$	$a/c = 7.14$	$(a/b)(b/d) = 9.64$
$a/d = 9.63$	$b/c = 1.57$	$(a/c)(c/d) = 9.64$
$b/d = 2.11$	$c/d = 1.35$	$(b/c)(c/d) = 2.12$

tains. Compute any three ratios, such as a/d, b/d, and c/d. The remaining three ratios can be obtained from them by multiplication or division. Thus, arbitrarily setting one item parameter at unity, say $d = 1$, I can obtain all six ratios from just three parameter values, $a = 9.6601$, $b = 2.1170$, and $c = 1.3526$. (As it happens, these values were the ones estimated from an actual set of data, one with the same observed score distribution as Simulation IV.) To make this property of the model entirely explicit, I show in Table 7-2 the simulated frequencies in each of the six item cross-classifications of one of the simulations. These are the frequencies actually used in computing the correlations that were fitted to the Spearman model. Notice that the correlation matrix would be in the 4 × 4 format of Table 7-2, but it is symmetric. Thus we have an obvious metaphor: the Spearman model factor analyzes the symmetric inter-item correlation (or covariance) matrix, reducing the 6 correlations to 4 factor loadings. The model I am using "factor analyzes" the inter-item asymmetries, reducing the 6 asymmetries to 4 item parameters, one of which may be assigned an arbitrary value. (In the Spearman case, if covariances are factor analyzed, one factor loading may be given a similarly arbitrary value.)

Although Table 7-2 is helpful in demonstrating the properties of the model I am using, to test the model's empirical suitability for a set of actual items, one must examine the 4-way (16-cell) cross-classification of the items for a sample of respondents. (It is—or should be—an embarrassment to proponents of factor analysis that their model is never tested against the facts of this detailed cross-classification.) I do not go into specific procedures for estimating and testing the model, inasmuch as another publication (Duncan 1984) deals with these matters. But I do want to sketch its rationale as I did earlier for factor analysis.

The measurement model is taken from Rasch (1960/1980; 1968), all of whose work pertained to cognitive tests, although his followers have done some research on attitude scales. It postulates that response to any item is probabilistic and depends *only* upon the additive combination of two parameters, one pertaining to the particular item (the same for all respondents) and the other pertaining to the particular respondent (the same for all items):

$$\log [p_{ij}/(1 - p_{ij})] = \theta_i + \beta_j$$

where log is the natural logarithm, p_{ij} is the probability of a positive response to the j–th item by the i–th respondent, θ_i is the person parameter that locates the respondent on the latent attitude scale θ and β_j is the item parameter that locates the j–th item on that same scale. The conceptual framework is much like that of Thurstone, which was summarized in Chapter 6, and the model might seem to have been designed to satisfy Thurstone's criteria of invariance and relevance (also mentioned in Chapter 6), although Rasch apparently did not use Thurstone's work. (Further on Thurstone and Rasch, see Andrich 1978a.) The probabilities p_{ij}, which differ from one individual to another, can hardly be estimated directly, since that would require many repetitions of each item to each respondent, with a "brainwashing" (as Paul Lazarsfeld used to say) between each presentation, so that memory of the previous response would not affect the present one. Moreover, the item parameters β_j, although roughly analogous to item "difficulties" in classical test theory, are not simple functions of the item response percentages (the item means in Table 7-1). In principle, it should be possible to estimate item parameters by a method like Thurstone's (described in Chapter 6) or an analogous magnitude-estimation procedure (also in Chapter 6). But Rasch has shown that item parameters can be estimated from the response data without a separate item-scaling procedure. (In this, as in some other ways, Rasch's approach is kin to the Likert method of test construction; see Andrich 1978b, 1982.) The same is true of the person parameters θ_i, although to secure much precision in estimating them requires a scale including a considerable number of items covering a range of parameter values.

The Rasch model is said to be "population-free" or "sample-free" in a particular sense of these terms (Andrich 1982). It contains no parameter that depends upon the frequency distribution $f(\theta)$ of the unobserved (latent) attitude dimension or upon the distribution of observed scale scores in a population or sample. Of course, the idea of "population" is relevant to the model in that variation in attitudes among individuals is expected, unless we are dealing with the limiting case of complete consensus, in which $\theta_i = \theta_0$, a constant for all i. And it is understood that any scale will apply—or, we may say, will have "validity"—only within a population of potential respondents who share a common understanding of the items.

Nothing I've said should be construed as a claim that scales can easily be constructed to Rasch's specifications. I only claim, following Perline, Wright, and Wainer (1979, p. 253), that "The Rasch model, when it holds, yields measures of person abilities and item facilities on an interval scale with a common unit," and, on the authority of the same authors (p. 237), that the model is a "special case of additive conjoint measurement" (Luce and Tukey 1964) when the conjoint measurement theory is appropriately modified to accommodate a stochastic response structure. By contrast, as I pointed out in Chapter 4, one cannot defend rigorously even the claim for mere ordinal measurement on behalf of instruments based on classical test theory. Incidentally, the raw score (number of items answered in the positive direction) for a set of items in a Rasch scale does provide an ordinal scale, and it is also the sufficient statistic for estimating the person parameter θ_i, which is a monotonic transformation of the raw score. I do not consider here the technical problem of making estimates of θ_i, since these estimates are very imprecise and of no great interest when we have a very few items. Nevertheless, it is important to note Wright's formulation of the uniqueness theorem, "The Rasch model is the *only* latent trait model for a dichotomous response that is consistent with 'number right' scoring" (1977, p. 102).

In survey research it is usually considered impractical to use scales with many items, and we cannot realize all the benefits of Rasch measurement if that presumption prevails. Nevertheless, we often confront the issue of whether some two, three, or four items can be said to measure the same thing. The model provides an answer to that question and, when the answer is affirmative, a justification for using raw score as an ordinal scale, as in Guttman scaling. For more on how Rasch's model realizes the stipulations on measurement proposed by Guttman while providing a more powerful instrument, see Andrich (1981). For further discussion of the prospects for scales of this kind in survey work, see Turner and Martin (1984, Ch. 6). I should also call attention to two helpful texts on psychometric applications of Rasch measurement (Wright and Stone 1979; Wright and Masters 1982). An important reference, although it is somewhat dated, in the social science literature is Mokken (1971), which may be the first work to demonstrate the conceptual affinity of Rasch's approach to that taken in Guttman scaling. The reader should also be aware of models (Lord 1980; Weiss and Davison 1981) that generalize the Rasch approach by including additional parameters to describe items and/or persons. However successful these may be as models for response structures—an especially interesting set of results for some attitude items is given by Reiser (1981)—they give up the attractive properties of the conjoint measurement framework, or the invariance criterion of Thurstone. In my view, what we need are not so much a repertoire of more flexible models for describing extant tests and scales (interesting as such models may be) but scales built to have the measurement properties we must demand if we take "measurement" seriously. As I see it, a measurement model worthy of the name must make explicit some conceptualization—at least a rudimentary one—of what goes on when an examinee solves test problems or a respondent answers opinion questions; and it must incorporate a rigorous argument about what it *means* to measure an ability or attitude with a collection of discrete and somewhat heterogeneous items.

Thurstone explicated the meaning of measurement as it might be accomplished by such an instrument. Rasch provided the formalization of that meaning. With techniques borrowed from the domain of log-linear statistical models, it is now possible to evaluate rigorously any attempt to realize the Thurstone-Rasch criteria in practice. While I am not optimistic that this can be readily accomplished, I really see no alternative to making the attempt. Surely the Rasch model, which synthesizes key features of the earlier contributions of Thurstone,

Likert, Lazarsfeld, and Guttman, deserves as much attention as the methods associated with those names received in their day.

REFERENCES

Advisory Panel on the Scholastic Aptitude Test Score Decline. *On Further Examination*. 2 vols. New York: College Entrance Examination Board, 1977.

Aigner, D. J., and A. S. Goldberger, eds. *Latent Variables in Socio-Economic Models*. Amsterdam: North-Holland, 1977.

Anastasi, Anne. *Individual Differences*. New York: Wiley, 1965.

Andrich, David. "Relationships Between the Thurstone and Rasch Approaches to Item Scaling." *Applied Psychological Measurement* 2 (Summer 1978a): 451–462.

Andrich, David. "Scaling Attitude Items Constructed and Scored in the Likert Tradition." *Educational and Psychological Measurement* 38 (Autumn 1978b): 665–680.

Andrich, David. "Rasch's Models and Guttman's Principles for Scaling Attitudes." Paper presented at conference, Objective Measurement in Honor of Georg Rasch. University of Chicago, 1981.

Andrich, David. "Using Latent Trait Measurement Models to Analyse Attitudinal Data: A Synthesis of Viewpoints." In *The Improvement of Measurement in Education and Psychology*, edited by Donald Spearitt, Ch. 5, pp. 89–126. Melbourne: Australian Council for Educational Research, 1982.

Berger, Brigitte. "A New Interpretation of the I.Q. Controversy." *The Public Interest* 50 (Winter 1978): 29–44.

Blalock, Hubert M., Jr. *Conceptualization and Measurement in the Social Sciences*. Beverly Hills, Calif.: Sage, 1982.

Boring, Edwin G. "The Beginning and Growth of Measurement in Psychology." In *Quantification*, edited by Harry Woolf, 108–127. Indianapolis: Bobbs-Merrill, 1961.

Coleman, James S., and others. *Equality of Educational Opportunity*. Washington, D.C.: GPO, 1966.

Committee on Ability Testing. *Ability Testing: Uses, Consequences, and Controversies*. 2 vols. Washington, D.C.: National Academy Press, 1982.

Cooley, Charles Horton. "Genius, Fame and the Comparison of Races," 1897. Reprint, in *Sociological Theory and Social Research*. New York: Augustus M. Kelley, 1969.

Duncan, Otis Dudley. "Rasch Measurement in Survey Research: Further Examples and Discussion." In *Surveying Subjective Phenomena*, edited by Charles F. Turner and Elizabeth Martin. New York: Russell Sage Foundation, 1984.

Eisenhart, Churchill. "Realistic Evaluation of the Precision and Accuracy of Instrument Calibration Systems," 1963. Reprint, in *Precision Measurement and Calibration*, edited by Harry H. Ku, NBS Special Pub., Vol. 1, pp. 21–47. Washington, D.C.: GPO, 1969.

Goslin, David A. *The Search for Ability: Standardized Testing in Social Perspective*. New York: Russell Sage Foundation, 1963.

Humphreys, Lloyd G. "Factor Analysis: Psychological Applications." *International Encyclopedia of the Social Sciences* 5: 281–287. New York: Macmillan, 1968.

Jöreskog, Karl G., and Dag Sörbom. *LISREL V: Analysis of Linear Structural Relationships by Maximum Likelihood and Least Squares Methods*. Uppsala: Department of Statistics, University of Uppsala, 1981.

Lord, Frederic M. *Applications of Item Response Theory to Practical Testing Problems*. Hillsdale, N.J.: Erlbaum, 1980.

Lord, Frederic M., and Melvin R. Novick. *Statistical Theories of Mental Test Scores.* Reading, Mass.: Addison-Wesley, 1968.

Luce, R. D., and J. W. Tukey. "Simultaneous Conjoint Measurement: A New Type of Fundamental Measurement." *Journal of Mathematical Psychology* 1 (1964): 1–27.

Lumsden, J. "Tests Are Perfectly Reliable." *British Journal of Mathematical and Statistical Psychology* 31 (1978): 19–26.

Lumsden, James. "Variations on a Theme by Thurstone." *Applied Psychological Measurement* 4 (1980): 1–7.

Mokken, R. J. *A Theory and Procedure of Scale Analysis.* The Hague: Mouton, 1971.

Perline, Richard, Benjamin D. Wright, and Howard Wainer. "The Rasch Model as Additive Conjoint Measurement." *Applied Psychological Measurement* 3 (Spring 1979): 237–255.

Rasch, Georg. *Probabilistic Models for Some Intelligence and Attainment Tests*, 1960. Reprint, with a Foreword and Afterword by Benjamin D. Wright. Chicago: University of Chicago Press, 1980.

Rasch, Georg. "An Individualistic Approach to Item Analysis." In *Readings in Mathematical Social Science*, edited by Paul F. Lazarsfeld and Neil W. Henry, 89–108. Cambridge: M.I.T. Press, 1968.

Reiser, Mark. "Latent Trait Modeling of Attitude Items." In *Social Measurement: Current Issues*, edited by George W. Bohrnstedt and Edgar F. Borgatta, Ch. 4, 117–144. Beverly Hills, Calif.: Sage, 1981.

Schuessler, Karl. *Measuring Social Life Feelings.* San Francisco: Jossey-Bass, 1982.

Sewell, William H., and Robert M. Hauser. "The Wisconsin Longitudinal Study of Social and Psychological Factors in Aspirations and Achievements." *Research in Sociology of Education and Socialization* 1 (1980): 59–99.

Thomas, Dorothy Swaine. *Research Memorandum on Migration Differentials.* New York: Social Science Research Council, 1938.

Turner, Charles F., and Elizabeth Martin, eds. *Surveying Subjective Phenomena.* Vol. 1. New York: Russell Sage Foundation, 1984.

Weiss, David J., and Mark L. Davison. "Test Theory and Methods." *Annual Review of Psychology* 32(1981): 629–658.

Wright, Benjamin D. "Solving Measurement Problems with the Rasch Model." *Journal of Educational Measurement* 14 (Summer 1977): 97–116.

Wright, Benjamin D., and Mark H. Stone. *Best Test Design: Rasch Measurement.* Chicago: MESA Press, 1979.

Wright, Benjamin D., and Geofferey N. Masters. *Rating Scale Analysis: Rasch Measurement.* Chicago: MESA Press, 1982.

8

SOCIAL MEASUREMENT: PREDICAMENTS AND PRACTICES

W E ARE CLOSE to the end of an oddly proportioned essay on social measurement and I have said precious little about the actual enterprise or industry of measuring things social. There isn't room to list in small type the names of the various "measures" proposed by social scientists: "There are literally thousands of scales and indexes to measure social variables," according to Miller (p. 207), who attempted something like an inventory and took over 250 pages to make annotations on "selected" and recommended scales, along with details on a few of them, under some 13 headings:

A. Social Status
B. Group Structure and Dynamics
C. Social Indicators
D. Measures of Organizational Structure
E. Evaluation Research and Organizational Effectiveness

F.   Community
G.   Social Participation
H.   Leadership in the Work Organization
I.   Morale and Job Satisfaction
J.   Attitudes, Values, and Norms
K.   Family and Marriage
L.   Personality Measurements
M.   Inventories of Sociometric and Attitude Scales

It will be noted that Miller's "M" provides references to still other compilations; several of them are even more compendious than his own. Not only these inventories but also the massive critical surveys of work on social indicators and social statistics sponsored by the Russell Sage Foundation (Sheldon and Moore 1968; Campbell and Converse 1972; Land and Spilerman 1975; Hauser 1975) relieve me of responsibility for providing specific information about how social measurement actually is done.

I am going to offer some generalizations on roughly the universe of scientific endeavor covered in these and other such publications. But my statements are only the impressions and reflections of one individual, albeit one preoccupied for over a third of a century with quantification and measurement in sociological research. Other views on what are usually called "methodological" issues will be found in the symposia on social measurement edited by Blalock (1974) and by Bohrnstedt and Borgatta (1981).

As I have tried to show, the social roots of social measurement are in the social process itself. This may be the best assurance we can have that there is ultimately something valid about our enterprise. But it may also be the key to our most serious difficulties in carrying that enterprise through to a truly scientific level of achievement. Other difficulties may stem from our willingness to adopt procedures other sciences have devised for predicaments crucially different from ours.

The sciences we think of as having made the greatest progress in the arts of measurement are—astronomy aside—for the most part laboratory sciences. It is customary to take note of the advantages they enjoy by virtue of the ability to control and to vary experimentally the conditions under which their phenomena are observed and measured. While this is indisputable, I wish also to emphasize that it is convenient if what you want to observe can be contained in a small space. By contrast, most of the things social scientists want to investigate are "spread out" in space and also in time, so that it is hard to observe complete "episodes" of even the simpler kinds of processes. In that respect their predicament is like that of geologists, meteorologists, and ecologists, among others. As I have already noted, there is a large overlap of the social sciences and the population sciences: we deal with smaller or larger numbers of intrinsically variable, more or less autonomous units. One consequence is that we look—we should look—to demography in somewhat the same way (if the analogy be not too strained) that physics looks to geometry. Many social scientists have little appreciation of the generality of demographic models, which can be put to use in a variety of problems, including ones in which the units of the population are groups, organizations, social relationships, and the like, and not necessarily human individuals. The writer who, perhaps, has been most persuasive in arguing for the study of populations and their interactions as the common framework for the social sciences is K. E. Boulding. His *Ecodynamics* demonstrates the possibility of erecting a general theory of societal evolution on the foundation of demographic and ecological concepts. On a more modest scale, McPherson (1983) derives interesting theoretical consequences from "a dynamic image of the births and deaths of organizations in a population." The investigation leads to new ways of looking at familiar data on organization memberships and to new quantitative concepts, such as "measures of the extent to which two organizations inhabit the same social space."

It is generally understood, I think, that social measurement has a kind of "special relationship" with statistics. Yet the reasons for this and its implications sometimes are not quite correctly understood. One fertile source of misunderstandings is the obiter dicta on "permissible statistics" that S. S. Stevens incorporated in the several articles on the theory of scales of measurement that I reviewed earlier. The supposition that his statements on the subject of statistical method have some special authority is widespread. (The author of a successful text on social statistics informs me that in preparing the second edition he and his co-author came under irresistible pressure from their publisher to include a summary of the Stevens discussion because of reader demand.) This is ironical in that Stevens (by his own admission) was no statistician, was antipathetic to the use of statistics in psychology, and made virtually no use of formal statistical models himself, preferring ad hoc methods of "averaging," on which he wrote an essay containing misinformation which he later was led to retract. In the first draft of this essay I included several pages documenting errors in Stevens's remarks about statistics and deploring our dependence on them for guidance in selecting appropriate statistical methods. But now it seems best to pass over these matters in silence in the hope that neglect will be better medicine for this infection than polemic. One need only examine the recent statistically sophisticated work in psychophysics (e.g., Cleveland, Harris, and McGill), on problems that Stevens himself opened up, to see what folly it would be to heed the carelessly enunciated injunctions of one who was a fine scientist in spite of his prejudices.

For the moment I want to focus on what I take to be the core of the modern conception of statistics. As Hacking (1965, p. 34) puts it: "Arithmetic is the theory of numbers, and geology, I suppose, is the theory of rocks. Statistics is the theory of chance." (The broader, classical idea of statistics as the collection and interpretation of numerical data about the condition or "state" of society is implicit in the earlier sections of this essay.) We have need of that theory whenever we encounter chance phenomena, whether they are actually generated by the measurement process itself or are merely disclosed by attempts at measurement. Any of the following four circumstances—which often occur in combination—will lead to such encounters (dare I say, of the third kind?): (a) *Errors of measurement.* Even when the quantity to be measured is hypothetically fixed—as, for example, the velocity of light in a vacuum—repeated independent measurements of it on a sufficiently fine scale will generate numerical values differing among themselves. Any rational attempt to reconcile the discrepancies or to arrive at a "best" value presupposes a theory of error that is applicable to the measurement process being used. How statistics may assist in arriving at a useful model of that process is a complex matter, but at least some of the leading ideas are made relatively accessible in a selection of papers from the National Bureau of Standards (Ku 1969, especially Part 1). Measurements made under conditions preventing strict replication can only be assumed to be subject to errors from a greater variety of sources. Statistical methods and research designs for

detecting and correcting for them are recognized to be underde-
veloped, but statistics nevertheless offers (for example, Mosteller 1968)
various options that are demonstrably better than resorting to un-
tutored common sense. (b) *Sampling*. Because our populations are
typically large and spread out, sampling is unavoidable. Rigorous inferences from samples are justified if the samples are designed and
carried out according to methods that are now well known (to sampling experts, if not the rest of us), having been under intensive development and widespread application for about half a century. (c) *Intrinsic variability*. One biological individual is never an exact copy of
another, even if they are monozygous litter mates. For that matter, no
two products of a physical production process are completely interchangeable. Variability in production is the subject of a distinct
branch of statistics dealing with quality control, which was pioneered
by W. A. Shewhart and is of about the same antiquity as probability
sampling. Variability of organisms, though obvious to everyday observation, began to be correctly understood by geneticists when Mendel's
ideas were rediscovered around the turn of the century, although their
integration with modern statistics by R. A. Fisher and others came two
or three decades later. Whereas statistics was once known as the "science of averages," it is better (though incompletely) described as the
"science of variation." An early formulation of the idea of variation,
implicitly linked to the idea of central tendency, is attributed by Plato
(*Phaedo*, 89) to Socrates: "There are not many very good or very bad
people, but the great majority are something between the two. . . .
Can you think of anything more unusual than coming across a very
large or small man, or dog, or any other creature? or one which is very
swift or slow, ugly or beautiful, white or black? Have you never
realized that extreme instances are few and rare, while intermediate
ones are many and plentiful?" An anticipation of the concept may also
be imputed to Thrasybulus, tyrant of Miletus, who, on the account of
Herodotus (*History*, Book 5), illustrated for a visitor the method of
governing a city. As they walked through a wheat field, Thrasybulus
cut off all the tallest ears of wheat and threw them away, thereby
sacrificing the best part of the crop. When the visitor recounted this
strange behavior to Periander in Corinth, the latter realized that the
point was to eliminate the outstanding citizens in his city, so there
would be no threat to his own influence. Despite these adumbrations,

means of actually quantifying variation were not developed until long after the Greeks. (d) *Random behavior.* Putting aside individual differences between organisms or other systems, the behavior of any one such system may be such that outcomes can only be described in terms of a probability distribution of values, not a unique value. Many examples pertaining to physical systems are given by Bendat and Piersol, who note that there can be no exact prediction of non-deterministic physical phenomena, observations on which produce random data that must be described by probability statements or parameters of statistical models rather than explicit equations. We have a good deal of data on human responses that can hardly be understood on any premise other than that they are generated by a stochastic (chance, probabilistic) mechanism. In some parts of the quantitative social sciences, notably econometrics and fields influenced by econometric ideas, a popular viewpoint is that the main features of a process (such as the market for a good) may indeed be described by exact equations, but these equations are "disturbed" by such a large number of additional unknown—and, practically, unknowable—causes that we must resort to models including stochastic error terms. The specific statistical assumptions appropriate in this connection are, however, often uncertain and sometimes controversial.

In all applications of statistical theory a crucial question is whether observations are produced by a constant system of chance causes or whether the system itself is changing. Quetelet already had some insights concerning this issue before the middle of the last century. Shewhart dealt with it by providing criteria for judging whether a production process is in what he called a state of "statistical control." And the measurement specialists at the National Bureau of Standards, regarding measurement itself as a production process, adapted Shewhart's approach to their material. (See the collection of papers edited by Ku.) A fundamental distinction in the branch of statistics that deals with stochastic models for time series concerns so-called stationary versus nonstationary series. It may be that some of this work will provide the stimulus social scientists seem to need in order to get beyond the notion of statistics as the calculation of numbers taken to be plausible summaries of data.

Notwithstanding the general recognition that empirical research in the social sciences requires statistical methods of some kind, there is a marked reluctance in some sectors of our enterprise to take statistics seriously. A few years ago, for instance, some quantity of ink was spilled on the so-called "significance-test controversy." One argument amounted to the claim that if sampling was done poorly enough, random variability could safely be ignored. Accordingly, entire monographs featuring displays of numerical data were published without any consideration of error whatever. In other sectors one can still see a slavish reliance on correlationology, over half a century after the obsession with correlation statistics began to disappear from biometrics, where it originated. Stigler (p. 295) reminds us of an earlier lag of "over a century" until Edgeworth proceeded in 1884–85 to "adapt the statistical methods of the theory of errors to the quantification of uncertainty in the social . . . sciences." Ignorant as we are about modern statistics—as distinguished from the statistics of, say, Karl Pearson— we are easily swindled by confidence men who peddle statistical nostrums in the form of packaged computer "software." It is almost impossible to persuade students not to speak of "computer analysis of data," even by holding out the threat that when such a thing becomes possible there will be no jobs for sociologists or any other human analysts.

Coupled with downright incompetence in statistics, paradoxically, we often find the syndrome that I have come to call *statisticism*: the notion that computing is synonymous with doing research, the naive faith that statistics is a complete or sufficient basis for scientific methodology, the superstition that statistical formulas exist for evaluating such things as the relative merits of different substantive theories or the "importance" of the causes of a "dependent variable"; and the delusion that decomposing the covariations of some arbitrary and haphazardly assembled collection of variables can somehow justify not only a "causal model" but also, praise the mark, a "measurement model." There would be no point in deploring such caricatures of the scientific enterprise if there were a clearly identifiable sector of social science research wherein such fallacies were clearly recognized and emphatically out of bounds. But in my discipline it just is not so. Individual articles of exemplary quality are published cheek-by-jowl with transparent exercises in statistical numerology. If the muck were ankle deep, we could wade through it. When it is at hip level, our most adroit and most fastidious workers can hardly avoid getting some of it on their product. It would be invidious as well as tedious to cite examples documenting this assessment. A few professional statisticians, however, have begun to take a close look at the abuses referred to in such sweeping terms and to speak out about the mess they perceive. I would hope this might lead to something like the famed Flexner report of 1910 that put the spotlight on the miserable state of medical education at that time.

One of the most egregious manifestations of statisticism merits separate attention because it represents a claim to get at the essence of the problem of social measurement. I mean the prevalent and mischievous presumption that we can "measure" anything to which a name can be given that somehow connotes variation in amount, intensity, or the like; and that measurement can be effected via such simplistic procedures as those typically incorporated in "scorecards," "inventories," and the like; and, finally, despite the lack of justification for such maneuvers from an established scientific theory, that the justification can yet be forthcoming from correlational estimates of "reliability" and the like. Is it really credible that sociologists in 1965 already knew how to *measure* 2,080 distinct sociological quantities— or even as many as one quantity for each of the 78 "conceptual classes" into which the 2,080 scales and indices cited by Bonjean, Hill, and McLemore were categorized?

Here, in brief, is a typical protocol of sociological "measurement" (Bonjean, Hill, and McLemore, p. 3):

. . . if an author measured religiosity by asking "How many times did you attend church last year?", the resulting numbers were regarded as indicators rather than as indices or scales, because they were based upon a single piece of information; and such indicators are, consequently, not included in this volume. If, on the other hand, religiosity was measured by combining information on church attendance, number of other church-related activities, proportion of income spent on religious matters, frequency of Bible reading, and so on, the measure has been included in this volume.

In a chemistry laboratory one learns to be a little cautious about "combining" substances. But, so far as I know, the somewhat analogous "combining" of information has not been widely recognized to have a property analogous to blowing up in the experimenter's face. That it could happen, though, seems evident: suppose Catholics attend church more often than Methodists but read their Bibles less often; which group then manifests the greater "religiosity"? The authors just cited mention that they found "435 attempts to measure socioeconomic status by techniques employing either occupational status or more than one piece of information" (p. 5).

> Divers weights are an abomination unto the Lord.

Synonyms for "indicators" and "indices" are "symptoms" and "composites." How to get from symptoms to a composite has seemed to many authorities to be the capital issue in sociological methodology. I do not hold with that view. Nor do I believe that index construction is, in general, measurement. (If anyone insists on citing some of my own writing to the opposite effect, I can only squirm.) Even so, we may continue to rely heavily on composite indices for a merely pragmatic reason, to achieve data reduction—data reduction at a terrible cost in scientific terms, on account of the conceptual ambiguity that is (almost) inescapable. Let me come at my argument historically.

Oberschall finds that within the German tradition of empirical social science Gottlieb Schnapper-Arndt was a pioneer in raising methodological issues. In his critique of survey methods published in 1888, he wrote: "For a given phenomenon whose extent one wants to capture, one must find more or less representative symptoms and delimit the area in which these symptoms are to be established statistically. . . . To determine the number of unhappy marriages . . . one might consider the number of divorces as a symptom . . . at any rate for purposes of comparison." After quoting this statement, Oberschall (p. 25) comments, "These ideas . . . are a precursor to the modern notion that concepts may be redefined and operationalized in terms of their indicators. . . . Schnapper-Arndt did not consider the possibility of combining several indicators into an index. . . . The term 'symptom' seems to have originated in the work of the moral statisticians." Niceforo (pp. 7–8) states that the seventeenth-century French economist P. Le P. Boisguillebert spoke of "marques sensible d'opulence" which might constitute "baromètres" of that opulence, and that Quetelet in his *Physique Sociale* of 1869 likewise gave examples of indicators that could be used in such a manner. In his dissertation on *The Division of Labor*, first published in 1893 but still studied today,

Durkheim provided an example of the use of "symptomatic" data that is familiar to sociologists. His proposal (p. 109) was to "measure the relative importance of . . . solidarity" due to the "common conscience" (as opposed to cohesion arising from the cooperation of differentiated social units) by "determining what fraction of the juridical system penal law represents," inasmuch as penal law is "repressive" (in contrast to "restitutive law"). Actually, Durkheim did not ascertain that "fraction" quantitatively; unlike his later study of suicide, the dissertation includes no statistical data.

According to Zeisel it was Niceforo who took the "decisive step" of defining his scientific objectives first and then searching for data suited to the development of indices. I am not sure if the claim for Niceforo's priority is accurate, but I follow Zeisel's lead nevertheless, because *Les Indices numériques de la Civilisation et du Progrès* was published in the year of my birth and is, therefore, old enough to be classic. Niceforo's idea of the scope of his inquiry was hardly less modest than the field modern exponents of "social indicators" think should be covered. By "civilization," construed according to "ethnographic" rather than "philological" usage, he meant the entirety of the material, intellectual, and moral life of a population, and its political and social organization. He recognized at the outset that many key facts about a civilization are not quantifiable and that statistics do not always refer to exactly the phenomena the investigator may be interested in. Hence, it is necessary to make use of "facts, susceptible of being measured, which can be considered, so to speak, as *symptoms* of the phenomenon" for which "it is evidently impossible to obtain a direct measure," such as the "degree of *morality* (and even of *religiosity*) of a population, the *intellectual level* of a group, its . . . degree of material welfare." With measures of the symptomatic facts in hand, one "finally, if one judges it useful to do so, will see if there is a means of reducing all the measures obtained to a single global or synthetic measure" (pp. 8–9). It is Niceforo's unsuccessful confrontation with the last-mentioned problem that is immediately relevant here, but I want to glance as well at the range of other issues he touched upon.

First, while he finds that there is a wealth of statistical information available about modern civilizations (albeit not evenly distributed over his five categories), he considers it essential to make careful selections from the store of quantitative facts, focusing on those to be regarded as "caractères signalétiques," those "which suffice to give the signalment of the whole" civilization (p. 56). If the reader is puzzled by the French "signalétique" and unfamiliar with the English "signalment," as I was, it may be helpful to give a formal definition of the latter: a systematic description of a person in an official or administrative document as, for example, a description for identification purposes according to the system of the French criminologist Alphonse Bertillon (whose work was recent at the time Niceforo, also a criminologist, was writing). Under each of his main rubrics, therefore, Niceforo will note the "signal" quantities. Because of their covariation with many other facts, qualitative as well as quantitative—he provides a little exposition of measures of correlation and concordance—these can serve the two main purposes Niceforo mentions: to ascertain, by cross-sectional comparisons, whether civilization in one region is more advanced than in another and, by analysis of time series, whether "amélioration" or "progrès" is occurring in a civilization. Proposals concerning a "unique" symptom of progress (such as the increase of knowledge) are examined and decisively rejected. But having a multiplicity of indicators entails a multiplicity of problems. Niceforo points to the ambiguity of many purported symptoms, the necessity for correcting or adjusting others for various distortions, the distinction between causation and covariation—"signs" are not necessarily either causes or effects—the virtual impossibility of measuring the "quality" of a civilization, the unavoidable conflict between enhancement of the welfare of individuals today and the improvement of society in the future, and the fact that no amount of improvement in conditions of life will be experienced by individuals as an increase in their happiness.

Approaching the climax of his pilot study on the "métrologie" (p. 204, his quotation marks) of civilization, Niceforo finds that the array of selected symptoms to which the statistical materials have been reduced by critical analysis has gaps and other inadequacies, but he still wishes to consider whether it is desirable to attempt "a measure of the *ensemble* of all these diverse manifestations" (p. 192). For an illustrative paradigm he considers the problem of measuring "progress" in Italy from 1884 (when his statistical series begin) to 1914. Here, without comment or explanation—although work of G. H. Knibbs on price indexes had been mentioned 20 pages earlier—he plunges into the calculation of index numbers. Each series, such as the consumption of tobacco or the homicide rate, is first expressed on a per capita basis for each year; then the value observed for 1914 is expressed as a percentage of the 1884 value. And now Niceforo gets hung up in a curious way when he asks whether "it would be possible to . . . totalize in a single index number all the index numbers that appear in the table" (p. 192), such as the 175 for tobacco and the 57 for homicide. The difficulty is that being above (or below) 100 does not mean the same thing for each of his individual indexes. Both the increase of tobacco consumption (because Niceforo is regarding it as a "symptom" of rising levels of consumption and not as a measure of the ingestion of poison) and the decrease of the homicide rate represent "améliora-tion," so that it would be misleading to average them. Moreover, there are index numbers, such as the 143 for theft, an increase in which represents the opposite of "amélioration," unless that increase is dis-counted for the even greater increase in opportunities for such crime which is suggested by the expansion of business, with an index of 224 in 1914. "In consequence, by an increase, the indices sometimes may attest to progress and at other times to retrogression; certain indices, on the other hand, can perfectly signal an amelioration by a decrease: how can we bring together in a unique measure this ensemble of measures each of which moves in its own way?" (p. 193) What Niceforo seems not to have realized—and one could say the same about many other uses of index numbers, such as those contemporaneously prepared by L. P. Ayres (1920) under the auspices of the Russell Sage Foundation for tracking educational progress in the several United States—is that the measurement problem must be solved *before* the "synthetic" index is computed. Averaging price indexes makes sense, of a kind—I must not get bogged down in the ultimate indeterminacy of even the best justified economic index numbers—because the amount of money spent on beef can be *added* to the amount spent on pork to get a meaningful total having the same units as its components. *Measure-ment* is accomplished on the scale of money, not on the scale of the index number as such. It should be carefully noted that Niceforo's problem is merely highlighted by the embarrassment he mentions, and the essential impossibility of aggregating incommensurables would re-main even if all his indexes happened to have the same "sense" and happened to move in the same direction, thereby concurring in regard to whether there was progress.

Contemporary proponents of composite indexes can, of course, quickly suggest a way around Niceforo's problem, such as the assignment of weights according to the pattern of correlation among the individual symptoms. If there is general "progress," homicide will be negatively correlated with consumption and will be weighted inversely in a composite. But notice that our paradigm has now shifted from that provided by the theory of price indexes—that subject does have a theory (see, for example, Allen, Ch. 1) and not merely a set of numerical recipes—to one that emulates the procedures of psychometrics. I have had my say about the psychometric paradigm in an earlier discussion. As far as I can see, it gives us no reason for complacency in the present situation. Resorting to that paradigm, under the circumstances, is a species of statisticism.

A few years after Niceforo, an eminently sensible discussion by Rice (1930) fingered exactly the distinction I am making: "It must be kept in mind that an index is a *representative* figure. It stands for some quantity, degree of activity, value, or situation, which cannot itself be expressed directly. . . . [I]ndex numbers are required, first, when the thing in which we are interested is intangible or poorly defined . . . and second, when we are attempting to make a net or total statement concerning a complex group of tangible things or events." A psychometric test score (an index of the intangible "intelligence") illustrates the former, a price index the latter. "Thus, there seem to be two types of index numbers, the term being usually reserved for the second—that which pertains to a group of related phenomena rather than to intangibilities" (pp. 11–12). Rice goes on to observe that an index of the kind that summarizes tangibles might have two distinct purposes. One would be simply to track the magnitude of some complex of problems for the sake of "bookkeeping." But another would be to aid in securing control over those problems. "An index is a tool which may be used in the effort to attain such control, provided it has been constructed with reference to the underlying forces which produce the problems. For this purpose, there must be homogeneity among the latter" (p. 15). But, of course, homogeneity of forces is an issue of substantive theory, not measurement methodology. It cannot be resolved by a merely statistical formula for "totalizing" (to use Niceforo's term) intrinsically heterogeneous components. What Rice's principle really means is that there is no fundamental solution to the problem of combining indicators (whether of "tangibles" or of "intangibles") until the system that generates them is correctly understood. Niceforo—although he alluded to variously defective theories of progress—evidently could not see that measurement by way of symptoms is an impossibility if one does not have a true theory of progress that explains its symptoms.

To come back to the example from Bonjean, Hill, and McLemore, an index of religiosity of the kind they suggest is justified only if (among other things) the causes of church attendance and of Bible reading "and so on" are exactly the same, work in exactly the same way, and affect all the indicators to exactly the same extent. Otherwise, we are into the problem (already noted by Niceforo) that I once had occasion to term that of the "single dimension with a two-way stretch." It can happen—it did happen in the research of the hapless investigator whose monograph I was reviewing—that one component goes up, the other down, over a period of time and that, absent a common *measure* for the two indicators, the net outcome is an utterly arbitrary result of the utterly arbitrary aggregation formula that has been imposed in computing the synthetic index combining the two.

Niceforo was right: the conclusion from a correct analysis of the problem of indicators and indices (or symptoms and composites) is none too optimistic. Nonetheless, *faute de mieux*, we shall continue to work for the foreseeable future with symptoms rather than direct measures; and, since our data collection machinery produces a continual increase in the volume of raw statistics, we shall either use "representative figures" or be inundated by numbers. I do not question that a kind of correlational discourse, propositions in which are rendered in plausible prose—prose that might have some heuristic or practical value, to be sure—can be produced by the fraternity of social scientists caught in this predicament, using the kind of recipes I call statisticism. (In previous publications I have said all I know, and a little bit more, about how this might be done.)

It could happen that some of the answers to questions about how to measure better will be found in a search for answers to the question of why we measure. If you ask an engineer interested in measurement systems—for example, Doebelin (Ch. 1)—he can give you a straightforward answer. Measuring instruments are used (1) to monitor processes and operations, as what was once called the Weather Bureau

monitors the weather or your friendly public utility monitors your
consumption of electricity; (2) to control processes and operations, as
your thermostat controls your furnace or air conditioner; and (3) to
provide data for experimental engineering analysis, where theory is not
available, where theory provides results that are not specific enough, or
theory requires excessively simplified assumptions or excessively complicated mathematics, or where the validity of theoretical calculations
must be checked against actual behavior. I have seen discussions of
econometrics that would fit comfortably into Doebelin's outline. But
the suggestion of a few years ago that a permanent national commission be set up to "monitor social trends" made some parties a little
nervous. The further proposal that "control" should follow upon
"monitoring" seemed to be lurking in the background, and it was not
wholly clear who would control whom and to what end. That very
issue is raised, if a trifle obliquely, in the recent essay of Alonso and
Starr on "The Political Economy of National Statistics," while Mac-
Rae, writing on "Democratic Information Systems," is not quite so
blunt on the issue of "control" but is even more explicit that social
measurements, if made public and used for policy purposes, should be
justified by reasoning similar to cost-benefit calculations pertaining to
their prospective uses.

I hope that the debates and inquiries flowing from such formulations will not be entirely preoccupied with the foreground, where what
looms so prominently is a Federal statistics bureaucracy grown huge
and—by the standards of the recent past—hugely competent on the
technical level, but struggling with political forces that seem to under-
mine the very idea of disinterested inquiry, observation, measuring, or
"monitoring." There is much we need to know about the background:
that long historical sequence that turned our society into an example of
what George Sand called the civilizations of quantity. As paraphrased
and quoted by Niceforo (pp. 118–119), she was contrasting people like
the French and Italians, who are guided by quality—by proportion
and harmony—with the northern peoples who love quantity and are
preoccupied with the dimensions of things, who "only appreciate intellectual grandeur after having calculated and measured material
grandeur . . . which always makes the artistic people of Italy laugh."

Let me not be stuck with the specific terms of Sand's comparison,
for I have already pointed out the Italian priority in demography and

the arithmetic that makes it possible. Menninger (pp. 191–192; also pp. 287, 442–443) suggests that with the institutionalization of the decimal notation the way was open to extend the number sequence with the greatest of ease, to recognize magnitudes without names, magnitudes far beyond the bounds of everyday experience, which had hitherto governed the development of the number *words* serving the arithmetic of daily life. Thus, around 1500, at the threshold of history's "modern" period, Europeans had the intellectual tools for dealing with quantities of any size in a purely abstract, technical way, thereby strengthening the power of quantitative reasoning relative to the older categorical logic. Mumford (p. 328) has an eloquent paragraph much to this effect, written in his distinctive style, which is so resistant to paraphrase. I take from him the further suggestion that quantification was not only crucial for material technique, but also led to the refinement of ethical discourse, when absolute qualities were gradually replaced by notions of how much is good and how good it is, as the difference between a medicine and a poison is seen to turn on the size of the dose. But measurement could be hoist on its own petard, if we grant that there could be too much of it. Pope thought so, when he wrote of vulgar criticism: "But most by numbers judge a poet's song." And Mark Schorer has found (pp. xiii, xvi) in a tale that was "very nearly the first English novel," Defoe's *Moll Flanders* (1722), the "classic revelation of the mercantile mind: the morality of measurement," built on the assumption that "Everything can be weighed, measured, handled, paid for in gold, or expiated by a prison term. . . . this is a morality in which only externals count since only externals show." In the end, despite its technical facility and reader appeal, the work falls short as a novel because the author does not provide a judgment of his material: "Defoe has apparently neglected to measure" the morality of measurement.

Closer to home, Cohen (in a study published as my essay was undergoing final revisions) reports an exploration of the "spread of numeracy" in early America and the concomitant "spread of the domain of number as things once thought of solely in qualitative terms become subject to quantification" (p. 12). "Numbers," she concludes (p. 224), "have immeasurably (*sic*) altered the character of American society."

But the "pantometry" of the seventeenth century, which Cohen identifies as the general cultural stimulus to social quantification in her period, has ancient antecedents in works familiar to educated persons from the Renaissance on. Shorey pointed out (pp. 176–177) that Plato's dicta on measurement resemble closely the encomia of measurement of Lord Kelvin, Kant, and Clerk Maxwell, although, Shorey maintains, Plato never imagined that all science could be reduced to mathematics. But Plato did not stop with the refutation of the purported motto of Protagoras, "Man is the measure of all things," which he carried through by demonstrating the unreliability of sense impressions and the need for specific measurement techniques to supplement man's capacities. He also prized a rational (or "coherent," as the exponents of the metric system call it) system of measures for its educational and disciplinary value as well as for the pursuit of knowledge and the facilitation of crafts and commerce:

So now we must endeavour to discern—after we have decided on our division into twelve parts—in what fashion the divisions that come next to these and are the offspring of these, up to the ultimate figure, 5,040, (determining as they do, the phratries and demes and villages, and also the coinage-system, dry and liquid measures, and weights), how, I say, all these numerations are to be fixed by the law so as to be of the right size and consistent one with another. Moreover, he should not hesitate, through fear of what might appear to be peddling detail, to prescribe that, of all the utensils which the citizens may possess, none shall be allowed to be of undue size. He must recognise it as a universal rule that the divisions and variations of numbers are applicable to all purposes—both to their own arithmetical variations and to the geometrical variations of surfaces and solids, and also to those of sounds, and of motions, whether in a straight line up and down or circular. The lawgiver must keep all these in view and charge all the citizens to hold fast, so far as they can, to this organised numerical system. For in relation to economics, to politics and to all the arts, no single branch of educational science possesses so great an influence as the study of numbers (*Laws* 746D–747A, Bury translation).

Plato does indeed sound a bit like some proponents of the metric system, and there is no place in his thought for the gentle suggestion of a Boulding that something of our system of "natural units" might be retained, for the sheer "pleasure in cultural diversity" if for no better reason. (A better reason than pleasure, we could also learn from Boulding, might be the ecological wisdom that diversity often, in unexpected ways, turns out to be the key to survival.) But the problem with a Platonic outlook on measurement may go a bit deeper. Popper, who showed us the fundamental identity of Plato's political program with that of modern totalitarianism, unfortunately did not discuss the specific passages in Plato's writing that I have cited on the topic of measurement. Nevertheless, it is not hard to see their affinity with the themes of "aestheticism, perfectionism, utopianism" that Popper analyzes, and we can certainly recognize the would-be "philosopher king"—"What a monument of human smallness is this idea" (Popper, p. 153)—in the proposal to center education on numerology.

A little before Plato's time, if Livy (IV.8) is to be believed, the Romans began an episode that could be an object lesson for someone interested in the "political economy of national statistics." It will be recalled that Livy repeats (I.42) the tradition according to which Servius Tullius originated the census around 550 B.C. Then in 443 it was noted that the census had not been taken for quite some time, but the consuls, who hitherto were the responsible officials, were preoccupied with military affairs. The Senate, upon consideration, decided that census taking was beneath the dignity of a consul. Hence they moved to designate a special magistrate, called "censor," to decide upon the form of the census and to keep the records. He was provided with a clerical staff to assist with the labors. Livy conjectures that the Senate favored the innovation because it meant an increase in the number of offices that would be held by the patricians. However, none of the leading personages in Rome desired the office, and it was given to Papirius and Sempronius, who had not been allowed to complete their year as consuls. From this "trivial origin," writes Livy, the censorship (which, as I noted, was much esteemed by Jean Bodin in later days) "grew to exercise jurisdiction over the whole range of our social proprieties, to determine membership of the classes of Senators or Knights according to property and desert and to have complete control over the regular state revenue and the location of public and private buildings."

Social measurement, I have tiresomely reiterated, is rooted in the social process, and a plant separated from its roots will wither. No information—least of all, decently quantified information—comes at zero cost; and costs are borne by somebody. Somebody who can pay can have that information. Therefore we have a polling industry that is designed to serve those who market products—goods, or the services of candidates for public office. Public enlightenment and data bases for scientific use are side benefits, sometimes. In the long run what will be measured will be what the society wants or allows to be measured and is able and willing to pay for. How it will be measured—or, in any event, the socially tolerable limits on concepts and methods of measurement—is also socially determined. That is as clear in the essays on the current U.S. situation I cited earlier as in Hughes's mordant summary of the vicissitudes of racial and religious categories in the German statistical yearbooks of 1932 to 1952 or Rice's outraged report on how statistics was conceived in the Soviet Union, 1950. (The Nazi Yearbook had no data on "religion" but much on "race," while the comrades in the Central Statistical Office of the U.S.S.R. would have no truck with the theory of probability.)

Less dramatic support for my point—but more obviously relevant to current issues of social measurement in this country—is found in the confrontations between alternative approaches to estimating the incidence of criminal offenses. Biderman and Reiss, in their ruminations on the problem of the "dark figure" of crime—occurrences not registered in standard statistical series—point out that any measure of crime must be built up from "institutional processing of people's reports." The concept of a "true" incidence rate not rooted in some institutional mechanism is not merely a fiction but a downright self-contradiction: "there are no rates without some organized intelligence system, whether that of the scientist, the police, or the jurist. . . . The criteria of knowing, defining, and processing lie in organization. . . . Concepts and operational definitions will differ depending upon formally organized or informal social processes, whether those of science, of operations or of social policy" (pp. 9, 14).

Let us, therefore, suppose a society like MacRae's, where systems of "end-value indicators" are designed to "maximize their usefulness" for public policy and are brought into being by a "democratic" process of choosing indicators with due but not exclusive regard to the views of social scientists. Further assume a society beginning to learn how to do this and comfortable with it, for the time being. Then, I ask, at what point should we begin to inquire whether the cost of the measurements needed to understand what is really at stake in policy issues is more than our—or any—society can afford? Or whether the measurements themselves, if they were made, would tell more than the society could afford to know about itself? (Cassedy reports that the Massachusetts Bay Colony refused to disclose statistics on mortality for fear of jeopardizing the project's future.) Or, perchance, whether what a society would need to know to make rational, and not merely "enlightened," policy choices exceeds what, in principle, can be known? In his day Niceforo found it impossible to know, in the sense of a single, numerically precise figure, just how much progress a civilization had made in three decades. Perhaps even deeper "impossibility theorems" await discovery by some intrepid thinker who looks hard enough at the paradoxes of social measurement.

Thanne hadde he spent al his philosophye
Chaucer

REFERENCES

Allen, R.G.D. *Index Numbers in Theory and Practice.* London: Macmillan, 1975.

Alonso, William, and Paul Starr. "The Political Economy of National Statistics." *Social Science Research Council Items* 36 (September 1982): 29–35.

Ayres, Leonard P. *An Index Number for State School Systems.* New York: Russell Sage Foundation, 1920.

Bendat, Julius S., and Allan G. Piersol. *Measurement and Analysis of Random Data.* New York: Wiley, 1966.

Biderman, Albert D., and Albert J. Reiss, Jr. "On Exploring the 'Dark Figure' of Crime." *Annals of the American Academy of Political and Social Science* 374 (November 1967): 1–15.

Blalock, H. M., Jr., ed. *Measurement in the Social Sciences.* Chicago: Aldine, 1974.

Bohrnstedt, George W., and Edgar F. Borgatta, eds. *Social Measurement: Current Issues.* Beverly Hills, Calif.: Sage, 1981.

Bonjean, Charles M., Richard J. Hill, and S. Dale McLemore. *Sociological Measurement: An Inventory of Scales and Indices.* San Francisco: Chandler, 1967.

Boulding, Kenneth E. *Ecodynamics.* Beverly Hills, Calif.: Sage, 1978.

Boulding, Kenneth E. "Numbers Count." *Sciences* 19 (October 1979): 6–9.

Campbell, Angus, and Philip E. Converse, eds. *The Human Meaning of Social Change.* New York: Russell Sage Foundation, 1972.

Cassedy, James H. *Demography in Early America: Beginnings of the Statistical Mind 1600–1800.* Cambridge: Harvard University Press, 1969.

Cleveland, William S., Charles S. Harris, and Robert McGill. "Judgments of Circle Sizes on Statistical Maps." *Journal of the American Statistical Association* 77 (September 1982): 541–547.

Cohen, Patricia Cline. *A Calculating People: The Spread of Numeracy in Early America.* Chicago: University of Chicago Press, 1982.

Doebelin, Ernest O. *Measurement Systems: Application and Design.* Rev. ed. New York: McGraw-Hill, 1975.

Durkheim, Emile. *The Division of Labor in Society*. Trans. by George Simpson. Glencoe, Ill.: Fress Press, 1947 (1st ed., 1893).

Hacking, Ian. *Logic of Statistical Inference*. Cambridge: Cambridge University Press, 1965.

Hauser, Philip M., ed. *Social Statistics in Use*. New York: Russell Sage Foundation, 1975.

Herodotus. *The Histories*. Trans. by Aubrey de Sélincourt. Harmondsworth: Penguin, 1972.

Hughes, Everett Cherrington. "The Gleichschaltung of the German Statistical Yearbook." *American Statistician* 9 (December 1955): 8–11.

Ku, Harry H., ed. *Precision Measurement and Calibration*. NBS Special Publication 300, Vol. 1. Washington, D.C.: GPO, 1969.

Land, Kenneth C., and Seymour Spilerman, eds. *Social Indicator Models*. New York: Russell Sage Foundation, 1975.

Livy. *The Early History of Rome*. Trans. by Aubrey de Sélincourt. Harmondsworth: Penguin, 1971.

MacRae, Duncan, Jr. "Policy Indicators as Public Statistics: Democratic Information Systems." In *Policy Analysis: Basic Concepts and Methods*, edited by William N. Dunn and Michael White. Greenwich, Ct: JAI Press, 1983.

McPherson, Miller. "An Ecology of Affiliation." *American Sociological Review* 48 (August 1983): 519–532.

Menninger, Karl. *Number Words and Number Symbols: A Cultural History of Numbers*. Cambridge: M.I.T. Press, 1969.

Miller, Delbert C. *Handbook of Research Design and Social Measurement*. 3d ed. New York: David McKay, 1977.

Mosteller, Frederick. "Nonsampling Errors." *International Encyclopedia of the Social Sciences* 5:113–132. New York: Macmillan, 1968.

Mumford, Lewis. *Technics and Civilization*. New York: Harcourt Brace, 1934.

Niceforo, Alfredo. *Les Indices numériques de la Civilisation et du Progrès*. Paris: Flammarion, 1921.

Oberschall, Anthony. *Empirical Social Research in Germany 1848–1914*. Paris: Mouton, 1965.

Plato. *Laws*. Trans. by R. G. Bury. 2 vols. Cambridge: Harvard University Press, 1967.

Plato. *Phaedo*. In *The Last Days of Socrates*, trans. by Hugh Tredennick. Harmondsworth: Penguin, 1969.

Popper, Karl R. *The Open Society and Its Enemies*. Princeton: Princeton University Press, 1950.

Quetelet, M. A. *A Treatise on Man*, 1842. Reprinted. New York: Burt Franklin, 1968.

Rice, Stuart A. "The Historico-Statistical Approach to Social Studies." In *Statistics in Social Studies*, edited by Stuart A. Rice, Ch. 1. Philadelphia: University of Pennsylvania Press, 1930.

Rice, Stuart A. "Statistical Conceptions in the Soviet Union Examined from Generally Accepted Scientific Viewpoints." *The American Statistician* 6 (June-July 1952): 12–15. Followed by unsigned report, Methodology Conference of Central Statistical Administration USSR, *idem*, 16–22.

Schorer, Mark. Introduction in *Moll Flanders*, by Daniel Defoe, pp. v–xvii. New York: Random House, 1950.

Sheldon, Eleanor Bernert, and Wilbert E. Moore, eds. *Indicators of Social Change*. New York: Russell Sage Foundation, 1968.

Shewhart, W. A. *Economic Control of Quality of Manufactured Product*. New York: Van Nostrand, 1931.

Shorey, Paul. "Platonism and the History of Science." *Proceedings of the American Philosophical Society* 66 (1927): 159–182.

Stigler, Stephen M., "Frances Ysidro Edgeworth, Statistician." *Journal of the Royal Statistical Society 141* (1978): 287–322.

Zeisel, Hans. "Afterword: Toward a History of Sociography." In *Marienthal: The Sociography of an Unemployed Community*, by Marie Jahoda, Paul F. Lazarsfeld, and Hans Zeisel. Chicago: Aldine, 1971.

ACKNOWLEDGMENTS

IT IS APPROPRIATE, I think, to propose a vote of thanks to the Russell Sage Foundation for sponsoring enterprises in social measurement throughout its history. The multi-volume reports on the Pittsburgh Survey (1909–1914) and the Springfield Survey (1918–1920) were among the early products of this enlightened policy. I have noted a few later ones in my text. Ransacking my memory, I was impressed by the realization that the Foundation has sponsored, in whole or in part, no less than half a dozen projects on social measurement preceding this one in which I have personally been involved. The opportunity for a career featuring this kind of endeavor is due in no small part to this support, and I am grateful for it as well as the invitation to prepare an essay to help celebrate the anniversary of the Foundation.

It was a good omen that the invitation was conveyed by Robert K. Merton, whose work on the sociology of science I have admired for nearly four decades. His part in initiating the project led me to think of it as a first step toward a sociology of measurement.

Two experiences in the immediate background strongly influenced the cast of my essay. One was my service with the Panel on Survey Measurement of Subjective Phenomena, whose report is also being issued by the Russell Sage Foundation. Clearly, I was still trying to answer for myself some difficult questions that arose in the deliberations of the panel, particularly those formulated by William Kruskal. Second was an informal seminar in which my colleagues at the University of Arizona, Robert L. Hamblin, Michael Hout, and Arthur L. Stinchcombe, heard me out on the subject of Rasch measurement models and did their best to teach me something about the theory and practice of measurement.

Specific suggestions or responses to queries were provided by Robert P. Abelson, Robert F. Boruch, James S. Coleman, Beverly Duncan, Churchill Eisenhart, Philip M. Hauser, Robert A. Johnson, Duncan MacRae, Jr., William H. Sewell, Jr., Bruce D. Spencer, Stephen M. Stigler, David C. Young, and Eviatar Zerubavel. The first draft of the entire manuscript was read by Clifford C. Clogg, A. Hunter Dupree, Robert L. Hamblin, Harold W. Pfautz, Albert J. Reiss, Jr., Karl F. Schuessler, William H. Sewell, Michael E. Sobel, and four anonymous reviewers. At a very late stage in my work, I was led to make substantial revisions of Chapter 7 by comments vouchsafed by a seminar at Indiana University organized by George W. Bohrnstedt, the director of the Program in Measurement at that institution, where on occasion for a period of a quarter century I have been privileged to try out ideas before audiences of stern but sympathetic critics. The reader will join me in my regret that the essay does not reflect more adequately the expertise invested in it by others.

NAME INDEX

A

Aaron, 46
Abelson, Robert P., 242
Abraham, 33–34
Achilles, 4, 69, 82–84
Adam, 34
Adams, Ernest W., 121, 145, 155, 170
Adams, John Quincy, 19, 36, 37
Adams, Robert McC., 117
Adler, H. E., 197
Aeschylus, 5, 71–72, 82
Afriat, S. N., 144, 155
Agamemnon, 5
Agasicles, 82
Ahrens, L. H., 152, 155
Aias, 4
Aigner, D. J., 206, 218
Alcibiades, 70
Allen, R. G. D., 232, 239
Allport, Gordon W., 133, 155
Alonso, William, 234, 239
Amasis, 45
American Metrological Society, 25–26, 36
Anastasi, Anne, 114, 201, 206, 218
Anderson, N. H., 186
Andrich, David, 215–217, 218
Antilochus, 84
Antipater, 44
Arbuthnott, John, 95, 113
Argeia, 61
Ariantes, 45
Aristodemus, 61
Aristophanes, 72, 114
Aristotle, 3, 6, 10, 13, 35–37, 48, 61, 90, 101, 103, 109, 113, 117, 118, 136, 148

Arrow, K. J., 7, 8, 10
Athena, 5, 83
Augustus Caesar, 49, 85
Ayres, L. P., 78, 81, 113, 231, 239

B

Badia, P., 156
Baker, Keith Michael, 7, 10
Barnard, F. A. P., 25–26, 58
Barnett, M. K., 120, 148, 155
Barrows, H. P., 110, 113
Beaufort, Francis, 136
Beccaria, Cesare, 91, 113
Bedell, G. H., 110, 113
Beloch, K. J., 51
Bendat, Julius S., 225, 239
Bentham, Jeremy, 110
Berger, Brigitte, 202, 218
Bergin, Thomas Goddard, 38
Berriman, A. E., 12, 36
Bertillon, Alphonse, 230
Bickerman, E. J., 130, 155
Biderman, Albert D., 238, 239
Binet, Alfred, 200
Black, Duncan, 7, 10
Blalock, H. M., Jr., 198, 209, 218, 221, 239
Bloch, Marc, 7, 10
Bock, R. Darrell, 174, 197
Bodin, Jean, 20, 36, 51–54, 58, 64–67, 85–86, 90–91, 113, 237
Boethius, 109
Bohrnstedt, George W., 219, 221, 239, 242
Boisguillebert, P. le P., 228
Bonjean, Charles M., 227, 233, 239
Booth, Charles, 107, 116
Borda, Charles de, 7, 8, 21, 140

Borgatta, Edgar F., 219, 221, 239
Boring, Edwin G., 106, 113, 172, 200, 218
Born, Ernest, 18, 37
Boruch, Robert F., 242
Boulding, Kenneth E., 23, 36, 160, 170, 222, 236, 239
Bowley, A. L., 107
Box, Joan Fisher, 98, 113
Boyd, Julian P., 18–19, 36
Bradburn, Norman, 208
Brahe, Tycho, 108
Breasted, James Henry, 45, 113
Brezzi, Paolo, 57, 116
Bridgman, P. W., 15, 16, 36, 165
Brodbeck, May, 15, 36–37
Bryant, William Cullen, 41, 113
Buckle, H. T., 96
Bugge, Thomas, 22, 29, 36
Bunge, Mario, 121, 126, 140–141, 147, 155
Burch, William R., Jr., 34, 36
Burch-Minakan, Laurel, 34, 36
Burn, A. R., 42, 113
Burrage, Michael C., 68, 114
Bury, R. G., 90, 117, 236
Bush, Robert R., 198

C

Caesar, 49, 57
Calchas, 31
Caldwell, Otis W., 79, 114
Callias, 70
Callimachus, 3
Campbell, Angus, 221, 239
Campbell, Donald T., 118
Campbell, Lewis, 96, 114
Campbell, N. R., 120, 122, 126, 155, 193, 197
Caplow, Theodore, 56, 114
Carnap, Rudolf, 120, 136, 155
Carnot, Nicolas Léonard Sadi, 149
Carroll, Lewis, 10
Cassedy, James H., 239
Cattell, James McKeen, 107, 200
Celsius, Anders, 124, 147–149
Chadwick, E., 77
Chadwick, Edwin, 99

Chapin, F. Stuart, 39–40, 114
Chapman, George, 31
Chaucer, Geoffrey, 239
Chave, E. J., 179
Cheops, 35
Christ, 33
Christ, Carl F., 160, 170
Churchman, C. W., 156
Cipolla, Carlo M., 27–28, 36, 54, 114
Clark, G. N., 106, 114
Clark, John, 118
Cleisthenes, 102
Cleveland, William S., 223, 239
Clogg, Clifford C., 242
Clytemnestra, 5
Coggins, R. J., 47, 114
Cohen, Morris R., 124–127, 137, 147, 155
Cohen, Patricia Cline, 235, 239
Coleman, James S., 97, 114, 151, 155, 186, 197, 198, 202, 218, 242
Coleman, Richard P., 185, 194–195, 197
Comte, Auguste, 23
Condorcet, Marquis de, 7–9, 11, 21, 140
Confucius, 73, 114
Converse, Philip E., 221, 239
Cooley, Charles Horton, 201, 218
Coombs, Clyde H., 142–143, 155
Copernicus, Nicolaus, 116
Corry, David, 68, 114
Courtis, Stuart A., 79, 114
Cox, Edward Franklin, 23–24, 26, 36
Cressey, Paul F., 73, 114
Croesus, 3
Crombie, A. C., 115
Crosland, Maurice P., 22, 29, 36
Cross, David V., 187, 194, 197–198
Cubberley, Ellwood P., 79, 114
Cyrus, 3

D

Danloux-Dumesnils, Maurice, 16, 29, 30, 36, 159, 170
Danto, Arthur, 156
Darius, 3–4, 43–44, 58
Darwin, Charles, 98, 116, 200

David, 33–34, 47–48, 52–53
David, F. N., 92–96, 114
Davis, H., 121
Davis, H. P., 110, 113
Davis, Harmer E., 166–167, 170
Davison, Mark L., 217, 219
Dawson, William E., 192, 197
Defoe, Daniel, 235, 240
de Grazia, Alfred, 7, 11
De Jong, Frits J., 161, 170
Deluc, Jean André, 149
Demaratus, 43
Den Boer, W., 33, 36
Dewey, Melvil, 26
Dionysus, 72, 82
Dodd, Stuart Carter, 161, 170
Dodgson, C. L., 10
Doebelin, Ernest O., 233–234, 239
Douris, 4–5
Dow, Sterling, 101–102, 114
Doyle, Kenneth O., 72, 114
Dresner, Stephen, 159–160, 163, 170
Drummond, Frederick, 68, 114
DuBois, Philip H., 72, 74, 114
Duncan, Beverly, 242
Duncan, Otis Dudley, 34, 36, 116,
    198, 215, 218
Dunn, William N., 240
Dupree, A. Hunter, 13, 15–19, 37,
    39, 114, 242
Durkheim, Emile, 99–100, 114, 117,
    192, 229, 240
Dutot, 107

E

Ebert, James D., 170
Edgeworth, Francis Ysidro, 108, 118,
    226, 240
Eisenhart, Churchill, 107, 203, 218,
    242
Ekman, Gösta, 172, 197
Electra, 5
Elliott, E. B., 25
Ellis, Brian, 120, 153, 155
Engel, Ernst, 40
Epstein, Richard A., 110, 114
Ethelbert, 87
Eumelus, 83

Euripides, 71–72, 82
Evans, J. A. S., 33, 37
Eversley, D. E. C., 115
Ezra, 48

F

Fagles, Robert, 115
Fagot, R. F., 145, 155
Fahrenheit, Gabriel Daniel, 124, 147–
    149
Fang, Achilles, 105, 114
Farquharson, Robin, 7, 11
Farr, William, 42, 49, 51, 114
Faustus, 42
Fechner, G. T., 106, 126, 172, 197
Feigl, Herbert, 15, 36–37
Fermat, Pierre de, 93
Ferster, Charles B., 94, 117
Festinger, Leon, 155
Fienberg, Stephen E., 101, 114
Figlio, Robert M., 185, 190–191, 197
Finkelstein, L., 121, 156
Finley, M. I., 38, 114, 130
Finnie, B., 179, 198
Fisch, Max Harold, 38
Fisher, George, 77–78
Fisher, R. A., 98, 224
Fitts, Dudley, 114
Fleetwood, W., 107
Flexner, Abraham, 227
Ford, R. N., 128, 155
Forester, T., 118
Frankfort, Henri, 55, 114

G

Galanter, Eugene, 187, 198
Galen, 134, 148
Galileo, 93, 148
Gallup, George H., 105
Galton, Francis, 80, 97–98, 107–108,
    114, 134, 200–201, 203
Gardiner, E. Norman, 69–70, 82, 114
Garnett, William, 96, 114
Garrett, Anne, 170
Geertz, Clifford, 129, 155
Georgescu-Roegen, Nicholas, 110,
    114, 191, 198

Gillispie, Charles Coulston, 9, 11, 96, 115
Glass, D. V., 115
Glassner, Barry, 38
Goldberger, A. S., 206, 218
Goldthorpe, J. H., 194, 198
Goode, William J., 86, 115
Goslin, David A., 202, 218
Gosnell, Harold F., 103, 115
Graves, Robert, 5, 11
Graunt, John, *viii*, 95
Green, Peter, 102, 115
Grierson, Philip, 16–17, 28, 37, 87, 115
Guerlac, Henry, 137, 155
Guttman, Louis, 128, 142, 155, 217–218

H

Haber, A., 156
Hacking, Ian, 40, 71, 92–93, 115, 223, 240
Hajnal, J., 54, 115
Haldane, J. B. S., 98
Hall, A. R., 37
Hall, Jerome, 88, 115
Hallock, William, 20, 37
Hamblin, Robert L., 185, 194–196, 198, 242
Hamilton, Alexander, 19
Harris, Charles S., 223, 239
Harris, H. A., 69–71, 115
Hasofer, A. M., 94, 115
Hatt, Paul K., 198
Hauser, Philip M., 116, 221, 240, 242
Hauser, Robert M., 202, 219
Hecataeus, 33
Helen, 42
Hellman, C. Doris, 19, 37
Helmholtz, Hermann von, 120
Hempel, Carl G., 120, 136, 155
Henry, Neil W., 219
Herodotus, *vii*, 2–4, 8, 11, 14, 27, 32–34, 37, 43–45, 55–56, 60–61, 65, 70, 82, 84, 90, 115, 224, 240
Herschel, John, 96–97, 115
Hill, Richard J., 227, 233, 239
Hipparchus, 188
Hobbes, Thomas, 89, 115

Holland, Paul W., 111, 115
Hölder, O., 120
Holmyard, E. J., 37
Homer, *vii*, 5, 31, 33, 42, 43, 56, 69, 84, 113
Hope, Keith, 194, 198
Horn, Walter, 17–18, 37
Hout, Michael, 242
Hubble, Edwin P., 165
Hughes, Everett Cherrington, 238, 240
Humason, Milton L., 165
Humphreys, Lloyd G., 207, 210, 218
Hunter, J. Stuart, 158, 163–164, 170

I

Isaac, 33

J

Jacob, 33
Jahoda, Marie, 118, 240
Jaques, Elliott, 34–35, 37
Jechonias, 33
Jefferson, Thomas, 18–20, 36, 37
Jencks, Christopher, 62, 115
Jesus, 33
Jevons, W. Stanley, 108–109, 115
Joab, 47
Johnson, Robert A., 242
Johnson, Samuel, 42
Jonah, 47
Jones, Lyle V., 174, 197
Jöreskog, Karl G., 206, 218
Joseph, 33–34
Joshua, 100

K

Kant, Immanuel, 236
Katz, Daniel, 155
Kaul, Jainath, 26, 38
Kelley, Truman Lee, 172, 198
Kelly, P., 12
Kelsen, Hans, 87–89, 115
Kelvin, *see* Thomson, William
Kemeny, John G., 141, 155
Kendall, M. G., 39, 51, 93–95, 107, 113, 115–116
Kennelly, Arthur E., 24, 37

King, W. I., 40, 116
Klein, H. Arthur, 16, 37, 112, 115, 163, 170
Klemm, O., 172
Knibbs, G. H., 230
Knolles, Richard, 36, 53, 66, 113
Knox, Bernard, 82, 115
Köbel, Jacob, 17
Kraeling, Carl H., 117
Krantz, David H., 110–111, 115, 120–121, 155, 187, 198
Kruskal, William, 103–104, 115, 153, 165, 241
Ku, Harry H., 171, 195, 198, 218, 223, 225, 240
Kuhn, Thomas S., 136, 168–169, 170

L

Lakeman, Enid, 8, 10, 11
Land, Kenneth C., 221, 240
Landtman, Gunnar, 87, 116
Lang, Albert R., 114
Langevin, Luce, 20–23, 37
Laplace, Pierre Simon de, 8–9, 21, 96, 140
Larsen, J. A. O., 3–4, 6, 11, 102, 116
Latham, Henry, 75, 116
Latimer, Charles, 26
Lazarsfeld, Paul F., 40, 95–96, 99, 107, 116, 118, 215, 218, 219, 240
Leaning, M. S., 121, 156
Lécuyer, Bernard, 40, 95, 116
Leeper, E. M., 72, 116
Lefebvre, Georges, 10–11
Leinhardt, Samuel, 111, 115
Le Play, Frédéric, 107
Leser, C. E. V., 192, 198
Lewontin, R. C., 98, 116
Lexis, W., 108
Lichtenstein, Murray, 94, 116
Liddell, H. G., 10
Lide, David R., Jr., 163–164, 170
Likert, Ronald, 215, 218
Lindley, Mark, 13, 37
Lindquist, E. F., 145, 156
Lipset, Seymour Martin, 36
Livy, 48–49, 63, 116, 237, 240
Lodge, Milton, 179, 180, 182–183, 195–197, 198

Lombardi, Vince, 83
Lord, Frederic M., 127, 156, 204, 217–219
Lorimer, Frank, 98, 116
Louis XVI, 9, 30
Loyseau, Charles, 67, 116
Luce, J. V., 4, 11
Luce, R. Duncan, 115, 155, 179, 187, 198, 216, 219
Luke, 33
Lumsden, James, 207, 219
Lycurgus, 1–2, 32

M

Macaulay, G. C., 55, 115
Macbeth, 68
MacRae, Duncan, Jr., 234, 238, 240, 242
Madison, James, 19
Maitland, Frederic William, 28, 37
Malthus, T. R., 98
Marks, Lawrence E., 133, 151, 156, 178, 186, 198
Marlowe, Christopher, 42
Martin, Elizabeth, 198, 217–219
Martindale, Don, 61, 116
Mary, 33–34
Masters, Geofferey N., 217, 219
Matthew, 33–34, 57
Mauldin, W. Parker, 128
Maxwell, James Clerk, 96, 236
McGill, Robert, 223, 239
McLemore, S. Dale, 227, 233, 239
McPherson, J. Miller, 139, 156, 222, 240
Meeks, J. G. Tulip, 191, 198
Megabyzus, 4
Mendel, Gregor, 98, 116, 224
Menelaus, 70
Menninger, Karl, 235, 240
Méré, Chevalier de, 92
Merton, Robert K., 27, 38, 40, 116, 198, 241
Middleton, W. E. Knowles, 120, 147, 149–150, 156
Miller, Delbert C., 220–221, 240
Miltiades, 3
Mizruchi, Ephraim H., 38
Mohs, Friedrich, 134, 165–166

Mokken, R. J., 217, 219
Montesquieu, Baron de [Charles Secondat], 20, 37, 58, 116
Montgomery, R. J., 75, 116
Moore, Wilbert E., 221, 240
Moreau, Henri, 20–24, 37
Morgenbesser, Sidney, 156
Morgenstern, Oskar, 125, 147, 156, 191, 199
Moses, 46
Moskowitz, H. R., 197
Mossberg, Sheldon, 67
Mosteller, Frederick, 103–104, 115, 224, 240
Mouton, Gabriel, 20
Muirhead, James, 63, 86, 116
Mumford, Lewis, 28, 37, 235, 240
Murray, Gilbert, 6, 11

N

Naddor, Eliezer, 162, 170
Nagel, Ernest, 119–120, 124–127, 137, 147, 155–156
Neale, Walter C., 57, 59, 116
Necker, Jacques, 20
Nehemiah, 48
Neugebauer, O., 15, 37
Newcomb, Simon, 26
Newman, James R., 119, 156
Neyman, Jerzy, 96, 98, 116
Niceforo, Alfredo, 228–234, 239–240
Nixon, Richard M., 180
North, Cecil C., 198
Noth, Martin, 46, 116
Novick, Melvin R., 204, 219

O

Oberschall, Anthony R., 39–40, 81, 95, 99, 114, 116, 172, 198, 228, 240
Ockeghem, Jean de, 13
Odbert, Henry S., 133, 155
Odysseus, 4–5, 56
Ogburn, William Fielding, 39–40, 116
Ore, Oystein, 93, 116
Orestes, 5
Otanes, 4

P

Pacioli, Luca, 71
Palmer, R. R., 11
Pangle, Thomas L., 62, 85, 117
Panites, 61
Paolucci, Henry, 113
Papirius, 237
Pareti, Luigi, 42, 57, 116
Parsons, Talcott, 162, 169, 170
Pascal, Blaise, 93
Pastorello, Thomas, 38
Patroclus, 82
Pausanias, 84
Pearson, E. S., 94, 115–116
Pearson, Karl, 97–98, 203, 226
Peirce, Charles Sanders, 19
Peleus, 83
Periander, 224
Perline, Richard, 216, 219
Perrin, Bernadotte, 1, 11
Petech, Luciano, 57, 116
Pfanzagl, Johann, 111, 116, 120, 156
Pfautz, Harold W., 107, 116, 242
Pheidon, 14
Phillips, Thomas R., 118
Piersol, Allan G., 225, 239
Pindar, 4–5, 71
Pipkin, Frances M., 163, 170
Pittendrigh, Colin S., 156
Plackett, R. L., 94–95, 108, 113, 115, 117
Plato, 55, 62–63, 85, 89, 110, 117, 138, 204, 224, 236–237, 240
Pleistolas, 130
Pleket, H. W., 36
Pliny the Younger, 7
Pliskoff, Stanley S., 94, 117
Plutarch, 1, 11, 32, 48
Pluto, 72
Polanyi, Karl, 56–57, 117
Pope, Alexander, 235
Popper, Karl R., 237, 240
Pound, Ezra, 114
Prell, Arthur E., 186, 198
Proclus, 27
Procrustes, 129
Protagoras, 236
Provine, William B., 98, 117

Q

Quetelet, Adolphe, 40, 80, 96–97, 108, 115, 225, 228, 240

R

Rabinovitch, Nachum L., 94, 117
Rabinowitz, Louis Isaac, 94, 116
Rainwater, Lee, 185, 194–195, 197
Rankine, W. J. M., 124
Rasch, Georg, x, 215–217, 219
Ratoosh, P., 156
Rawlinson, George, 43, 115
Réaumur, René Antoine Ferchault de, 149
Reiser, Mark, 217
Reiss, Albert J., Jr., 194, 198, 238, 239, 242
Resnick, Daniel, 81, 117
Reynolds, M. Lane, 132, 156
Rice, Stuart A., 105, 116–117, 232, 238, 240
Riley, J. W., 155
Riley, M. W., 155
Ritter, Rogers C., 163, 170
Roberts, Fred S., 111, 117, 120, 122, 151, 156, 187, 198
Robinson, Claude E., 104–105, 117
Robinson, R. E., 145, 155
Rommel, George M., 110, 117
Rose, Arnold M., 186, 198
Ross, W. D., 11, 37, 113, 117
Rossi, Peter H., 195, 198
Rowe, John Howland, 31, 37, 49–50, 63, 117
Rowlinson, J. S., 170
Runyon, R. P., 156

S

Sadie, Stanley, 37
Sabagh, Georges, 32, 37
Sambursky, S., 94, 101, 117
Samuel, 47
Sand, George, 234
Savage, Leonard J., 153
Scarr, A. J. T., 168, 170
Scharf, B., 197
Schepartz, Bernard, 160, 170

Schiffman, Susan S., 132, 156
Schnapper-Arndt, Gottlieb, 228
Schorer, Mark, 235, 240
Schuessler, Karl F., x, 34, 37, 207–210, 212, 219, 242
Schwartz, Richard D., 118
Scott, Christopher, 32, 37
Sechrist, Lee, 118
Secondat, Charles, see Montesquieu
Sélincourt, Aubrey de, 37, 115, 116
Sellin, Thorsten, 185–186, 188–189, 198
Selvin, Hanan C., 99, 117
Sempronius, 237
Seneca, 52
Seth, 34
Sethos, 32
Sewell, William H., 201–202, 219, 242
Sewell, William H., Jr., 9–11, 67, 117, 242
Shakespeare, William, 68
Sheldon, Eleanor Bernert, 221, 240
Shewhart, W. A., 166, 170, 224–225, 240
Shinn, Allen Mayhew, Jr., 184, 194, 198
Shorey, Paul, 236, 240
Siegel, Paul M., 194, 198
Simpson, George, 114
Simpson, George Gaylord, 136–137, 156, 170–171
Singer, Charles, 37
Sjöberg, Lennart, 172, 197
Skinner, F. G., 16, 38
Small, Albion W., 93, 117
Smallwood, Mary Lovett, 76–77, 117
Smelser, Neil J., 36
Smith, Adam, 57
Snell, J. Laurie, 141, 155
Snow, John, 99
Sobel, Michael E., 242
Socrates, 82, 110, 224, 240
Solomon, 48
Solon, 3, 45, 48, 61–62, 82
Somervell, D. C., 38, 118
Sommerhoff, G., 169, 171
Sophocles, 71, 82, 115

Sörbom, Dag, 206, 218
Sorokin, Pitirim A., 27, 38, 88–89, 117
Spaulding, John A., 114
Spearitt, Donald, 218
Spearman, Charles, 201, 203–204, 206, 211, 213–214
Spencer, Bruce D., 242
Spencer, Herbert, 23, 38
Spilerman, Seymour, 221
Spuhler, J. N., 111, 117
Srole, Leo, 208
Stahl, W. R., 160, 171
Stanford, W. B., 4, 11
Starr, Paul, 234, 239
Staveley, E. S., 6–7, 11, 102, 117
Stern, William, 201
Stevens, J. C., 197
Stevens, S. S., viii, ix, 121–129, 132– 156, 172, 176–184, 186–189, 191– 193, 196–199, 222–223
Steward, Julian H., 37, 117
Stewart, John Hall, 10–11, 21–22, 29, 38
Stigler, Stephen M., 108, 118, 226, 240, 242
Stinchcombe, Arthur L., 35, 38, 242
Stone, Mark H., 217, 219
Straffin, Philip D., Jr., 7, 11
Suetonius, 49, 85, 118
Sumner, William Graham, 92, 118
Suppes, Patrick, 115, 153, 155, 156
Susser, Mervyn, 99, 118
Swift, A., 7, 11
Sydenham, P. H., 13, 38, 71, 118– 120, 156
Sydenstricker, Edgar, 40, 116

T

Talleyrand-Périgord, C.-M. de, 22, 29
Tanenhaus, Joseph, 198
Taylor, C. C. W., 110, 117
Taylor, Lily Ross, 6, 11
Themistocles, 8
Thomas, Ivor, 28, 38
Thomas, Dorothy Swaine, 201, 219
Thompson, E. H., 110, 118
Thompson, Gerald L., 141, 155

Thomson, Alexander, 118
Thomson, J. A. K., 109, 113, 118
Thomson, William [Lord Kelvin], 124, 147–150, 165–166, 171, 236
Thrasybulus, 224
Thucydides, 32–33, 38, 42, 70, 118, 130, 156
Thurstone, L. L., ix, 172–176, 178– 180, 184, 199, 206, 215, 217–219
Tiffany, Lewis H., 156
Toby, J., 155
Todhunter, Isaac, 8, 11
Tomasson, Richard F., 54, 118
Toops, H. A., 128, 156
Torgerson, Warren S., 127, 143, 156, 162, 171
Toynbee, Arnold J., 23, 27, 29–31, 38, 72, 87, 118
Treat, Charles F., 23, 26, 38
Treiman, Donald J., 65, 118, 194, 199
Troxell, George Earl, 170
Tukey, J. W., 216, 219
Tullius, Servius, 48, 52, 63, 86, 237
Turgot, Anne Robert Jacques, 9
Turner, Charles F., 198, 217–219
Tursky, Bernard, 179, 198
Tversky, Amos, 115, 155

V

Valentinian II, 44
Vegetius, 44–45, 60, 118
Verman, Lal C., 26, 38
Versnel, H. S., 36
Vico, Giambattista, 31, 38
von Neumann, John, 125, 147, 156, 191, 199

W

Wachsmann, Klaus, 13, 37
Wade, Herbert T., 20, 37
Wagner, Adolph, 80–81, 118
Wainer, Howard, 216, 219
Walton, J. Michael, 71, 118
Warner, Rex, 38, 118
Warren, Bruce L., 111, 118
Washington, George, 18–19

Webb, Eugene L., 61, 106, 118
Weber, Eugen, 24, 38
Weber, Max, 13, 38, 51, 59, 73–74,
  92, 118, 172
Wegener, B., 197
Wehler, Hans-Ulrich, 117
Weiss, David J., 217, 219
Wes, M. A., 36
White, Michael, 240
Whitla, D. K., 156
William the Conqueror, 28, 50
Willcox, Walter F., 50, 118
Winfree, Arthur T., 30, 38
Wiskocil, Clement T., 170
Wittfogel, Karl A., 44, 49–50, 74,
  118
Wolfe, A. B., 49–50, 118
Wolfgang, Marvin E., 185–186, 188–
  189, 197, 198
Wolins, Leroy, 144, 146, 156
Woolf, Harry, 113, 116, 126, 155,
  156, 218
Wren, Christopher, 20

Wright, Benjamin D., 216–217, 219
Wright, Lawrence, 28, 31, 38
Wright, Sewall, 98

X

Xanthias, 72
Xerxes, 8, 34, 43–44, 60, 82

Y

Yeats, W. B., v
Youden, W. J., 163, 171
Young, David C., 70, 82, 118, 242
Young, Forrest W., 132, 156

Z

Zabell, Sandy, 94, 118
Zebrowski, Ernest, Jr., 157–158, 171
Zeisel, Hans, 40, 118, 229, 240
Zerubavel, Eviatar, 27–31, 38, 242
Zupko, Ronald Edward, 12, 16, 38

SUBJECT INDEX

A

Absolute scale, *ix*, 147, 149, 151–153, 191
Acceleration, 159–160
Accuracy, *see* Error
Addend, 128
Age, 31–32, 34, 50, 53, 54, 61, 144, 150, 201
Ammain, 40
Angle, *ix*, 26, 158, 168
Appraising quality or performance, *see* Athletics, Contest, Examination, Grading, Poetry, Test
Arithmetic, 42, 139, 235
Athletics, *viii*, 31, 69–71, 81–84
Attenuation, 205
Attitude, 173–176, 197, 203, 215, 221
Average, 17, 78, 80, 107–110, 143, 174, 180, 193, 196, 223–224, 231; *see also* Mean
Awards, *viii*, 55, 84, 86; *see also* Reward

B

Bookkeeping, 51, 232
Bureaucracy, Bureaucratization, *vii*, 26, 60, 73; *see also* Census

C

Calendar, *see* Time
Calibration, *viii*, 17, 60, 78, 91–92, 159, 165, 191, 195
Catalog of Ships, 41, 43
Category scaling, 135, 178, 180, 188, 194–195, 197
Censor, 49, 52, 54, 237

Census, 19, 26, 31–34, 41, 45–54, 62–63, 103, 105, 111, 131, 150, 192, 237
Chance, *viii*, 62, 85, 91–92, 104, 223, 225; *see also* Lot, Probability
Change, social, *vii*
Chinese, *viii*, 15, 27, 61, 72–74
Class, *vii*, 48, 50, 59, 61, 102, 122, 129, 131–132, 148
Class conflict, *vii*, 7, 9–10, 102
Coinage, *see* Money
Computer, 226
Consensus, social, *ix*, 178, 197
Contest, *v*, *viii*, 31, 69–72
Coordination number, 152
Correlation, *x*, 97, 111, 153–154, 162, 173, 201, 203–206, 209–213, 226–227, 230, 232–233
Counting, *v*, *vii*, *ix*, *x*, 6, 33, 41–55, 59, 99, 111, 112, 131, 139, 150–152, 160
Cross-modality matching, 181, 183, 186–187, 196

D

Degree, *viii*, 68, 124, 126–127, 134, 137, 147–148, 154
Demography, 50, 54, 160, 222, 234
Dimension, *vii*, *ix*, 2, 14–16, 30, 35, 89, 133, 159–162, 177, 187, 210–211, 234
Distance, *see* Length
Distribution, *viii*, *x*, 76, 80, 96, 111, 112, 129, 145, 208, 211–212, 225

E

Econometrics, Economics, *ix*, 110, 160–162, 191–192, 225, 234, 236

Egyptians, 14, 26–27, 32–33, 42–43, 55–56, 61, 65
Elasticity, 192–193
Election, *see* Voting
Electric current, *ix*, 158, 160
Empirical equations, 159, 166, 168, 177, 193
Empirical sciences, *ix*, 119–120, 162, 168
Energy, 159
Error, *x*, 16, 31–32, 42, 108, 121–122, 165, 176, 192, 196, 203–204, 206, 223–224, 226
Examination, *viii*, 72–74, 79; *see also* Test

F

Factor analysis, *x*, 161, 203, 205–208, 210–214
Feelings, *x*, 203, 207–209; *see also* Happiness
Flow, 160
Force, 159
French Revolution, *vii*, 9–10, 20–23
Fundamental inventions, *vii*, 106, 110–113, 120; *see also* Invention

G

Games, *viii*, 69; *see also* Athletics
Gifts, 55–56
Grading, *viii*, 76–81, 109, 141, 143, 167
Greeks, *viii*, 1–8, 14, 31–35, 41–44, 51, 56–58, 61–62, 65, 69–72, 81–85, 94–95, 101–103, 224

H

Happiness, 135; *see also* Hedonimeter, Utility
Hardness, *ix*, 134, 141, 165–167
Hedonimeter, 110–111, 191
Honors, *viii*; *see also* Awards, Reward
Hydraulic state, 44, 49–50

I

Inca, 49–50, 63, 72
Index number, *v*, *x*, 26, 59, 107, 111, 112, 143–144, 188, 227–233

Indicator, *x*, 35, 70, 161, 174, 220–221, 227–229, 233, 238
Inflation, 25–26, 58, 85, 144
Interval scale, *viii*, 30, 141, 143–148, 150, 153
Invariance, *x*, 125, 175–176, 187, 213, 215, 217
Invention, *vii*, 2, 3, 10, 28, 39–41, 55, 59, 72–73, 78, 79, 87, 91, 102–103, 106, 110; *see also* Fundamental inventions

J

Jews, 33–34, 45–48, 65, 94, 100–101; *see also* Religion
Jury, 5–6, 28, 94, 101–102

K

Kelvin scale, *ix*, 124, 149, 158; *see also* Temperature
Kleroterion, 101–102

L

Latent trait, 2, 174, 212, 216
Length, *ix*, 14–15, 17, 18, 20–21, 71, 87, 106, 158–160, 162, 163, 165, 167
LISREL, 206, 210
Lot, 2, 4, 13, 62, 85, 94, 100, 104; *see also* Probability, Randomization
Luminous intensity, *ix*, 158

M

Magnitude estimation, *ix*, 133, 175, 177–179, 182–183, 187–189, 191, 194–197, 215
Mass, *ix*, 158–160, 162
Mathematical social science, *vii*, 7–8, 90
Mathematics, 119, 120, 141, 149–150, 161–162, 169, 193, 236
Mean, 96, 107–109, 140, 177, 180, 191; *see also* Average
Metric system, *vii*, 19–27, 29, 158, 236
Metrology, *v*, *vii*, 12, 14, 21, 26, 35, 39, 87, 155, 167, 230

Military, *see* Warfare
Modulus, 180, 189–192
Money, *v*, *viii*, 14, 18, 20, 22, 24, 26–27, 28, 55–59, 65, 82, 84, 85, 87, 91, 112, 160–162, 185–186, 193, 235–236
Movement, social, *vii*; *see also* Metric system

N

Network, *viii*, 111–112
Nominal scale, *viii*, 30, 123–140, 148, 154
Numbers, *xi*, 42, 44, 50, 53, 55, 97, 110, 124–125, 131–133, 137, 150, 152, 169, 235–236
Numerology, 237

O

Offense, *viii*; *see also* Punishment, Seriousness of crime
Ordinal scale, *viii*, 30, 59–60, 123–125, 140–143, 148, 151, 153, 216
Organization, social, *viii*, 27, 30, 238
Ostracism, 5

P

Pantometry, 106, 235
Paradox, *vii*, 7–9, 239
Physical measurement, *vii*, *ix*, 10, 19, 35, 106, 132, 144, 147, 157–171, 193
Pitch, 13
Poetry, *viii*, 71–73, 81–82, 106
Poikilitic function, 153, 179
Population, *v*, *ix*, *x*, 44–45, 49, 51, 54, 59, 95–96, 98–99, 102–103, 112, 137, 160, 161, 200, 205, 211–212, 216, 222, 229
Power, 159
Power function, *ix*, 177–178, 181, 183–184, 186–187, 193–194
Precedence, 68
Prediction, 93
Prestige of occupations, *ix*, 65–67, 139, 178, 194–195
Probability, *viii*, *ix*, 40, 91–100, 104, 108, 112, 140, 152–154, 175, 215, 225, 238; *see also* Chance, Lot, Randomization, Sampling
Process, social, *v*, *vii*, *x*, 13, 30, 36, 40, 221
Psephology, 4
Psychometrics, *v*, *x*, 75, 77–79, 81, 107, 144, 197, 200–219, 232
Psychophysical law, *ix*, 177, 186–187
Psychophysics, *v*, 2, 106–107, 110, 112, 147, 152, 172–200, 223
Punishment, *v*, *viii*, 7, 53–54, 62, 85–91, 112, 185–186, 188, 193, 235

Q

Quantification, *v*, 36, 71, 107, 112, 126, 131–132, 148, 152, 154, 162, 166, 169, 178, 188, 221, 229, 235–236
Quet, 40
Quipu, 50

R

Randomization, *v*, *viii*, 2, 94, 100–102, 127; *see also* Lot, Sampling
Rank, Ranking, *v*, *viii*, 7–9, 59–68, 80–81, 112, 123, 139–140, 173
Ratio scale, *viii*, *ix*, 17–18, 19, 30, 57, 60, 62, 122, 145, 147–149, 153, 167, 178, 184–187, 192, 194, 196
Relevance, *x*, 176, 215
Reliability, 204, 211–212
Religion, 92, 128, 138
Representation, 6, 102–106
Reward, *v*, *viii*, 70, 81–86, 90, 112; *see also* Awards
Romans, *viii*, 6, 7, 16, 17, 20, 24, 31, 33, 44, 48–49, 51–54, 60, 63, 65, 86–87, 130

S

Sampling, *viii*, 17, 72, 102–106, 112, 175–176, 206, 224, 226
Scale, Scaling, 77–78, 80, 88–89, 112, 120–122, 125, 128, 142, 147, 167, 173, 178, 180, 186, 188, 194, 203, 207, 211, 216–217, 220–221, 231
Scale type, *v*, *viii*, 59, 121–155, 222

Scientific method, *v*, 2, 106
Score, Scoring, *viii*, 71, 76, 79, 109–110, 140–146, 195, 203, 208, 211, 216, 227
Sensation, *ix*, 121–122, 147–148, 172, 176, 186–187, 189
Seriousness of crime, *ix*, 87–89, 178, 185, 188–193
SI units (International System of Units), 158–159, 163–164; *see also* Metric system
Simulation, *x*, 211–214
Social Life Feeling Scales, *x*, 207–209
Sociology of knowledge, measurement, *vii*, 13, 27, 238, 241
Sone scale, 121–122
Standards, *vii*, *viii*, 12, 13, 14, 16, 19, 28, 55, 71, 73, 75–76, 78–79, 87, 91, 144–145, 149, 157–159, 162, 164, 168, 204
Statisticism, 226–227, 232–233
Statistics, *x*, 21, 25–26, 49, 54, 77, 95–96, 99, 108, 111, 121, 125, 146, 159, 161, 164, 166, 168, 173–174, 183, 192, 206, 209, 221–227, 229, 232, 234, 237
Status, social, 194–195, 201–202, 220; *see also* Class, Rank
Stochastic behavior, *x*, 215, 225; *see also* Probability
Stock, 160
Substance, *ix*, 158, 163
Survey, 107, 131, 167, 216, 241

T

Tactus, 13
Taxation, 48, 51–52, 54, 55–58, 63
Taxonomy, 136–139

Temperature, *ix*, 2, 23, 26, 96, 106, 110, 120, 136, 147–150, 158, 164, 187
Test, *viii*, *x*, 72, 74, 78–79, 107, 112, 141–146, 152, 173, 200–206, 215–217, 232; *see also* Examination, Score
Theory, 147, 151, 162, 169, 186, 204, 206, 209–210, 222
Thermometer, *see* Temperature
Time, *viii*, *ix*, 14, 15, 18, 25–27, 28, 30–35, 71, 97, 106, 107, 129–130, 158–160, 162
Typology, 136–137, 200

U

Units, *vii*, *viii*, 6, 12, 14, 16, 23, 29, 40, 59, 79, 145–147, 153, 158–159, 162, 163, 189, 191, 193, 216, 222, 231, 236
Unobtrusive measures, 61, 106
Utility, *viii*, 110, 112, 160, 191

V

Valuing, *viii*, 20, 26, 52–53, 55–59, 191; *see also* Money
Variability, *x*, 80, 122, 163, 175, 179, 200, 222, 224–225
Voting, *v*, *vii*, 1–10, 59, 63, 101, 103–105, 112, 152

W

Warfare, 42, 44–49, 51–53, 60, 63, 66, 80, 84–86, 101, 201
Weights and measures, *vii*, 10, 12, 13, 16–21, 23–24, 27, 30, 55, 71, 87, 97, 158, 228, 235–236

WESTMAR COLLEGE LIBRARY